THE BRUSHBACK REPORT

THE BRUSHBACK REPORT

ALL THE SPORTS NEWS THAT'S UNFIT TO PRINT

DAVE SARAIVA

Creator of
TheBrushback.com

BALLANTINE BOOKS ▥ NEW YORK

A Ballantine Books Trade Paperback Original

Copyright © 2006 by Dave Saraiva

Published in the United States by Ballantine Books, an imprint of The Random House Publishing Group, a division of Random House, Inc., New York.

BALLANTINE and colophon are registered trademarks of Random House, Inc.

ISBN 0-345-49284-6

Printed in the United States of America

www.ballantinebooks.com

2 4 6 8 9 7 5 3 1

BOOK DESIGN BY CASEY HAMPTON

PHOTO CREDITS

Gutierrez. P. 161, Teen at Party: Bryanne Hamill. P. 163, Kordell Stewart: AP Photo/Markus Schreiber. P. 172, Man Playing: Dave Saraiva. P. 177, Hamstring Injuries: AP Photo/Chuck Burton. P. 180, Controversial Female: Kate Hamill. P. 181, NFL Cornerbacks: AP Photo/John Gaps III. P. 183: One More Bet: Dave Saraiva. P. 186, Chess Club: Kate Hamill. P. 188, Little Leaguer: Dave Saraiva. P. 192, Vince Young: Dave Saraiva. P. 195, Greyhound: Stuart Bauer. P. 199, Seven-Dollar Ballpark: Dave Saraiva. P. 200, Jim Brown: AP Photo/Wilfredo Lee. P. 201, New Girlfriend: Kate Hamill/Dave Saraiva. P. 203, Griffey Completes: Dave Saraiva. P. 206, Former X Games Champ: Kate Hamill. P. 209, Spelling Bee Champ: Harry Newton.

INTRODUCTION

When *The Brushback* first hit newsstands in July 1978, it was nothing more than a free weekly paper covering the world of "brushback dancing," a unique style of dance popular in Trinidad and Tobagoan wedding ceremonies. The dance is usually accompanied by tambourine music and consists of one step forward and two steps back. Sadly, brushback dancing never took off in the States, and by 1979 *The Brushback*'s readership had dwindled to zero.

Discouraged, The Brushback editor threw away his typewriter and swore off writing forever. He was a man of many interests, however, and soon found he could write about things other than brushback dancing. In 1981 a new craze was sweeping the nation: "sports," or recreational activities carried out for enjoyment or competitive purposes. The editor found great pleasure in these activities and became increasingly obsessed with the games, and, more specifically, the people who played them. His favorite sports quickly became baseball (a game derived from cricket, which involves a wooden bat, a leather glove, and a stitched-together ball), basketball (a game that involves depositing a ball though a hoop, and which seemed to be dominated by members of the economically disadvantaged lower class), hockey (a game played on ice that nobody cares about), and football (a thrilling game that mixes the grace of ballet dancing with the savagery of jazz dancing).

In 1983 The Brushback editor decided America needed a newspaper dedicated to covering sports stories; from the action on the field to the personal lives of the players. His friends thought he was crazy. "Nobody wants to read about something so trivial," they said. "Americans have other things to worry about, like the infiltration of communism into Central America, and who shot JR." Like so many of the athletes he loved, The Brushback editor ignored the naysayers and believed in himself.

And so, on June 23, 1983, the first issue of the *The New Brushback Sporting Sheet* (changed to *The New Brushback Sporting Sheet For The Masses* in 1990, and then later shortened to *The Brushback*) appeared. The cover story for that first issue was entitled "Why Rookie Sensation Dan Marino Will Never Win a Super Bowl." It also contained an editorial suggesting that the National Hockey League stage a work stoppage in 2005.

Among the highlights of *The Brushback*'s early years was a controversial article alleging mass steroid use in Major League Baseball. It predicted a user named Jose Canseco would write a tell-all book called *Juiced,* which would blow the whistle on other steroid users and unleash a massive scandal that would result in congressional hearings. The nation completely disregarded *The Brushback*'s predictions, mostly because nobody at the time could fathom a Latino being one of the most prominent ballplayers in the nation. This, of course, was prior to the discovery of the Dominican Republic, a small island of baseball players.

Throughout the 1990s, *The Brushback*'s readership grew, and by 2000 the newspaper had a loyal cult following. In 2003 the paper was awarded the Saunders Prize for Excellence in Free Sports Papers. Sportscaster Bob Costas called it "a beacon of light in a world of pain, isolation, and loneliness." The Dalai Lama said it was "essential reading for anyone seeking to know the universe and, more important, the self." Baseball player Barry Bonds called it "a fucking piece of shit."

Today *The Brushback* has more than 7 billion readers, most of whom get their *Brushback* fix from the paper's home page: TheBrushback.com.* *The Brushback Report* is a compilation of *The Brushback*'s finest articles. Freshly edited and typed in a snazzy new font, the sports stories herein will make you laugh, cry, and most of all, think. Between these covers you will find not just news articles, but a comprehensive, penetrating account of the past 839 days in the world of sports, both professional and amateur. And oh, what an 839 days it has been. . . .

—*The Brushback*
January 2006

* N.B. This is a book and not a web page, so be sure to turn the pages manually, as clicking a mouse will do nothing.

THE BRUSHBACK REPORT

Bill Belichick Forced to Cut Daughter From Cash-Strapped Family

FOXBORO, MA — New England Pariots coach Bill Belichick has made some difficult decisions during his storied career. Last year he axed fan favorite Lawyer Milloy four days before the start of the season. This year, Belichick has taken a hard-line stance with cornerback Ty Law and Antoine Smith, the tailback who brought him two Super Bowls.

Those choices were certainly painful, but they were nothing compared to the decision Belichick made this weekend, when he decided to cut his 10-year-old daughter from the family for financial reasons.

"This is one of the toughest decisions I've ever had to make," said a cold, steely-eyed Belichick at a press conference afterward. "Jessica was a great kid and I wish her all the luck in the world. If I had my way, I'd keep all my kids forever, but if my family wants to remain financially viable in the future, we have to make some hard choices. Therefore, Jessica is being granted her unconditional release from the Belichick family, effective immediately."

Jessica was sent packing Sunday evening

"THERE ARE PLENTY OF KIDS AT THE ORPHANAGE WHO COULD DO ALL THE THINGS SHE DID, BUT CHEAPER AND WITH A LOT LESS ATTITUDE," SAID MRS. BELICHICK.

and last seen hitchhiking down I-95 South in Rhode Island.

"Jessica should understand that this isn't a personal thing at all," continued Belichick. "But this family isn't about just one person. We have a son to think about, too, as well as my wife, a German shepherd puppy, a cockatiel, and me. By eliminating Jessica, we save thousands a year."

According to family financial records, Jessica was costing close to $20,000 annually to feed, clothe, educate, and entertain. On the

see BELICHICK, page 4

> BELICHICK, continued from page 3

contrary, 6-year-old Justin costs only half that amount.

"I can't let my personal feelings get in the way of my decision-making," said Belichick. "That's just not a good way to do business, and it's not a good way to operate a family. To be honest, Jessica was starting to get a little selfish. She had to have her own phone line, her own Internet account—it was getting a little ridiculous. We can't have everyone on a different page. Cutting her will definitely streamline things a bit."

When Belichick sat down to do his 2003 taxes, he knew that changes would have to be made in order to save the family from financial ruin. Rumors swirled about Jessica's impending release, but it was still a shock when it actually happened.

"She was real surprised," said an emotional Helen Belichick, Jessica's mom. "In all honesty, I think she overestimated her value to this family. Sure, she's a great daughter, but she's not bigger than the family unit. We have another child, and there are plenty of kids at the orphanage who could do all the things she did, but cheaper and with a lot less attitude."

As expected, young Justin was shocked and furious upon learning of his sister's release, and wonders when his time will come. Belichick insists that Justin is safe for now, and that the youngster will benefit greatly from the release of his sister.

"I'm sure he'll understand why we did what we did next Christmas," said Belichick. "When he looks under the tree and sees that new GameCube, he'll forget about Jessica pretty quick."

Despite his family's disappointment, Belichick drew high praise from around the NFL for his efficient handling of the Jessica release. And with the family in excellent financial shape heading into the new fiscal year, Belichick plans to start shopping around for another daughter in order to round out the family unit once again.

"We'll probably look for something practical," Belichick said. "Like one of those Guatemalan orphans—you know, like those kids Angelina Jolie keeps adopting. Whoever she is, she'll really have to embrace the team concept. She'll come cheap, or she won't last very long. Believe me, I didn't win two Super Bowl rings by being sentimental and compassionate."

Clubhouse Cancer Requests Different Nickname

NEW YORK—Kenny Lofton of the New York Yankees, who has been called a clubhouse cancer several times during his career, has formally requested a different nickname since his current one is "a little grim." "I know 'clubhouse cancer' has a nice ring to it, but I was thinking of something else," said Lofton. "Like 'K-Lof.' That rolls right off the tongue, doesn't it? Or how about 'the Silent Assassin'? I'd even settle for something simple, like 'Swifty' or 'Speedy.' Anything, really, other than 'clubhouse cancer.' " Lofton's teammates have obliged his request for a new nickname, and are now referring to him as "dickhead."

Lance Armstrong Sells Uranium to Iran Just to Piss Off France

AUSTIN, TX—Tour de France champion Lance Armstrong, eager to piss off French authorities, sold a large quantity of uranium to Iran yesterday. The uranium will probably be used to build a nuclear weapon, ensuring that Armstrong gets the last laugh in his ongoing feud with France.

"Yep, I think I finally stuck it to those snotty bastards," said a satisfied Armstrong from his home in Texas. "You want to accuse me of doing steroids? You want to tarnish my reputation? Fine, then I'm selling highly enriched uranium to the country that you're trying to prevent from having nuclear weapons. Good luck with those negotiations, suckers!"

Armstrong and the French have had a rocky relationship for years. His seven Tour de France victories have been tainted by the French media's repeated allegations that he used performance-enhancing drugs. Now Armstrong is striking back.

"I can't tell you how much damage the French media has done to my image," Armstrong said. "I thought long and hard about the best way to get back at them. That's when it hit me: Since they're in these negotiations with Iran, trying to stop them from building nukes, wouldn't it be funny if I threw a wrench into the whole thing? Don't worry, though. The Iranians have assured me they will use that highly enriched uranium for peaceful purposes only."

French officials were outraged when they heard the news of Armstrong's dealings with Iran. The nuclear talks have been completely derailed, and the matter will probably have to be referred to the UN Security Council. President Jacques Chirac called Armstrong's actions "totally irresponsible," and in a press conference held yesterday, Tour de France chief Jean-Marie LeBlanc vowed never again to let Armstrong race in his country.

"This man is a nuclear arms dealer," said LeBlanc, who has long suspected Armstrong of using steroids. "Mr. Armstrong has gone too far in his personal war against our nation. He gave one of the most dangerous regimes in the world a canister of highly enriched uranium. He is an enemy of the state, an ally of extremists, and worst of all, he may have once used steroids."

In the meantime, the International Atomic Energy Agency is wondering where exactly Armstrong got the uranium.

"Enriched uranium is not something you buy at the corner store," said Mohamed El Baradei, head of the IAEA. "It would be nice if Mr. Armstrong could tell us where he acquired this dangerous substance, so we can be assured that no more of it falls into the wrong hands. If the Iranians build a nuclear weapon, God help us all. I must admit, though, even as head of the IAEA, that the expression on Jacques Chirac's face when he found out was priceless."

THE BRUSHBACK GLOSSARY

AUTOGRAPH: A priceless treasure that can be acquired by a) begging; b) sending a letter; or c) being anywhere near a television camera when an athlete walks by.

Nation's Jobless Receive Emergency Airlift of *Madden 2006*

GILES, TN—Federal aid workers, in conjunction with state unemployment offices, coordinated an emergency airlift of the video game *Madden 2006* to jobless people across the nation yesterday. Over two million unemployed males received free copies of the hit game, which should keep them busy at least until Christmas.

"We got two million copies out. We'll send more in the coming days," said Marsha Rothstein, director of the Red Cross. "The 2006 version of the game, which features a new 'superstar mode' and an enhanced franchise mode, should be just what the doctor ordered for these unfortunate people. You know, sometimes we forget that there are folks out there who can't afford to buy *Madden*. And they're the people who need it most. They're unemployed. What else are they going to do with their time?"

Rothstein painted a bleak picture of the nation's jobless, unable to make ends meet and unable to purchase the single greatest video game ever invented.

"Those of us who have jobs and a steady income probably take it for granted," she said. "But imagine if August rolled around and you couldn't afford to buy the new *Madden*? You got laid off from your job, you've got a wife and kids to feed, you've got to put food on the table, and you're looking at a long, harsh winter without the most kick-

ass game in history. Worse yet, maybe you're stuck playing *Madden 2005,* or—God help me—*Madden 2004.* For some people, this nightmare is a reality."

Dozens of cargo planes fanned out across the country and dropped boxes of *Madden 2006* on some of the poorest sections of the country. The South and Midwest, where unemployment is rampant, received the bulk of the aid.

Doug Harley, a 45-year-old resident of Linden, TN, fell to his knees and wept upon receiving the complimentary video game.

"Oh thank you, thank you, thank you!" he shouted to the sky as the plane flew away. "Whoever you are, thank you. I've been out of work for six months now, with no sense of purpose, no source of income. On top of all that I've been playing *Madden* with last year's rosters. Dammit, Randy Moss is still on the Vikings! And the San Diego Chargers aren't even any good. I might as well move to Niger and live in one of those refugee camps."

Despite the success of the first airlift, Rothstein says the job is far from over. The Red Cross will apparently spend late winter and early spring preparing for the airdrop of the next *Grand Theft Auto* game.

Mike Ditka Won't Stop Talking About New Erection

CHICAGO, IL—After fifteen years of trying everything from psychotherapy to smoked oysters, Mike Ditka finally has an erection. The venerable old football player has signed an endorsement deal with Bayer AG, which produces Levitra, and is traveling the nation preaching its virtues to anyone who will listen.

"If you ever need help getting back in the game, you should try Levitra," said Ditka to his brother-in-law, Phil Bartlett, at his son's birthday party. "Lots of men have erectile problems. It's nothing to be ashamed of. When I tried Levitra, it changed my life. Now my sex life with [wife] Linda is as healthy as ever."

The ad campaign is causing a stir with friends and family, who wish that he was a little less open and honest about his erectile dysfunction.

"Don't get me wrong. I'm thrilled that Mike can get it up now," said his brother-in-law Phil. "But to be honest, I kind of miss the old Mike who was ashamed to talk about his penis. Nobody ever knew he had a problem, and we didn't need to know. Now the whole damn country is hearing about it over and over again."

Ditka's Levitra spots air repeatedly during football broadcasts, in order to reach the target male demographic that the drug is made for. In the ads he uses thinly veiled football analogies to communicate the power of Levitra. He does the same thing off camera.

"Mike is so sincere. He's not acting at all," said his longtime friend Carl Roney. "Even when he's off camera he says stuff like 'Hey, pal, if you ever need help making that big push at the line of scrimmage, you should try Levitra. Sometimes, when the clock is winding down, you just need a little edge to come

through in the clutch.' I'm like 'Yea, Mike. You told me that already about a hundred times.' There was a time when men didn't go on television talking about their boner problems. That time is gone. Please, someone build me a time machine."

Ditka's new erection has been a mixed blessing for his marriage.

"I'm glad he's 'cured' and feels better about himself," said his wife, Linda. "But there are drawbacks. First, he talks about it all the time. The other problem? I'm a 68-year-old woman and don't want my husband mugging me every five minutes because he can finally spring a woody. Where was this stuff fifteen years ago?"

Though many of Ditka's friends and wife are annoyed by his sudden frankness, none are more disturbed than his own children. His daughter, Amy, claims to be mortified by her father's admission and frequent television spots.

"Oh, God help me. You do not know shame, embarrassment, and nausea until your father starts telling you about his penis," said the 29-year-old Amy. "He tells me how he's 'back in the game' now, and that he's off the 'injured reserve list.' Great, Dad. You're screwing Mom a lot better now. That's just what I needed to hear.

"And its not just me," she added. "It's my friends, too. Do you know how much shit I've gotten because of these commercials? My boyfriend, Tom, actually went up to my father the first time he met him and said, 'How's your penis, Mike?' And you know what? Dad didn't even get upset. He said, 'I'm glad you asked' and started going into his spiel again. That's it. Hand me a razor blade. Somebody. Now."

Heat Concerned by Shaq's Request to Be Paid in Pancakes

Report: Some Americans Do Not Own Sports Blogs

Nobody Notices Bullpen Coach Hasn't Shown Up for Three Weeks

"IF HE CAN APPLY THE SAME INTENSITY TO THE GOOD BOOK THAT HE APPLIED TO LYING AND CHEATING, HE'LL GO STRAIGHT TO HEAVEN," SAID RELIEVER TODD JONES.

Pete Rose Wondering If It's Too Late to Find Jesus

CINCINNATI, OH—Pete Rose has tried everything to get back into baseball. After initially denying allegations that he gambled on the game, he reversed course and admitted to the problem. He later offered a public apology to the league. Nonetheless, his chances of reinstatement are slim. His last remaining option is to find Jesus and rehab his image, but Rose is wondering if it's too late even for that.

"Boy, that's a last resort, but desperate times call for desperate measures," said Rose, the all-time hit leader, who would be a shoe-in for the Hall of Fame if not for his suspension. "I could just say I've overcome my problem and turned my life over to the Lord Jesus Christ and my mission is to give all glory to him. You know, getting into the Hall of Fame would be just one more way for me to glorify Him. If they don't induct me, obviously they hate God."

Rose is in dire need of an image makeover. The release of his autobiography *My Prison without Bars* sparked outrage around the baseball world. Though its purpose was to tell Rose's side of the story, many found it offensive, arrogant, and unrepentant. With

see JESUS, page 10

> JESUS, continued from page 9

his reputation all but destroyed, only Jesus, King of Kings, may be able to save him now.

"My Lord Jesus Christ is looking over me right now, and he's telling me to spread his Gospel to everyone," said Rose. "I no longer want to be reinstated into baseball for the glory. I want back in so I can use my high-profile position to draw attention to the Scriptures and tell everyone the good news of the Messiah. Furthermore, in the Bible it says that gambling is okay as long as you don't bet on your own team. It's on page 324."

A Jesus makeover will be a hard sell for Rose, but it hasn't stopped him from trying. He even contacted MLB Commissioner Bud Selig, who promptly informed him that a religious conversion would have no effect on his chances for reinstatement.

"Finding Jesus isn't going to cut it at this point," said Selig. "That would be the height of hypocrisy. Rose's window of opportunity has closed as far as I'm concerned. Nobody's gonna buy it if he suddenly goes all Kurt Warner on us."

Despite Selig's criticisms, several major leaguers have voiced their support for Rose's desire to be born again.

Reliever Todd Jones is a member of Baseball Chapel, a loose organization of Christian ballplayers that meets during the season in nearly every major league city, and spoke out in favor of Rose.

"Tell Pete if he wants to join us, to call me," said Jones. "We'd love to see him at our Bible study sessions. If he can apply the same intensity to the Good Book that he applied to lying and gambling, he'll go straight to heaven."

But Rose pointed out that he hasn't converted just yet. While he appreciates Jones's kind words, he understands that a total religious conversion is not to be taken lightly.

"Jesus Christ, I said I was *thinking* about converting. I haven't joined the fucking seminary yet," he said. "So lets take a deep breath and calm down boys, okay? I've already told Bud that I'm willing to find Jesus, but only if it helps me get back into baseball. Otherwise, what would be the point? I'm not sitting around in Bible study meetings with those freaks for nothing."

God to Professional Athletes: "Please Stop Pointing at Me"

HEAVEN—In an unusual and unprecedented move, God, Creator of the Universe, publicly demanded that professional athletes stop pointing at Him when they score a touchdown, hit a home run, dunk a basketball, or perform other athletic feats. God explained that pointing is rude and that a deity like Himself deserves better treatment. "Please, please stop pointing at me," God said. "Do you know how rude that is? Every time someone does something on the field, they have to stop and stick their little fingers in my face. Yes, I know. I'm great. I heard you the first time. Now hand the ball to the referee and act like you've been there before, for Christ's sake."

Fallujah Devastated After Losing Out on Summer X Games

FALLUJAH, IRAQ—Officials from the city of Fallujah were devastated upon learning that they were rejected in their bid to host the 2005 Summer X Games. The event's organizers decided to hold the games in Los Angeles instead of the war-torn Iraqi city, leaving the city's mayor at a complete loss.

"I don't understand it," said Mayor Hamid al-Kafi. "Fallujah is a very cosmopolitan city with lots of hotel space and some wonderful restaurants. Plus, it is a hotbed of extremism, and that is what the X Games are all about, isn't it? We are the most extreme place in the world . . . dude."

Al-Kafi said he was "99 percent positive" that his city would be awarded the games after coalition forces cleared the area of insurgents.

"The U.S. Marines came in and retook the city. Now there are no more insurgents," he said. "The corpses have all been cleaned out of the soccer stadium, and we have installed a half pipe in the town square, right next to the giant smoking crater that used to be a police station. Also, since the majority of the cars have been used for car bombings, we have ample parking all over the city."

Now that they have lost out on the games, the citizens of Fallujah are left with a brand-new skate park, several half pipes, a giant bicycle ramp, and a large expanse known as Ahman bin Sadish Memorial X Games Park.

"Just like Olympic host cities must build a central location for athletes and fans to gather, we have built a beautiful recreational area to serve as our own 'Olympic Park,'" said al-Kafi. "It is named after bin Sadish, a former mayor of Fallujah who was killed by insurgents, or the coalition, or possibly random bandits looking for money. There are many ways to die in Fallujah, and death stalks you at every corner, but so what? X Gamers are supposed to be brave, bold people unafraid to risk life and limb. If they are not, then the Mountain Dew people have been lying to us all this time. Infidels!"

X Games coordinator Richard Pemulis defended his decision to keep the games in Los Angeles, saying that L.A. was better equipped to deal with the popular event than a terrorist-infested insurgency hotbed.

"I was impressed with the efforts of the people of Fallujah," said Pemulis. "I'd say in thirty or forty years that place will be a strong candidate to host the X Games. Right now, however, they're not quite there yet. After all, they had thirty-two beheadings in Fallujah last year alone. By contrast, Los Angeles had only ten."

DID YOU KNOW?

In 1991, despite the pleas of his agent, teammates, and fans, Barry Bonds left the Pittsburgh Pirates to go fight for his country in Operation Desert Storm.

Identity Thief Disappointed to Get Mike Tyson's Identity

CLINTON, NJ—Kevin Katz, an identity thief from Clinton, NJ, was disappointed to learn that he had gotten Mike Tyson's identity. Katz purchased the Social Security and credit card numbers from an associate who was able to hack into  the database of a large financial institution.

"Of all the goddamn people to get, I get Mike frigging Tyson. Great," said Katz, 29. "The guy's in debt like $38 million. I'm already in debt a few thousand myself. The idea of identity theft is to get someone who has *more* money than you. I couldn't even get a Blockbuster card with this guy's information."

Katz is an unemployed postal worker who has fallen on hard times. After divorcing his wife of ten years, he was forced to move out of his home and rent an apartment on the outskirts of town. Being saddled with Tyson's identity is just another blow for the hard-luck Katz.

"I tried setting up an account with Cingular with the intention of running up the bill and never paying it, but they turned me down," said Katz. "They said I already had an account with them and that it was way past due. I called Verizon, Sprint, T-Mobile, and some company called Hank's Wireless, and they all told me the same thing: that I owe tons of money and should stay on the line. Then they asked me if I wanted to pay with an online check. What nerve. I was, like, 'I'm Mike Tyson, bitch. Screw you.' "

As a last resort, Katz attempted to open a bank account using Tyson's name and Social Security number.

"Holy shit, I didn't realize how much trouble this guy was in," he said. "I gave all the information to the customer service rep, and she plugged it into the computer. Then she got this look on her face like she just saw a ghost. She said, 'Excuse me a moment, Mr. Tyson,' and came back with the bank manager. He took one look at my information and told me I could not open a bank account and should leave immediately or he would call the police. I started to argue, but then I remembered I was stealing someone's identity and it probably wouldn't be that great an idea."

Across the country in Phoenix, where Tyson is training for an upcoming fight, the 38-year-old expressed surprise that his identity had been stolen. According to Tyson, all his debts are tied up in court and he is unable to purchase anything with credit.

"I cannot believe someone would steal my identity," said Tyson while working out at Central Boxing in downtown Phoenix. "If he had just asked me for my identity, I would have given it to him. How much is he in debt? $12,000? I see. I would like to trade identities with him. I will be Kevin Katz, regular guy from Jersey, and he can be Mike Tyson, broke, middle-aged boxer who is about to get his head crushed by some anonymous guy from England. He can have my criminal record, too. And this tattoo on my face. Nobody told me these things don't come off."

Plan to Drink One Beer for Each Lap of Daytona 500 Falls Far Short

DAYTONA BEACH, FL—An ambitious plan to consume one beer for all 200 laps of the Daytona 500 fell far short yesterday as both participants lost consciousness after lap twenty. The coengineers of the plan, Jimmy Hillsboro of Little Rock, AR, and Hal Kniptick of Macon, GA, started off with a bang but ended prematurely, sleeping through the last 180 laps of the famed car race.

"Hoo boy, we almost made it," said Hillsboro. "I hit my stride right around the tenth lap, but then I started to get a little tipsy, and the last thing I remember is finishing beer eighteen and peeing my pants. I didn't wake up till the race was over. Great race, though."

Kniptick didn't last much longer. He lost consciousness minutes after Hillsboro, and the two spent the rest of the race sprawled out on the metal bleachers amidst a crowd of enthusiastic fans. NASCAR fan Karl Veazie, 38, who was sitting behind the men, described the scene:

"These two fellas, they just kept drinkin' and drinkin'. Real fast, too. Every lap they'd get up to go get more beer. Then they started urinating and puking all over the place. And finally they passed out. I was pretty disgusted with their behavior until around lap forty, when I passed out myself. Kick-ass race, though."

According to sources close to the two men, the idea was hatched by Hillsboro, an avid NASCAR fan and alcoholic. Known as a chronic binge drinker, he once consumed an entire thirty-pack of Old Milwaukee during a tractor pull. The challenge of drinking one beer for every lap of the Daytona 500 was too tempting to pass up.

"Like Tony Stewart and Dale Earnhardt Jr., I love a challenge," said Hillsboro. "I also love drinking, so drinking all those beers during a race seemed like the best of both worlds. Only, I didn't really stop and think about the logistics. Two hundred beers is a lot, even for me."

Kniptick is not the drinker that Hillsboro is, but he was determined to keep pace with his friend and rival.

"Me and Jimmy, we're real competitive about everything. If he gets a rear spoiler on his car, I've got to get a rear spoiler on my car. If he knocks up his girlfriend, I gotta knock mine up. And if he drinks himself to a state of catatonia, well, I'll be right behind him. And I held my own, too. But now my liver hurts. It's actually aching. Is that normal?"

THE BRUSHBACK GLOSSARY

CAUTION FLAG: In car racing, a warning flag that is waved after a car has been devoured by a ball of flame.

According to officials at the Daytona 500, Hillsboro and Kniptick weren't the only people to drink themselves nearly to death that day. In fact, the majority of people in the area were either dead asleep or ill.

"Yeah, they were all pretty much done," says Walt Gunderson, head of security for the event. "It looked like one of those mass suicides or something. I hope these two enjoyed themselves and come back next year. Only, I hope they control themselves a little next time. Two hundred laps is a lot of laps, and a lot of beer. My suggestion would be to drink a beer every other lap. That works out to only one hundred."

see DRUNKS, page 14

> DRUNKS, continued from page 13

But Hillsboro and Kniptick are undeterred. The two have vowed to continue to push the boundaries of common sense and human endurance at NASCAR events in the future.

Says Hillsboro: "I failed, and I'm ashamed of myself. If I can't drink two hundred beers, then I need to build my tolerance. Maybe I was shooting a little too high with the Daytona 500. I should've started with Brickyard 400. That might've been a little more reasonable. How many beers is that, anyway?"

Fat Fuck Has Tremendous Upside

HOUSTON, TX—Roy McCardell, fat fuck from the University of Texas, has tremendous upside, scouts reported Saturday. The 393-pound defensive lineman is said to be a potential run-stuffer if he could only improve his mobility. He currently runs a forty-yard dash in just under ten minutes. "McCardell is basically immobile right now, but he does have some serious upside," said one NFC scout, who witnessed McCardell's workout at the combine. "If he could learn to move slightly to the left or right, and stand erect for more than one play at a time, he could make someone a great situational defender, especially in the 3-4." McCardell must work on his footwork and coordination before he becomes a serious candidate, but run-stuffers are so highly valued that he has a real chance of making an NFL roster next season. "I know a few teams that could use him," the scout said. "There's always going to be a market for somebody who can plug a gap or fill a hole. I'd say this guy could have a good three-, maybe four-year career before his inevitable coronary. Once that happens, his salary comes off the salary cap and it's no harm done."

Loser Says It's Only a Game

WORCESTER, MA—Hal Incandenza, loser of a game of one-on-one basketball against his friend and archrival, Tim Hatch, said later that it was only a game, even though he spent all week boasting that he was "gonna destroy" Hatch and send him home "crying to Mommy." "It's only a game. No big deal. So you beat me in one-on-one. I've got a lot more important things to worry about than putting a ball through a hoop," said Incandenza, who days earlier had dubbed the match "The Battle to End All Battles." "I don't know why you're bragging about it so much. It's just a stupid basketball game. It doesn't mean shit." Later, Incandenza challenged his rival to a rematch, which he said, would "finally determine the ultimate master of the hardcourt."

Stoned Person Finds Himself Watching Figure Skating

PORTLAND, OR—Tim Kesey, a Portland-area stoned person, found himself watching figure skating last Saturday afternoon. Too tired to switch channels, the 30-year-old sat through the entire U.S. Figure Skating Championship and found it strangely relaxing and enjoyable.

"Well, I did a bunch of bong hits and then I was just sitting there on the edge of my bed," said Kesey, an unemployed graphic designer. "Figure skating was on and my first inclination was to change the channel, but I couldn't bring myself to do it. I kept thinking, 'I'll pick up the remote control in a minute.' But a minute turned to two minutes, two minutes turned into half an hour, and before I knew it, it was all over. I guess time flies when you're completely immobile.

"I could see myself watching it again," he continued. "But next time I might try something a little different. I bet if you put on *Dark Side of the Moon*, and cue it up right when the figure skating starts, you would see some pretty cool shit. On the other hand, that's a lot of trouble to go through."

Tim's roommate, Doug Pierson, rolled his eyes when told of Kesey's newfound interest in figure skating. According to Pierson, Kesey doesn't have high standards when under the influence of marijuana.

"Tim's not the most demanding person while he's smoking pot and channel surfing," said Pierson. "I've seen him sit through fili-bustering on C-Span. I've seen him watch junior high talent shows on local access cable.

The only thing that rouses him out of his trance is when a Domino's commercial comes on. He'll say something like, 'Man I'm starved,' look over at the phone, and contemplate calling. Then you can actually see the resignation appear on his face as he realizes that it's not going to happen."

Officials from the figure skating world acknowledged that the majority of their TV viewers are stoned people too tired to change the channel. Still, the sport welcomes any new fans.

"This incident doesn't surprise me at all," said Chuck Foster, president of U.S. Figure Skating. "Figure skating has a few real, hard-core fans, but our studies show that most people who watch us are stoned. They get a kick out of the acrobatics and the moves, plus they can't summon the energy to channel surf. Still, we'll take any fans we can get, even the ones who are catatonic."

Dominican Republic Renamed "Southern Regional MLB Farm System"

Latrell Sprewell's Pet Parrot Won't Stop Cursing

German Army Decides Against Retro Uniforms

Bush to Use Steroid Scandal as Pretext for Invading Iran

WASHINGTON, DC—President Bush will use the steroid scandal as justification for an invasion of Iran, White House sources reported today. The president has been searching for a reason to install a new regime in Iran, and the epidemic of performance-enhancing drugs may be just the excuse he needs.

"We do have intelligence that performance-enhancing drugs are being used in professional baseball as well as the NFL," Secretary of State Colin Powell told reporters during a press briefing. "This horrible scourge is running rampant and must be stopped. Steroids

see BUSH, page 18

> BUSH, continued from page 17

are a gathering threat, and the president will not sit idly and wait for them to destroy us."

Powell added that President Bush would do anything in his power to protect the people of the United States, even if it means a pre-emptive strike.

"The lessons of 9/11 are clear: The best defense is a good offense, and we will not sit on our hands while the Iranians plot to destroy our freedoms. If this steroid scandal has taught us one thing, it's that Iran must be liberated."

While most public figures agree that performance-enhancing drugs have no place in professional sports, many are wondering how they relate to the situation in Iran.

"This is just another excuse for Bush and his big business buddies to raid a weaker country and install a puppet regime," said documentary filmmaker Michael Moore. "What is the connection between Iran and steroids? There is none, and my next documentary will prove it—or at least imply it, using circumstantial evidence and hearsay."

According to a high-ranking White House official, President Bush will formally introduce a UN resolution calling for an end to the widespread use of performance-enhancing drugs in professional sports. The details of the resolution are not known at this time, but the source indicated that it would require every professional athlete in the nation to pass a steroid test.

"That's the gist of it, yes," the source reported. "They'll have a small time frame in which to get themselves clean—all of them, every last one. It's a zero tolerance policy. Of course, it will be more effective if backed up by the threat of force. Therefore, if we have one positive test, Iran is going down."

CIA director George Tenet backed up Bush's claim that Iran is a threat to America's security. At a debriefing today before Congress, Tenet cited the recent widespread use of THG as living proof that the people of Iran need to be given the gift of freedom.

"We have intelligence saying that steroids are being used in nearly every major professional sport," Tenet said. "We feel that this intelligence is highly credible. People keep asking about the connection between Iran and steroids. Well, is it a coincidence that the Iranian hard-liners partook in a sham election at the same time the steroid allegations were coming to light? I don't think so. Don't try to understand. Just go with the flow. That's what I do."

Confused Canadians Turn to Bryan Adams

TORONTO, CANADA—The Canadian people, frustrated and confused by the loss of the NHL season, have turned to singer Bryan Adams for comfort and assurance. Adams is one of the nation's most beloved artists, and his heartfelt ballads have soothed Canadians for decades. "Please, Bryan, your country is suffering," said Prime Minister Paul Martin. "We need your soulful, earnest, and passionate songs to warm our hearts during this time of great confusion and loss. Bryan, your country needs you. Please answer the call." According to Adams's representative, Canada is about to get its wish. The singer is said to be working on a new single, "The Lockout of My Heart (Will End Someday)," which is due in stores by Christmas.

Chinese Athlete Gets English-Language Tattoo

MIAMI, FL—Miami Heat center Wang Zhizhi showed teammates his new tattoo today after practice. The design, drawn on his right shoulder, consisted of a black circle with the word "tranquility" written inside it in ornate English lettering. Zhizhi told reporters he got the tattoo because "he's really into English stuff." "I've always been fascinated with the English language," he said. "I think it's quite beautiful. So when I went for my tattoo, I knew it had to be something written in English. See, it says 'tranquility.' But you probably already knew that. Oh well, it's really dark and mysterious in China."

14-Year-Old Soccer Phenom Proves Soccer Really Isn't All That Hard

WASHINGTON, DC—When 14-year-old Ghana national Freddy Adu signed with DC United, he became the youngest person in over a century to play with an American professional sports team. Surprisingly, the so-called child prodigy has made a seamless, effortless transition from precocious kid to seasoned pro, proving beyond the shadow of a doubt that soccer really isn't all that hard.

"All these years, I thought I was playing an incredibly difficult, high-skill game," said Jaime Moreno, forward for United. "I used to tell people how soccer was one of the most physically strenuous, mentally exhausting games in the world, but now I realize I was wrong. If a fourteen-year-old kid can do it, how hard can it be?"

Of the four major sports in America—basketball, football, hockey, and baseball—none has ever featured a player under the age of seventeen. Wayne Gretzky was a well-known hockey phenom at 16, but didn't play his first professional game until age 18, probably because hockey is a man's sport.

"I've heard a lot of comparisons to Gretzky, but come on, that's just bullshit," said Don Cherry, analyst for *Hockey Night in Canada*. "You won't see a fourteen-year-old playing hockey, I can tell you that much. In hockey, you have to shoot into a tiny net with a huge goalie standing in front of it, while evil thugs are slashing at you with wooden sticks. Oh, and you're on skates, too. Throw me on a soccer field, and I'll show them how it's done."

Though Adu's arrival on the U.S. soccer scene has been greeted with widespread enthusiasm, some soccer officials have voiced concern about the impact a 14-year-old star will have on the sport's credibility.

"Freddy's great and all, but we're trying to sell soccer as a blood-and-guts, high intensity sport whose athletes are gritty warriors," said one MLS general manager. "Now we've got some kid coming in, and he's playing on the same level as some of the so-called greatest players in the world. I'm afraid the lid has been blown off our little charade."

Walt Weiss Wondering Why Nobody Ever Told Him About Steroids

BOULDER, CO—Walt Weiss, former teammate of Jose Canseco and Mark McGwire, is wondering why nobody introduced him to steroids back in the early nineties. The shortstop with the slight build and a paltry twenty-five career home runs could have used an edge but was left out of the loop, leaving him scratching his head and asking, "Why?"

"I don't get it. I'm hearing all this stuff about steroids being done in the clubhouse, and apparently it was all done behind my back," said Weiss, who retired from baseball in 2000. "Look at me. I'm tiny. I remember being envious of those guys for hitting all those home runs. I guess they just didn't want to spread the word around that they were doing steroids. Still, it hurts to know that while I was sweating my ass off fielding grounders, they were in the clubhouse jamming needles into their asses. Some guys have all the fun."

Weiss hit a total of eight home runs in his six seasons with the A's while his teammates were hitting homers at a record pace. Now that the lid has been blown off steroid use, Weiss is demanding answers from both Canseco and McGwire.

"I would like to sit down with those guys, especially Canseco," Weiss said. "Oh, I hear him on *60 Minutes* talking about how rampant steroid use was back then, but did anyone let me in on the secret? No, I was the

"IT HURTS TO KNOW THAT WHILE I WAS SWEATING MY ASS OFF FIELDING GROUNDERS, THEY WERE IN THE CLUBHOUSE JAMMING NEEDLES INTO THEIR ASSES," SAID WALT WEISS.

dependable little shortstop who was good for a bloop single every now and again. I'm telling you, this steroid scandal will not die, my friend, not until I find out why the hell I wasn't involved."

Former A's manager Tony LaRussa has publicly stated that none of his players ever used steroids. When questioned about Weiss, LaRussa was even more adamant.

"Weiss? Walt-fucking-Weiss?" LaRussa laughed. "Ha. Yeah, right. Walt used a ton of steroids. You can tell by the way he hit those dribblers up the middle."

LaRussa also noted that steroids are illegal and that Weiss should be proud of never having tried them.

"I'm surprised he's so upset," he said. "He

see WEISS, page 21

> WEISS, continued from page 20

should just take pride in the fact that everything he accomplished was done without the assistance of performance-enhancing drugs. He hit all two hundred of his dingers with his own power. What? Twenty-five? He had twenty-five for his whole career? Holy shit, what a waste of time. If I was him, I would've demanded McGwire share some of his shit—

that is, if he was indeed doing it, which he wasn't."

The current media firestorm over steroid allegations has left Weiss wondering what his career would have been like had he been exposed to the drugs. The former shortstop often fantasizes about being a bulked-up Neanderthal with an oversized head and shrunken testicles. But sadly, that dream will never come true.

Hacky Sack League Rocked by Doping Scandal

PORTLAND, OR—The Portland Community College Hacky Sack League, once considered a paragon of clean living and virtue, has been rocked by a recent doping scandal involving every single one of its members. Dean Kopeski, commissioner of the league, said he was "saddened" by the scandal, but stopped short of taking any disciplinary action. "Dude, I can't believe this shit," Kopeski told reporters at a press conference. "It's like everyone in the whole league is totally toking it up all the time. This is really going to hurt our image. We're not going to punish anyone, though. That would be hypocritical. Ever hear that old saying about passing out speeding tickets at the Indianapolis 500? That would apply here."

Air Ball Shooter Pretends He Was Fouled

PHILADELPHIA, PA—The 76ers' Allen Iverson pretended he was fouled after shooting an air ball Monday night during a game against the Indiana Pacers. Although no defender was in sight, Iverson winced and grabbed his wrist, scowling at Joe Crawford for not making the call. Crawford, a veteran official, had this to say after the game: "That's an old trick. Everybody does it. Throw up a shitty shot and then pretend you got hit in the arm. Why can't these guys just own up to it when they throw up an air ball? When I make a lousy call, I own up to it. Just kidding. What I actually do is insist it was the right call and give the guy a technical foul for arguing with me."

Fat Girl Accidentally Included in Beer Commercial

LOS ANGELES, CA—Coors Brewing Company executives rushed to do damage control yesterday after a fat girl inexplicably appeared in one of their commercials. The girl, unidentified at press time, is seen wandering into the shot holding a boom mike, then quickly retreating.

A statement released today by the Coors brass said, "We're working diligently to figure out exactly how this happened. It would appear that the fat girl in question is indeed an employee of Coors. While we do have a strict policy prohibiting fat girls from appearing on camera, that policy does not pertain to off-camera employment positions. This policy is currently under review."

The next step for Coors will be to pull all of its commercials off the air and go over them "with a fine-tooth comb" to make sure that the same problem hasn't already occurred in other spots.

"We're currently reviewing every ad we've put out for the past year to make sure nothing slipped by during editing," said Bob Parker, vice president of advertising. "We haven't found anything yet, but we're going to err on the side of caution."

Meanwhile, women's groups are outraged by the perceived sexism and weightism on the part of Coors brass.

"This is ridiculous," said Martha Burke, president of the National Council of Women's Organizations. "I've never seen anything like it. These commercials are sexist in the first place. The way they portray women as dumb, attention-starved sluts is offensive in every way. But to not allow women who happen to be overweight to appear in the ads is downright cruel. It's not their fault that doughnuts are so tasty."

Despite the public outcry Parker announced that the commercial would undergo "significant editing" before appearing on television.

Ron Artest Stomps Puppy to Death Just for Fun

DETROIT, MI—NBA bad boy Ron Artest stomped a puppy to death yesterday, just for fun. The Pistons forward, known for his abrasive personality and short temper, snatched the adorable puppy from a young child and jumped up and down on it. He then casually tossed the puppy corpse in a nearby trash can, leaving the youngster crying hysterically. "Every once in a while I like to do something like that, just for the hell of it," said Artest. "It's just the kind of guy I am. I get bored and I think up cruel things to do to people and animals. Then I sit back, rub my hands together, and laugh my diabolical laugh. I'm such a prick." Artest also announced plans to push an elderly woman down a flight of stairs and taunt the crippled kids at the hospital.

Pistons Fans No Longer Allowed to Smoke Crack at Games

DETROIT, MI—In the aftermath of the violent melee at Friday's Pistons game, NBA commissioner David Stern demanded that the Palace vendors halt the sale of crack during games. "The selling and smoking of crack is believed to have been a major contributing factor in the fans' ugly behavior during the brawl," said Tom Wilson, Pistons president and chief executive of Palace Sports and Entertainment. "Though crack-smoking has been a tradition at Pistons games in the past, we have been asked by the league to stop selling the drug. Unfortunately, some of our fans could not handle the intense and exciting buzz, and have ruined the fun for the rest of us. Now you'll just have to get it in the parking lot like everyone else."

Crippled Athlete Loses Swagger

PHOENIX, AZ—Rich Johnson, left-fielder for the Arizona Diamondbacks, was crippled for life when he was involved in a car accident last weekend. He lost all use of his legs and now requires a wheelchair to get around. Since the accident, teammates have noticed a decided lack of swagger in the third-year player. "Richie used to come strutting in here like he was king of the world," said teammate Shea Hillenbrand. "He was confident, cocksure—he had swagger. Now that swagger is gone, probably because swagger requires fully functioning legs. Oh well, at least he still has his mental swagger, which I'm sure will come in handy when he's playing solitaire."

Fucking Packers Fail to Cover Spread

CHULA VISTA, CA—The fucking Packers failed to cover the spread Sunday, reported bookie Jay Knowles, of Chula Vista, CA. According to Knowles, Brett Favre is a washed-up pussy and Ahman Green is overrated. Plus, the bitch of it is, they had a chance to win the game in the last minute, but Favre had his head too far up his ass to notice Dexter Jackson waiting for the goddamn ball. In addition, Knowles reports that he is through betting on the Packers and is focusing his efforts on teams that have a set of balls and know how to cover a goddamn spread.

Poker Officially Ceases Being Cool

LAS VEGAS, NV—Old-school poker players from around the world expressed dismay recently upon learning that their beloved game, once dominated by brooding, chain-smoking cowboys and gritty Vegas hustlers, has been overtaken by teenagers and computer nerds, removing the air of mystery and rebellion that once made it so cool.

"When I first started playing poker in the fifties, it was still an unbelievably cool thing to do," said Lyle "Six-Shooter" Watson, a professional gambler for over forty years. "Very few people really understood how to play, how to read someone's face, and how to bluff. I learned it from the great Tex Winthrop, who once shot a man to death for skipping out on a debt. Now you can see Texas Hold 'Em tournaments on ESPN every other day. That's the death knell for anything cool and dangerous. ESPN could make Russian roulette seem like a bland, prepackaged leisure activity."

Furthermore, the explosion of popularity has created millions of new players, watering down what was once an elite fraternity of hard-core professionals.

"In the old days no kid from the suburbs could win the World Series of Poker," Watson said. "No kid from the suburbs would even be playing in the World Series because he would be out of his league. Now we've got that dipshit Chris Moneymaker showing up at every tournament like he's a card shark. He's just some young fool who got lucky by bluffing his ass off. In my day, if a guy bluffed me out of a million bucks, I'd take him out

"IN MY DAY, IF A GUY BLUFFED ME OUT OF A MILLION BUCKS, I'D TAKE HIM OUT BACK, BREAK BOTH HIS ARMS, AND SHOVE A POOL CUE UP HIS ASS," SAID LYLE "SIX-SHOOTER" WATSON.

back, break both his arms, and shove a pool cue up his ass."

Adding to the humiliation is the stunning amount of media coverage dedicated to a game that was once relegated to casinos and smoky basements. The past week alone has seen *The Celebrity Poker Showdown* on Bravo, starring female soccer player Brandi Chastain, *Poker Royale 2: Battle of the Sexes* on the Game Show Network, and *Family Funtime Poker Party* on Nickelodeon.

While television has played a large part in bringing poker to the mainstream, the Internet has played an even larger part. Hundreds of new online gambling sites are springing up every day, giving casual players

see POKER, page 25

> POKER, continued from page 24

a place to sharpen their skills before competing professionally.

"The Internet is the worst thing to happen to poker," said Lawrence "Red" Philips, 70-year-old professional gambler. "Half of these Internet gamblers don't even know what they're doing, and they still walk away with your money. And the worst part is, you can't even shoot them for it anymore. Poker has truly lost its innocence."

Philips may not want to know what TV producers have in store for next year. Officials from the cable channel Animal Planet have announced plans to develop a weekly series called *Pet Poker*, in which dogs, cats, hamsters, and other domesticated animals will participate in a high-stakes game of Texas Hold 'Em. The show's producers say *Pet Poker* will bring the fun of Texas Hold 'Em to the only market on earth that has yet to be tapped—the animal kingdom.

Shaquille O'Neal Awfully Boastful in New Rap Song

MIAMI, FL—According to record company sources, Shaquille O'Neal comes across as "awfully boastful" in his new rap song "You Not the Fightin' Type." The song, which calls out several of O'Neal's enemies and features numerous bits of blatant self-promotion, will hit record stores next week. But the negative buzz has already started, with many people describing Shaq's lyrics as "conceited."

"Shaquille is really going to offend a lot of people with these lyrics," said Darnell Z, vice president of Jive Records, which is distributing the new album. "When he says, 'Even with wings you never as fly as me,' I think he's being a little bit boastful, don't you? And then when he says, 'You remind me of Kobe Bryant, tryin' to be as high as me,' that's very confrontational and arrogant. I'm sorry, but the whole thing is just a turnoff, and I don't think the rap world is going to take too kindly to it."

Pop-Up Ad Inspires Man to Join Army

LOUISVILLE, KY—A man visiting ESPN.com was inspired to join the U.S. Army after an exciting pop-up window reminded him of the Army's existence. The man, Paul Granger, of Louisville, went directly to the nearest recruitment office to enlist. He is leaving for basic training next month. "I'm so pumped about joining the army and being an Army of one," said Granger, 22. "I never really thought about it before, but after seeing that pop-up ad, I really want to go help protect our freedoms. Plus I've always wanted to learn how to program computers while being shot at. I have a friend who joined the army years ago and he loves it. I hear he got a free lifetime membership. What more could I ask for?"

Todd Bertuzzi Headed to Hospital to Finish Off Steve Moore

DENVER, CO—Todd Bertuzzi has been suspended by the NHL for the duration of the 2004 season and the play-offs for his cheap shot on Steve Moore last week. The sucker-punch provoked outrage across the nation and in Canada, but that hasn't stopped Bertuzzi from honoring hockey's sacred code of revenge and retribution. That's why he's headed to Denver General Hospital, stick in hand, to finish the job he started that fateful night in Vancouver.

"I know I hurt him pretty bad, but there's still work to be done," said Bertuzzi. "He knocked out my teammate, Markus Naslund, for three months. I heard Moore could be back on the ice within two months. That's unacceptable. I must uphold the sacred code of honor of the NHL. If I don't do this, the natural order of things will be thrown into a tailspin."

Players around the league, including the majority of Moore's teammates, have voiced no opposition to Bertuzzi's quest for justice. Though they sympathize with Moore, they realize Bertuzzi has a score to settle, and there's only one way to do it.

"Stevie's my teammate and I support him 100 percent, but I wouldn't stand in Todd's way," said Avs defenseman Rob Blake. "It would be the height of hypocrisy. This league is founded on the concept of retribution—an eye for an eye and a tooth for a tooth—you know, just like al-Qaeda."

Avalanche coach Tony Granato also expressed sympathy for Moore, but said he won't be the one to break with hockey tradition.

"We all know it's part of the game. It's an ugly part of the game, but it's something that's been with us for decades," said Granato. "Who am I to mess with tradition? As a coach and former player, I understand that the forces of the NHL code of honor have been set into motion, and Bertuzzi won't stop until justice is served. We're self-policing here. We don't need any cops with billy clubs messing with us. That's what hockey sticks are for."

To capitalize on the massive amount of publicity generated by the looming assault, ESPN has sent a camera crew to the hospital. The crew will tape the event and broadcast it live during prime time. The broadcast will be followed by a roundtable discussion of the brutality of hockey and what must be done to stop it.

As for Moore, he's taking it all in stride. The courageous young forward is not afraid of his upcoming beating and understands that it's all just part of the game.

"It's tough being beaten up. I'll be the first to admit it," said Moore, his voice soft and weak. "But I did attack Naslund a while back, and I had this coming. A lot of people wonder why I would allow this to happen. Well, if I allow my attack on Naslund to go unpunished, how will I be able to justify having my teammates bludgeon Bertuzzi mercilessly in retribution for what he's about to do to me?"

> "THIS LEAGUE IS FOUNDED ON THE CONCEPT OF RETRIBUTION—AN EYE FOR AN EYE AND A TOOTH FOR A TOOTH—YOU KNOW, JUST LIKE AL-QUEDA," SAID ROB BLAKE.

Major League Soccer's Only Soccer Ball Kicked Onto Neighbor's Roof

SAN JOSE, CA—Major League Soccer was forced to hold an emergency meeting when the league's only soccer ball was kicked onto a neighbor's roof by the San Jose Earthquakes' Landon Donovan. The incident occurred at the Earthquakes' practice facility, where the team was engaged in its off-season workouts.

"It was our turn to use the ball," said Donovan, from his off-season home in San Diego. "We wanted to get in some quality practices in preparation for the new season. Unfortunately, I booted the ball and it went high in the air and landed on Old Man McDougle's roof. It's way up there stuck in his gutter, and nobody on the team wants to go over there and ask him for it. The guy's nuts."

Donovan's teammates are irate at him for his carelessness with the league's only ball and are calling for disciplinary action against the star scorer.

"Landon's such a fucking show-off," said one teammate, speaking on condition of anonymity. "He always has to show people he's got the strongest leg, and he can kick the ball farthest. Did it ever occur to him that Old Man McDougle's place is right next door and he should be careful with the ball?

"HOW ARE WE SUPPOSED TO AFFORD ANOTHER BALL? WE'RE NOT THE NBA, YOU KNOW," SAID ONE TEAMMATE.

How are we supposed to afford another ball? We're not the NBA, you know."

An emergency meeting of the MLS brass was held at commissioner Don Garber's apartment in Sacramento. They reportedly discussed contingency plans for next season, as the prospect of raising enough money for a new ball by the start of the 2006 campaign looks bleak. For now, the league is planning to use a volleyball until it is able to afford another soccer ball.

Freshman Gets Laid in Hazing Ritual Gone Great

Yankees Insist Nuclear Reactor for Peaceful Purposes Only

Yao Ming Asks Permission to Grab Rebound

Chad Johnson Tramples Small Child to Get to Television Camera

Story of Gay Lacrosse Player Inspires Other Gays to Play Lacrosse

Lance Armstrong Laughing His Ass Off at Paris Riots

White Person Bravely Ventures Into YMCA Pickup Game

COLUMBUS, OH—Don McCullough, a white guy, showed the courage of a thousand men yesterday when he ventured into a pickup basketball game at a Columbus-area YMCA. The 26-year-old McCullough scored 0 points and had just one rebound during the twenty-minute game. "Holy shit, those guys are good," a winded McCullough told reporters. "How can you play full-court basketball for that long? It's just running back and forth over and over again. I couldn't get a shot off. Every time I squared up, this big guy kept coming over and slapping it out of my hands. It was a great workout. I just wish I could have kept some of my dignity."

Guy in Motorized Wheelchair Wins Wheelchair Marathon Again

BOSTON, MA—The 29th annual Boston Wheelchair Marathon was won, once again, by a guy in a motorized wheelchair. Thomas Ripp, a 33-year-old investment banker from Schaumburg, IL, outlasted his competition in what has become a yearly tradition. As was the case the previous two years, Ripp used his motorized chair to gain a decided edge in stamina and fatigue.

"I'd just like to thank God for giving me the talent to compete in this race," said an emotional Ripp after he crossed the finish line. "It was a tough one, that's for sure. These other guys don't give up easily, and it took all I had to win this thing. I'd also like to thank E & J Wheelchairs, who provided me with my motorized chair. I think that really gave me an edge at the end."

Ripp also thanked his personal trainer, Ed, for recharging his battery every five miles along the 26.2-mile course.

"Ed is a lifesaver. We went through some rigorous training to get through this race," said Ripp. "You know, these batteries don't stay charged forever. Plus, I get carpal tunnel syndrome in my thumb and forefinger from pushing that little lever forward. A lot of people don't realize it, but I was racing in pain the whole time."

Ripp said the most difficult part of the race was the beginning, when he was forced to watch the other racers whiz by on the downhill slope as he rolled along at a leisurely pace. But his patience and professionalism kept him going until the halfway point, when other racers were slowing down.

"Eventually a fatigue factor sets in for the other guys," he said. "It's always a little scary at the beginning when everyone is flying by, but my trainer has taught me how to be patient and stay focused. Right around mile thirteen, a lot of guys started dropping off. But not me. I was holding steady at ten miles an hour."

see WHEELCHAIR, page 31

> WHEELCHAIR, continued from page 30

The other competitors are all too familiar with Ripp and his motorized wheelchair. Charles Keaton, who has finished second to Ripp the past three years, voiced his opposition to Ripp's technique after the race.

"I don't mean to be a complainer, but it just doesn't seem fair," said Keaton. "The rest of us have to practically kill ourselves to get to the finish line, and all this guy has to do is sit back and enjoy the ride. I'm tired of it. Today I was really struggling toward the end, really huffing and puffing, and there's Ripp buzzing down the street like it's a Sunday drive."

So far, race officials have not protested Ripp's chair. But if fellow racers continue complaining, the issue will have to be addressed.

"Technically, he's really not doing anything wrong. There is no rule that says the chair cannot be motorized," said Wayne Guaret, wheelchair marathon organizer. "I think that calling so much attention to Mr. Ripp's mode of transportation undermines how much hard work he puts into winning this race. Everyone knows that equipment doesn't win races. Winning comes from the heart, and Mr. Ripp truly has the heart of a champion—and the wheelchair of a champion."

Tom Brady Receives Yet Another Blow Job

FOXBORO, MA—Tom Brady, quarterback for the Super Bowl champion New England Patriots, received yet another blow job yesterday, this time from a female fan outside a St. Louis nightclub. The incident marked the 364th blow job Brady has received this year, breaking the previous mark held by the 49ers Joe Montana. "I was walking out of this club and I got approached by a female fan," said Brady, recalling the incident on *Real Sports with Bryant Gumbel*. "I just assumed she wanted to blow me, so I pulled my pants down right there and waited. Sure enough, I was right. I'm just glad someone is keeping track of these things. This is the kind of record that you dream about breaking when you're a kid."

Swimsuit Model Concerned About *Sports Illustrated* Cover Jinx

NEW YORK, NY—Veronica Varekova, cover girl for the 2004 *Sports Illustrated* swimsuit issue, is concerned about the legendary *SI* cover jinx. The 26-year-old has heard about the jinx from various sports stars and is watching her step lest she fall prey to it. "I am hoping that I don't get jinxed by being on the cover," said the Czech Republic native. "I have heard about people who got on the cover and then had some bad luck. I know I am not an athlete in the traditional sense, but I am concerned that I may suffer some malady or tragedy in my future. I just hope it does not involve my breasts, because they are brand-new."

Player Who Left Everything on Field Forced to Drive Home Naked

PHILADELPHIA, PA—Reggie Walker, a hard-nosed, hustling utility infielder for the Philadelphia Phillies, was forced to drive home naked Sunday after leaving everything he had on the field. Walker later admitted that he was just trying to impress his manager, Larry Bowa. "I know that's the kind of player Larry was, and I know that's the kind of player he wants on his team," said Walker. "I just wanted to make a name for myself, and after coming off the field buck naked, I think I probably did." Unfortunately for Walker, he was demoted to Triple A the next day. Bowa called him a "hard-nosed" player, but said he tends to take things "a little too literally."

Deaf, Dumb, and Blind Kid Terrible at Pinball

PEORIA, IL—Timmy O'Brien, a deaf, dumb, and blind kid from Peoria, is said to be "terrible" at pinball, standing in stark contrast to the cool deaf, dumb, and blind kid from the Who's famous rock musical *Tommy*. "Kid can't even find the door let alone play pinball," said Paul Bezeldik, who witnessed the disgraceful showing at Great Times Emporium in Bartonville. "He had no skills, no Zen-like concentration, no heightened sense of awareness, nothing. And he tripped over some hot chick on his way to the bathroom and made a total ass out of himself. I guess deaf, dumb, and blind kids aren't as cool in real life as they are in rock operas."

Jamal Lewis Headed to Zihuatanejo to See His Friend

PORTLAND, ME—Ravens running back Jamal Lewis is finally a free man, but his journey is just beginning. For the second time in his life, Lewis is about to commit a crime: parole violation. He is headed to the Mexican resort town of Zihuatanejo to see his friend, Andy Dufresne. But he doesn't think the authorities will kick up too much fuss, not for an old crook like him.

"I'm excited," said Lewis while riding south in a Greyhound bus. "But it's the excitement only a free man can feel—a free man at the start of a long journey whose destination is unknown. I hope I get across the border without any problems. I hope to see my friend and shake his hand. I hope the Pacific is as blue as it has been in my dreams. I hope I can get this ankle bracelet off without electrocuting myself. I hope."

Lewis met Dufresne while serving time for a drug violation. Before long, he befriended the lanky, mysterious man, who claimed to be in jail for a crime he didn't commit. Years later, when his friend and confidant escaped from prison, Lewis experienced dual feelings of joy and sorrow.

"I was happy for him, but at the same time I missed him," he recalled. "I just had to remind myself that some birds weren't meant to be caged. Their feathers are just too bright. When I think about the stuff he pulled, I just laugh. Like when he locked himself in the warden's office and put on that Italian opera music. It wasn't my kind of music, but still I felt something when I was listening to it. I felt free. And to tell you the truth, a little gay. But mostly free."

Soon after Dufresne escaped, Lewis received a postcard from Zihuatanejo, a place Andy had mentioned to him months earlier. When Lewis was let out on parole a few years later, he wasn't sure he could make it on the outside. But he knew he had to fulfill a promise he made to Andy.

"Before he escaped, Andy made me promise him something," Lewis said. "He made me promise to go to this field in Maine and

see ZIHUATANEJO, page 34

> ZIHUATANEJO, continued from page 33

dig under a bunch of rocks. He said there would be something there waiting for me. When I got out of prison, I fulfilled that promise, and found under those rocks in Maine a whole bunch of money. Apparently Andy forgot that I'm a highly paid professional athlete."

Lewis also found a letter, a bus ticket, and an invitation . . . to Zihuatanejo.

"When I found the letter, I knew I had to go. I had to go see my friend," said Lewis. "It was my destiny. The hard part was hitching a ride in Maine. Jesus Christ, you'd think those people had never seen a black guy before."

Now that he is on the long bus ride to Mexico, Lewis can think of nothing else except for his new life and his friend, Andy Dufresne.

"I just can't believe he was able to escape like that," he said. "It's really amazing. He dug a hole in his prison wall with a rock hammer. Then he crawled through a sewage pipe to get out of there. Andy Dufresne, who crawled through a river of shit and came out clean on the other side. Andy Dufresne, who had group sex with a gang of homosexual ruffians. Andy Dufresne, fixing a boat instead of just buying a new one. Andy Dufresne."

College Hoops Player Nails Game-Winning 3-Pointer, Your Daughter

MIAMI, FL—University of Miami point guard Damon Wallace was the hero Monday night after he hit the game-winning 3-pointer against division rival Boston College. The tattooed, dreadlocked ex-con then celebrated the victory by having sex with your daughter, who was reportedly "hammered" after drinking nine Zimas. "I was smokin' a blunt at some frat party and this bitch started hangin' all over me," said Wallace. "She was trashed. I recognized her from earlier in the night when she was making out with some other chick. I thought, 'Hey, why not just nail her?' And so I did." Your daughter was also seen lifting up her shirt and exposing her breasts for the *College Girls Gone Wild* cameraman, who attended the party. The DVD should be available on the Internet in time for the holidays.

Every Single Receiver in League Not Getting Enough Catches

INDIANAPOLIS, IN—The young football season has already had its share of controversy and drama, but nothing looms larger than the epidemic of wide receivers being dangerously underfed. According to several league sources, every single wide receiver in the league is not getting enough catches.

"It looks like it's reaching epidemic proportions," says ESPN analyst Michael Irvin. "Terrell Owens, Marvin Harrison, Peerless Price. What are they waiting for? They need to get these guys some catches fast."

Even successful teams are not immune to the current crisis. A recent poll of NFL receivers conducted by *Sports Illustrated* reveals that no wide receiver in the entire league believes he's getting the ball enough.

"According to our poll, 100 percent of receivers believe they are not getting fed the ball enough," said *Sports Illustrated*'s Peter King. "The number is astounding. And what are offensive coordinators in the league doing about it? Nothing, it seems. Just look at Terrell Owens. The poor guy's cracking up."

In addition to Owens, Indianapolis Colts wide receiver Marvin Harrison voiced concerns last week over his lack of involvement in the team's offensive game plan. The normally reserved Harrison publicly stated that he, too, needed to get the ball more.

"It's getting a little ridiculous," said Harrison. "I'm not out there to block or run patterns or be a decoy. This team needs to get me the ball, immediately."

The fact that Harrison's Colts are 4–0 certainly clouds the issue. But Irvin claims that regardless of how the team is performing, these receivers need to be fed.

"If someone is hungry, you feed him," said Irvin. "Marvin's hungry. The team's record doesn't matter. What matters is that we have a crisis on our hands. Are we going to address it? Are we going to take action?"

While Price, Owens, and Harrison are the most vocal of the group, the problem doesn't end with them. It's a league-wide epidemic, and it may get worse before it gets better.

ON THIS DAY...

In 1926, Gertrude Ederle became the first woman to swim the English Channel. She went missing halfway through her trip and is presumed to have drowned. No, wait a minute. That's Amelia Earhart. Ederle survived and went on to tour the vaudeville circuit.

Nation's Prostitutes Gearing Up for Start of NBA Season

Team With Lots of Heart Beaten by Team With Lots of Money

Hook-Wielding Maniac Terrorizes Local Fish Community

Iraq Constitution Fails to Address Steroid Issue

BAGHDAD, IRAQ—The new Iraqi constitution, slated to be completed by the end of this week, fails to address the steroid issue, sources reported Tuesday. The exclusion of language dealing with the hot-button issue has perplexed U.S. lawmakers, who saw it as a crucial element in the formation of a new Iraq.

"This is extremely confusing," said Rep. Cliff Stearns (R-FL), chairman of the Commerce, Trade and Consumer Protection Subcommittee, which held hearings on the steroid scandal earlier this year. "Why would a fledgling democracy not want to address an issue that is threatening the integrity of sports? They have stuff about federalism, security, oil, women's rights—everything you can think of, but no steroids. The Iraqi people deserve better than this."

Thomas M. Davis (R-VA) also criticized the Iraqis, saying the constitution is incomplete without an antisteroid bill.

"I have to voice my displeasure with this document," said Davis, himself chairman of the Government Reform Committee. "It pains me to think that the leaders of Iraq spent months working on this constitution and never once considered the impact of performance-enhancing drugs on their nation's youth. This is why the Middle East is so screwed up. We should just nuke the whole place and start over again."

Davis reminded the Iraqis of the tumultuous year Major League Baseball has had

see IRAQ, page 38

> IRAQ, continued from page 37

and expressed regret that they took no steps to avoid the same fate.

"They had an opportunity and they blew it. That's what kills me the most," said Davis. "I'm sure if the forefathers of America knew about the steroid problem, they would have made it their number one priority while writing the Constitution. We are trying to make up for their appalling lack of foresight and now, sadly, future generations of Iraqis will have to do the same thing."

The U.S. Congress has been actively involved in the steroid crisis for the past few years. When Iraqi lawmakers began work on their constitution, it was widely assumed that they would address the issue of performance-enhancing drugs in sports. However, that issue was low on their list of priorities.

"Yes, it is true that we neglected this so-called 'hot-button' issue," said Saleh al-Khalizad, member of the Shiite constitutional committee. "But that is only because we had many other topics to discuss, such as the role of Islam, Kurdish autonomy, security, and, of course, the rights of women. We did not get to the steroid thing. We were too busy trying not to get blown up. Perhaps someday our nation will be prosperous enough that we can spend our time worrying about urine."

Even if a law was introduced to deal with steroids, al-Khalizad says there would be no guarantee that all sides would agree to implement it.

"Before we address this, we must make sure all parties are in agreement," he said. "You know how the Sunnis are. They disagree with everything. We would probably have to twist their arms just to acknowledge that steroids exist. Then there is the logistical issue. We don't even have a usable pen right now. It ran out yesterday and we are waiting for a new one to be shipped from India. Why do you think we had this delay?"

Martina Navratilova Admits to Being Distracted by Opponent's Tight Little Ass

NEW YORK — Martina Navratilova's Wimbledon comeback bid ended Thursday in a second round match against 19-year-old Argentine Gisela Dulko. The 47-year-old Navratilova was defeated 3–6, 6–3, 6–3 by the 59th-ranked Dulko. When asked about the reason for her loss, Navratilova was quick to point out that her opponent is a hot little teenage vixen with a tight ass. "She was very quick and strong, but that's nothing new to me," said Navratilova. "The biggest challenge, I think, was her tight little ass. Did you see the skirt she was wearing?" Navratilova then pointed out that when she was in her prime, most women tennis players looked like out-of-shape schoolteachers.

Rasheed Wallace Vaguely Aware of Own Charity Foundation

PORTLAND, OR—Rasheed Wallace, power forward for the Portland Trail Blazers, is vaguely aware of the existence of the Rasheed Wallace Foundation. The charitable organization was created by Wallace's agent, Arn Tellem.

"Believe me, Rasheed is very active in the organization," said Tellem. "But he's also very busy with the basketball and can't work here full-time. Occasionally he shows up and signs some autographs for the sick kids. He doesn't like to be around the contagious ones for obvious reasons, but he does send them each an eight-by-ten glossy signed by his secretary."

The Rasheed Wallace Foundation was founded in 1997 when Wallace signed a long-term deal with the Portland Trail Blazers. According to Tellem, as soon as Wallace had inked the deal, he inquired about ways he could help the community.

"He asked if I had any suggestions about how he could do the most good for the most people, and I suggested he set up a charitable foundation," said Tellem. "He didn't have time to do the legwork himself, so he left me in charge of the Rasheed Wallace Foundation, and we've built ourselves a nice little staff here."

It is not unusual for high-profile players to set up charity foundations after signing long-term deals. It's an effective way for the athlete to establish himself as a pillar of the community and reach out to those in need. Incidentally, there is one additional benefit.

"A lot of cynical people will call the foundation a mere tax write-off," Tellem pointed out. "But it's more than that—much more than that. For example, the sick kids provide many good photo opportunities for Rasheed. I'm confident that Rasheed would be really proud of the organization. That is, if he had any clue it existed."

> "I'M CONFIDENT THAT RASHEED WOULD BE REALLY PROUD OF THE ORGANIZATION. THAT IS, IF HE HAD ANY CLUE IT EXISTED," SAID ARN TELLEM.

DID Y●U KNOW

In 1905, eighteen professional football players were killed during games. Our thoughts and prayers go out to them and their families.

LeBron James Buys Cavaliers, Trades Self to Lakers

CLEVELAND, OH—In a move that stunned the basketball world yesterday, teenage phenom and top draft pick LeBron James purchased the Cleveland Cavaliers and promptly traded himself to the Los Angeles Lakers, where he will join Karl Malone, Gary Payton, Kobe Bryant, and Shaquille O'Neal on a team destined for the finals.

"I've always wanted to own an NBA team," says James. "I've also wanted to play for the Lakers. Now I can do both."

The move was announced yesterday afternoon at a press conference held jointly by the Lakers and Cavs. According to team officials, James swooped in to purchase the Cavaliers at a price of $200 million and then wasted no time in pulling the trigger on the blockbuster deal.

"LeBron made me an offer I couldn't refuse," said Gordon Gund, former owner of the Cavs. "$200 million is three times what I paid for the team. How could I say no?"

The Lakers reported that immediately after purchasing the Cavs, James phoned Lakers GM Mitch Kupchak and offered him a deal *he* couldn't refuse.

"He offered to trade himself to the Lakers for next to nothing," said Kupchak. "Well, not exactly nothing. He did ask for a bag of basketballs, but that was it. I discussed it with my staff and decided it was a sound deal."

There was no immediate report on how many basketballs were in the bag, but James insists the deal was a fair one.

"We're talking about Spalding basketballs, very high quality. The best money can buy.

"I'VE ALWAYS WANTED TO OWN AN NBA TEAM," SAYS JAMES. "I'VE ALSO WANTED TO PLAY FOR THE LAKERS. NOW I CAN DO BOTH."

Plus, they're already pumped up. They can use these things at practice, during games, whatever. They certainly have a lot of options there."

James went on to say that as the new owner of the Cavs, he isn't finished making bold moves to improve the club.

"I'm not going to sit idly by as owner of the Cavs. In fact, I'm working on deals now to get rid of some of the dead weight on the team and bring on some people who want to compete. For example, we're looking to move Jason Kapono, our second draft pick. We'll probably move him to the Lakers, too, since we have a good relationship with them. It's time for the Cavs to start rebuilding."

Special Olympics Targeted by Special Terrorists

SCOTTSDALE, AZ—Homeland Security officials warned today that the Special Olympics could be targeted by special terrorists. Precautions are being taken by local and federal law enforcement agencies to protect athletes and spectators.

"As you know, we take every threat to our nation seriously," said Homeland Security chief Tom Ridge. "These terrorists are gunning for the Special Olympics, and we're doing everything we can to stop them. The good news is: It shouldn't be too hard, since they're retarded."

Ridge cited increased security checkpoints, random searches, and bomb-sniffing dogs as some of the precautions being taken against the latest threat. Traps are also being set as a way to lure the special terrorists into exposing themselves.

"One thing we're working on is going to take place at the main entrance to the games," said Ridge, standing in front of a multicolored chart depicting the layout of the Olympic grounds. "There are two main entrances, but we will add a third as a deceptive ploy to trick these murderous thugs. It will read 'Crazed Islamic Suicide Bomber Entrance.' Hopefully, the terrorists will see this sign and head right in, then we got 'em. And don't give me any of that shit about 'leaks' or 'compromising security.' These are retards, people. They're not watching the news."

The terror threat against the Special Olympics was first reported last week, after an audiotape received from an Islamic militant group threatened to turn the event into "a river of blood." The tape, aired by al-Jazeera, is believed to be authentic.

"Oh, you evil Zionist pigs, we are the Very

see TERRORISTS, page 42

Extreme Bass Fishing Pretty Much the Same as Regular Bass Fishing

BRISTOL, CT—According to sources, ESPN's new *Extreme Bass Fishing* is pretty much the same as regular bass fishing, except the competitors wear wraparound sunglasses and shout things when they catch fish. "Extreme Bass Fishing is um . . . well, it's a lot like regular bass fishing except more extreme," said Shelly Stegemen, producer. "See, regular bass fishing doesn't have a slamming heavy metal soundtrack and trash-talking fisherman. It's so boring. This is not your granddaddy's fishing show, so if you can't handle some hard-core, in-your-face fishing action with lots of attitude, then. . . . Oh, forget it. I can't even do this anymore."

> TERRORISTS, continued from page 41

Special Islamic Mujahideen Death Squad," the voice on the tape began. "We will attack you where you live, where you sleep, and where you gather. The Special Olympics will be a bloodbath, God willing. Our holy warriors will strike at the heart of the enemy to receive their everlasting gift of martyrdom. Yaaaaayyyyyy!"

The Very Special Islamic Mujahideen Death Squad (VSIMDS) is believed to be a new terrorist group with indirect ties to Osama bin Laden's al-Qaeda network. Its existence was unknown prior to the airing of last week's audiotape, but now investigators believe it is a very real, and very lethal, group.

"Many retarded people in the Middle East are disenfranchised by American policies, just like their nonretarded counterparts," said Muhammad al-Atef, author of *Inside al-Qaeda* and an expert on international terrorism. "These people want to show the world that they are capable of carrying out suicide attacks just as well as anyone else. They probably chose to target the Special Olympics for their symbolic value, and because attacking the real Olympics would require half a brain."

An al-Qaeda commander, known only as "Wahid," recently spoke out on behalf of the VSIMDS.

"Just because they have mental deficiencies doesn't mean they're unable to strap explosives to their bodies and blow themselves to pieces," said Wahid. "They just want to be treated the same as any other suicide bombers. They aren't looking for a handout or charity, just a fair opportunity to enact revenge on the infidel Satans."

LeAnn Rimes Clearly Not Wearing Panties During National Anthem

PHILADELPHIA, PA—LeAnn Rimes, pop superstar, clearly was not wearing panties during her stirring rendition of the national anthem at Lincoln Financial Field in Philadelphia Sunday night. Dozens of players on both teams observed that Rimes had no panty line whatsoever. "She's definitely not wearing panties," said Todd Pinkston of the Eagles. "Look, you would see some kind of line or something wouldn't you?" Even the commentators, Al Michaels and John Madden, couldn't help but notice. Said Michaels: "Stirring rendition of the national anthem by LeAnn Rimes, even more so because you can see a little camel toe. Wow. Come to Daddy. Do you believe in miracles? Yes I do."

Lance Armstrong's Kids Touched By How In Love He Is

"WHENEVER I SEE HIM AND SHERYL ON TV, I GET SO EXCITED! I SAY, 'LOOK! THERE'S DADDY AND THAT WOMAN HE LIKES BETTER THAN MOM,'" SAID JENNIFER ARMSTRONG.

PAU, FRANCE—Ever since divorcing his wife in 2003, cyclist Lance Armstrong has been on a whirlwind romance with rock star Sheryl Crow. The famous couple seems to be everywhere these days, and nobody is happier for them than Armstrong's two children, who are touched by how in love their dad is.

"I'm so happy for my dad," said Armstrong's 8-year-old daughter, Jennifer. "He's finally found someone he can spend the rest of his life with. Whenever I see him and Sheryl on TV, I get so excited! I say, 'Look! There's Daddy and that woman he likes better than Mom.' And they're so cute together. It took a little getting used to at first, but now I'm just so happy that Daddy's found his soul mate."

Armstrong's son, Jared, is equally excited for his dad.

"Yay, Dad! He's so in love right now. It's awesome!" said Jared, 9. "Every time I turn on the TV, I see them together. They look so glamorous! I remember last year when he won the Tour de France and Sheryl got up on the podium with him. Mom used to do that with him, but it's obvious that Sheryl is way better. It's just nice to know that a person his age can still find true love."

When the children first heard the news of their dad's new sweetheart, they were saddened. But after a while they realized that Crow and their dad were meant to be together.

"It was hard at first," admitted Jennifer. "Just knowing that my parents didn't want to be together anymore made me really sad. Then when I found out that he was with somebody else, I got upset. But that didn't last long. I learned that when a grown man finds a person that completes him, everyone needs to step aside and let that love blossom—including the children. I guess I was just being selfish at first."

This year will be Armstrong's last at the Tour de France. The seven-time champion plans to retire so he can spend more time with his children and Sheryl Crow.

"My kids, they've been terrific. What can I say?" Armstrong told reporters at a press conference. "I'm sure it was pretty shocking for them at first to see me on TV every five minutes snuggling with someone who isn't their mom. But they dealt with it pretty well.

see ARMSTRONG, page 44

> ARMSTRONG, continued from page 43

In a way I think it helped them. It helped to drive home the point that their mom and me would never, ever get back together and that our family would never be the same again. I just can't say enough about how supportive they've been. Anyway, enough about them. Let's talk about Sheryl."

Some experts, however, say that the current situation is unhealthy and could be trau-matic for the Armstrong children for years to come.

"This is an unusual situation for those children," said psychologist Dr. Leonard Hunt. "One day you've got a normal family life and the next day your dad and mom don't love each other anymore and your dad is running around town with some rock star. To add insult to injury, it's Sheryl Crow, who hasn't had a decent song in, like, five years."

Fat Guy Bagging Groceries Looks a Lot Like Brian Bosworth

VAN NUYS, CA—According to witnesses, a fat guy bagging groceries at a Stop & Shop in Van Nuys, CA, looks an awful lot like ex-footballer Brian Bosworth, a former top draft pick for the Seattle Seahawks. "That guy looks just like the Boz," said Barry Gearson, 32. "The same facial expression, the same kind of hair, only much, much fatter. As soon as I saw him, I knew. I guess after football he didn't have anything to really fall back on." To confirm his suspicions, Gearson asked him directly. "I asked if he was Boz, and he looked at me and said, 'What's it to you?' Talk about a dead giveaway. It was obviously him, or he wouldn't have said that."

Bowling Tournament Raises $68 For Breast Cancer

EVERGREEN, AL—A local bowling tournament raised $68 to fight breast cancer Saturday night. The money was immediately sent in check form to the National Breast Cancer Foundation (NBCF) to be used in the fight against breast cancer. Edna Herbert, the hero who organized the event, said that it was a "roaring success" and that donations shattered last year's record of $63. "It feels good to give something back to the community," said Herbert, 67, whose impressive résumé also includes donating two dozen cans of lima beans to the tsunami relief effort. "Breast cancer is such a worthy cause. It's great to join the battle against it."

Free Agent Narrows Choices Down to Whichever Team Has the Most Money

Scientist Turns Into Mutant Superhero Following Exposure to Barry Bonds' Urine Sample

Obscenity Uttered at College Basketball Game

NHL Adds Two New Franchises During Lockout

TORONTO, CANADA—In the midst of a lengthy lockout, NHL owners have taken bold steps to increase revenue and tap into new markets across North America. Undeterred by the lack of a collective bargaining agreement and a downward spiral in fan interest, the league has announced the creation of two new franchises—the Mississippi Ice Cats and the New Mexico Frost.

"This is a great day for the NHL and another example of how diverse our product really is," said commissioner Gary Bettman at a press conference on Friday. "The Ice Cats and the Frost represent our first venture into two lucrative new markets, New Mexico and Mississippi. The NHL is one of the fastest-growing sports in the country. Watch out, women's lacrosse! We're snapping at your heels!"

Bettman scoffed at suggestions that the league should curtail expansion due to the current work stoppage.

"We're not going to let this labor strife stop us from spreading our game all over North America," he said. "Unbridled expansion is the key to success in any sport. That's what made the NHL so great. In the nineties, we just expanded and expanded and expanded and pretty soon everyone in America was crazy for hockey. Just think, if it wasn't for expansion, there would be no Phoenix Coyotes or Columbus Blue Jackets. What a chilling thought."

Players' union head Bob Goodenow expressed mild surprise at the decision to expand the league. With negotiations currently at a standstill, there might not even be hockey next year.

"Um . . . we're expanding? Wow, that's an interesting approach, I guess," said Goodenow. "You think they would've learned their lesson from all the expansion they did in the nineties that pretty much ruined the sport. Apparently they feel that the southern United States is a region ripe for NHL expansion."

Goodenow is not sure how the league expects to generate enough revenue to support two more teams, especially with the current financial climate.

"Plenty of franchises out there are struggling just to stay afloat," he said. "Half the teams that were added ten years ago are on the verge of being contracted. This just proves that NHL owners are delusional. They have no idea how limited the appeal of their sport actually is. But, hey, at least they're not as delusional as the players' union. We still think it's okay to hit one another over the head with sticks."

But in Jackson, MS, citizens are gearing up for a new NHL franchise. According to club officials, a total of nine people have already inquired about Ice Cats season tickets.

Over in New Mexico, officials admitted that fan interest is extremely low, but they have been reassured by commissioner Bettman and the other owners that things will pick up.

"Things have been a little slow, but that's to be expected," said Bettman. "Obviously with the lockout, things have been slow, but we're in this for the long haul. If history shows one thing, it's that expansion works. I didn't get this far by making bad decisions. I got this far by making great decisions that went terribly wrong. There's a difference."

> "I DIDN'T GET THIS FAR BY MAKING BAD DECISIONS. I GOT THIS FAR BY MAKING GREAT DECISIONS THAT WENT TERRIBLY WRONG," SAID GARY BETTMAN.

Red Sox Players Tell Bostonians to Get a Life

BOSTON, MA—Boston Red Sox fans are known as the most intense baseball fans in the country. Each year the Fenway faithful follow their team with a passion and zeal normally reserved for Islamic fundamentalists. With interest in the club at an all-time high, Sox players and coaches have a message for Boston residents: Get a life.

"When I first came here from Oakland, people told me the fans here were rabid, but I didn't expect this much," said outfielder Johnny Damon. "It's all they talk about, even during the off-season. They live and die with us. Jesus, we're just a baseball team. Maybe it's time for these people to get their priorities straight.

"And what's up with the eighty-one straight sellouts at Fenway?" he continued. "Eighty-one straight? Don't these people have anything better to spend their money on?"

Sox fans are so committed that some have confessed to ruining their marriages or

see RED SOX, page 48

> RED SOX, continued from page 47

neglecting their children in order to follow the team more closely.

Owner John Henry has heard his share of stories from obsessed Bostonians.

"Every Boston fan has a story," Henry told *The Boston Globe.* "And they're usually pretty pathetic. One guy told me he decided against buying his girlfriend an engagement ring after he got a chance to get season tickets to the Sox. I laughed while he was telling me, but inside I was thinking, 'Grow the fuck up.' Another guy told me he was really concerned that his son might grow up a Yankee fan because his wife, the child's mother, is from New York. He said he stays up at night worrying about it. If I were him, I'd be more concerned that the kid will grow up to be an emotionally crippled man-child like his father."

Most members of Red Sox nation are proud of their unflagging support for the home team. In fact, obsessing over the Sox has turned into a game of one-upmanship, with fans comparing stories about their disturbing levels of commitment.

"I had to blow a guy to get tickets to last weekend's series against the Yankees," said 21-year-old college student Jason Zimmerman. "He was a scalper, and I just didn't have enough money to buy the ticket. I was going to walk away, but then I remembered that Pedro was pitching, and there was just no way I was going to miss it. So I figured, 'What the hell?' It's something I've always wanted to do . . . watch Pedro pitch, that is."

As it turned out, the players weren't impressed at all.

"Grow up, get a grip—how many different ways can I say it?" asked first baseman Kevin Millar. "Go read a book. Spend some time with your kids. Watch the news, for God's sake. It's like having a needy girlfriend who won't leave you alone, and she's always asking where you're going and who you're going with, and she gets mad at the stupidest little things, and she's totally clingy, and you just wanna say, 'Get a life, bitch!' "

U.S. Hoping al-Qaeda Doesn't Find Out About Olympics

WASHINGTON, DC—Due to global instability and lingering security concerns, the United States is hoping that the al-Qaeda terrorist network does not get wind of the upcoming Olympics in Beijing, China. The administration has issued a warning to its allies to keep a stiff upper lip with regard to the games. "We'd like to remind our friends and allies not to tell anyone from al-Qaeda about the Olympics," Attorney General Alberto Gonzalez told reporters at a press conference today. "If we can keep a lid on this thing, we'll have a better chance of preventing an attack. Those people are everywhere, and if they find out about this thing, we could all be in some serious trouble. Remember, loose lips sink ships. And yes, I'm talking to you, Belgium."

55-Year-Old Rudy Still Carrying On About That One Stupid Play

AURORA, IL—Rudy Ruettiger, 55-year-old retired construction worker, is still carrying on about that one stupid play he got into during a Notre Dame game in 1970.

"Big fucking deal," says Rudy's son-in-law, Terrence. "I'm sorry, but I'm just not all that impressed. Sounds like he just had an unhealthy obsession with Notre Dame and the coach threw him a bone because he felt bad for him. Congratulations."

According to sources close to the Ruettiger family, the elder Ruettiger spends most of his days in a large easy chair musing over his one moment of glory.

"The guy's just living in the past," says Terrence. "I feel sorry for him, actually. The whole story is a little sad if you ask me. And if I have to sit through that corny-ass movie one more time, I'm gonna jump out the window."

Among those who have been annoyed by Ruettiger's incessant reminiscing are his grandchildren.

"Grandpa's always tellin' us that same story," said granddaughter Sally, 8. "I don't understand why all the people were yelling his name 'n stuff. All he did was run on the field for one play. So what?"

Not only is he irritating family members with his anecdotes, Ruettiger is currently touring on the lecture circuit, commanding close to $10,000 a speech and boring listeners nationwide. Most recently he spoke at the Brown University commencement, where he disappointed more than a few graduates.

"Yale gets Hillary Clinton, and we get Rudy?" lamented Mark Godfrey, a member of Brown's class of 2006. "The only interesting thing about it was seeing how he could stretch one lame-ass story into an entire speech. I wasn't sure he could do it, but he did. The kid sure is scrappy."

In addition to his speaking engagements, Ruettiger is brainstorming about more Rudy-themed future ventures, including a Rudy Saturday morning cartoon, a Rudy music album featuring duets with popular stars like 50 Cent and Justin Timber-lake, and even a *Rudy* reality TV show.

"The reality TV show is something I'm really looking forward to," said Ruettiger. "It'll just be me going through my daily life and encountering various travails and difficulties along the way. That way America can see first-hand my trademark earnestness, persistence, and determination. Actually, it really is trade-marked. So don't repeat that."

One of Ruettiger's former teammates claims that by making a full-length feature film out of Rudy's life, Hollywood created a monster.

"Talk about blowing something out of proportion," said Roy Boynton, linebacker for the '70 Notre Dame team. "The kid runs on the field for one play, maybe twenty people in the crowd are chanting his name because they feel sorry for him, and that was it. It wasn't like he found the cure for polio or something. If I hear the name 'Rudy' one more time, I'm going to shoot someone."

> "TALK ABOUT BLOWING SOMETHING OUT OF PROPORTION . . . IF I HEAR THE NAME 'RUDY' ONE MORE TIME, I'M GOING TO SHOOT SOMEONE," SAID NOTRE DAME'S ROY BOYNTON.

Allen Iverson Just Five Years Away From Regretting All the Tattoos

"THESE TATTOOS . . . SYMBOLIZE WHO I AM AND STUFF," SAID IVERSON.

PHILADELPHIA, PA—Allen Iverson may be proud of his tattoos now, but that will change in a few years. According to psychologists, people who cover themselves with tattoos in their early twenties generally experience overwhelming feelings of regret around the age of 35. At age 30, Iverson is just five years away from such remorse.

"Allen is a typical example of a person who, at a young age, was unable or unwilling to consider the consequences of littering his body with bad body art," said Dr. Arthur Straub, psychologist. "I'm afraid he is facing a bleak future of regret and horror at the fact that his sagging, aging skin is cluttered with unsightly pictures and ridiculous slogans. It's kind of funny, really, the way bad decisions come back to bite you in the ass."

Straub said that laser surgery would not be an option for Iverson because of the sheer number and size of the tattoos on his body.

"There's nothing at all that he can do. He's powerless to change his appearance," said Straub. "And that's too bad because some of those tattoos are pretty lame. He has one that says 'Cru Thik.' That's the name of his record company. On his right arm is a picture of a soldier's head. The words 'east end' run vertically down his left leg. Oh, and on his right leg he has another 'Cru Thik' tattoo. What a mess. It does make me feel better about that big Spin Doctors tattoo I have on my back, though."

When reached for comment, Iverson scoffed at the notion that he would regret his tattoos.

"To say that I'm going to regret these tattoos is just ignorant," said Iverson. "I love my tattoos. They symbolize who I am and stuff. There is no way I will ever feel any different about things than I do right now. In fact, I'm thinking of getting another one. I heard this great expression the other day that really blew me away. Ready? 'When the going gets tough, the tough get going.' Wow. That one's going on my forehead."

With the tattoo fad now reaching into the college game and even the high school game, Straub has suggested an awareness program to educate young athletes on the pros and cons of tattoos. However, he realizes getting the message across will be difficult.

"It's so widespread now. Kids really think it's the thing to do," said Straub. "Even perfectly normal, well-adjusted kids feel the need to get at least one tattoo. Maybe we could tell them that if they're not careful, they'll end up looking like Kenyon Martin. Talk about being scared straight."

Husband Joins Wednesday Night Drinking League

ITHACA, NY—Charles Clifton announced today that he has joined a Wednesday night drinking league, which meets every week at the Golden Pin in Ithaca. His wife, Mary Clifton, is glad to see her husband get a social life. "It's good for a man his age to get out at night and be with his friends," she said. "It's good that he's being honest with me, too. There's no need to lie and say that it's a 'bowling league' when I know damn well he's only there to get wasted. Plus, him being away gives me a chance to sit at home and drink vodka."

Hunter Proud of Outsmarting Elk

JACKSON HOLE, WY—Hunter J. B. Geary of Jackson Hole, WY, was extremely proud of being able to outsmart an elk during a weekend hunting trip, even though he is a heavily armed adult human being and the elk was an unarmed wild animal with a brain the size of golf ball. "That, my friend, is how to outsmart an elk," Geary, 40, told his son after shooting one down. "See, it's not enough just to hide behind the tree. You also have to keep dead silent, and make sure he can't see your hands or the muzzle of your gun. Then when he gets into view, take aim and—boom—you got your trophy." Last week Geary outsmarted a duck by luring it with a whistle and then shooting it.

Zack Jealous of Slater's New Job

LOS ANGELES, CA—Zack Morris of Bayside High School is jealous of his friend Slater's new job, sources reported Tuesday. Slater has been named cohost of *ESPN Hollywood*, a show that mixes sports news and celebrity gossip. According to their friends, the two haven't spoken since third period yesterday. "Zack is really upset right now," said Kelly Kapowski, 17. "He's jealous that Slater got that job hosting *ESPN Hollywood*. You know how those two are. They are so competitive! Zack just has to learn that being friends with someone means supporting them, not being jealous of them. Besides, he has no reason to be jealous. I saw the show last night and it's the gayest piece of shit I've ever seen."

Hospitalized Fighter Pilot Endures Three-Hour Visit From Arizona Cardinals

LANDSTUHL, GERMANY—During a grueling six-month tour of duty in Iraq, Sgt. Lance Peterson went through hell. His chopper was shot down by insurgents in Tikrit and he narrowly evaded capture by crawling on his hands and knees one hundred miles through the desert and across the border into Iran, where he sought refuge. Now recovering from surgery, Peterson longs to be back on the battlefield. During his long stay in the infirmary, he's had to endure weeks of painful rehabilitation as well as a grueling three-hour visit from the last-place Arizona Cardinals.

"Rehab is hard, and that crash landing sure was awful," said Peterson. "But I'd take any of that over another visit with those guys. I didn't even know any of them. It was just three hours of weird, awkward silence."

In recent months the U.S. military has been working with the NFL to organize meetings between players and wounded members of the armed forces.

"As soon as I heard about it, I was pretty psyched," Peterson said. "I was praying for the Packers because I really love Brett Favre. The Eagles would have been good, too. But no, I got the Arizona Cardinals. And Emmitt Smith wasn't even there. He sent an auto-graphed picture, which I clung to tightly while somebody named J. J. Arrington told me his life story."

Players from the Arizona Cardinals say they were "humbled and honored" to visit the fallen soldiers.

"It was such a great experience," said offensive guard Leonard Davis. "Those people are the real heroes. What we do is just a game. These guys are out there protecting our freedoms. They deserve all the attention and fame, not us."

"Who the fuck is Leonard Davis?" Peterson asked after speaking with the guard for over thirty minutes. "Nice guy and all, but I could've been talking to the janitor and it wouldn't have made one bit of difference. I was afraid to ask him his name because I didn't want to be rude, so I just waited till he signed my cast. He wrote 'Lenny.' I thought it said 'Larry.' So I said 'Thanks, Larry' and he corrected me. That may have been the single most uncomfortable moment of my life."

Peterson was able to endure only two hours and thirty minutes of the three-hour visit before he escaped the only way he knew how.

"I have a permanent morphine drip stuck into my arm. I'm not big into drugs, but with thirty minutes left in that snooze-a-thon, I decided I couldn't take it anymore and started pressing the button like crazy. I think I gave myself enough morphine to down a rhinoceros. I didn't wake up till three days later."

Running back Marcel Shipp was alarmed by Peterson's sudden loss of consciousness.

"I was telling him about our 44–6 loss to the Cleveland Browns when all of a sudden his eyes rolled to the back of his head and he just lost it. He was gone—out like a light. I thought he was dead, but it turns out he was just sleeping. Poor guy must've been exhausted from all the excitement."

Fugitive al-Qaeda Leader Forced to Get NFL Scores by Courier

MIRANSHAH, PAKISTAN—According to a letter intercepted by U.S. forces in Iraq, Ayman al-Zawahri, the second-ranked al-Qaeda leader in the world, is being forced to get his NFL scores and fantasy stats by courier camel. The letter, which was sent to al-Qaeda's leader in Iraq, inquired about the current state of the insurgency and hinted that the terror network's communication system had completely broken down.

"My brother, our communications have been destroyed by the infidels," the letter began. "We are able to get information only by courier camel, and that can take weeks. So I must ask you: How goes the insurgency? Are the crusaders retreating into their foxholes? Also, how are the Chicago Bears doing? The last I heard they were 1–1 and Kyle Orton was starting at QB. Can this be? Please inform. The courier camel is not expected to arrive for another two weeks."

The letter also detailed the workings of the terror mastermind's crude communications network.

"Every month, a boy on a camel is sent to Kabul to get the NFL scores and stats from Ahmed over at al-Jazeera," al-Zawahri said. "Once Ahmed prints them off his computer, he gives them to the boy, who tucks the document into his pants and journeys through the tribal region to bring it to me. My brother, I cannot tell you how I long for that document every day. It is all I have left. Damn the fat Americans and their cell phones that receive up-to-date scores from around the league. We will have no such problems, my brother, when we achieve our pan-Islamic state across the Middle East. That should happen within a week or so, yes?"

Finally, al-Zawahri inquired about the NFL power rankings.

"Have you seen any power rankings lately? I was wondering where my beloved Oakland Raiders were ranked. They have recently signed that snake, Randy Moss. He is a godless infidel, and the sword of Islam will

see AL-QAEDA, page 54

> AL-QAEDA, continued from page 53

someday crush him, God willing, but he does provide a much-needed deep threat. Anyway, good luck with the car bombings and such. At this rate, you'll probably run out of cars. LOL."

U.S. officials say that the letter is a "fascinating glimpse" into the everyday life of al-Zawahri and the inner workings of the al-Qaeda network in Afghanistan. The fact that the terrorist mastermind is unable to attain NFL scores is proof that the U.S. strategy is working, says one intelligence source.

"We have completely destroyed their communications network," said the source, speaking on condition of anonymity. "I mean, who the hell can't get NFL scores? I can't walk down the street without being hit over the head with them. Clearly this guy is living in a pretty isolated state and his communication is severely limited. Actually, I kind of feel sorry for him. Poor bastard thinks the Raiders are doing well this year. Boy, is he in for a rude awakening."

When told of the terrorist commander's inability to get up-to-the-minute scoring updates, NFL commissioner Paul Tagliabue offered a helping hand. The league is planning to work with Afghan authorities to provide al-Zawahri with stats, analysis, and rankings at the earliest date possible.

"We have heard the cries for help from Mr. al-Zawahri," Tagliabue said. "It has always been our policy that nobody, not even the worst criminals, deserve to be deprived of the National Football League. Therefore we will be working with Afghanistan and the Taliban remnants to bring relief to the lawless tribal region of Pakistan as soon as possible. He can also get some quality NFL merchandise—caps, sweatshirts, and shorts—at a discounted rate, since they're all manufactured about three miles from where he's hiding."

Popular Sports Cliché Celebrates One Millionth Utterance

LOS ANGELES, CA—A popular, time-tested sports cliché celebrated its one-millionth utterance yesterday when the Dodgers' Shawn Green uttered it at a press conference after a game with the Houston Astros. "We're just gonna take it one game at a time," said Green, unaware that he had spoken the famous cliché for the millionth time in MLB history. As soon as the words came out of his mouth, noisemakers sounded, confetti fell from above, and Commissioner Bud Selig emerged from out of nowhere to shake his hand and inform him of the milestone.

"Wow, this is quite an honor," said Green. "That cliché has served me and my fellow players quite well over the years, and it's great to be part of this special day." The cliché was first uttered by the Yankees' Mickey Mantle in 1961, in reference to his and Roger Maris's pursuit of Babe Ruth's home run record.

Brazilian Soccer Fan Trampled For Third Time This Month

Budweiser Targets Tailgaters with New Meat-Flavored Beer

Ricky Williams Formally Apologizes for Being Lenny Kravitz Fan

Chain-Smoking, Alcoholic Little League Coach Not So Funny in Real Life

BARRON, WI—Larry Mueller is not your typical little league coach. The 42-year-old unemployed construction worker drinks, smokes, and curses, often right in front of the children. Parents often compare his behavior to the lovable curmudgeon portrayed by Billy Bob Thornton in *The Bad News Bears*. Unfortunately, those parents learned that a chain-smoking, alcoholic little league coach is not so funny in real life.

"Jesus, that guy is an asshole," said Sandy Tucker, whose son Taylor is a pitcher on Mueller's team. "He swears right in front of the kids. Plus he's constantly drinking and smoking. I thought it was funny in that *Bad News Bears* movie, but in real life it's not funny at all."

Tucker was especially irritated when Mueller arrived at a game last week heavily intoxicated and barely able to stand up. He spent the first three innings yelling at the children and the last three sleeping on the bench.

"That was the last straw," Tucker said.

"All the parents cornered him afterward and told him to straighten up his act or we'd get him fired. He just laughed in our faces and took another sip of whiskey. Then as he was walking away, he threw the empty bottle at my son. It hit him right in the head. Talk about un-funny. I'll never look at alcoholism the same way again."

Mueller was named coach of the Hal's Bait Shop team earlier this year as part of his community service for his drunk driving conviction. He accepted the position as an alternative to a sixty-day jail sentence.

"I don't know why these parents get so irritated with me," Mueller said. "Haven't they ever seen *Bad News Bears*? I'm a lovable old oaf, just like Walter Matthau or Billy Bob Thornton. I'm not politically correct. I'm a little rough around the edges, but underneath it all I've got a heart of gold. The only difference between me and coach Morris Buttermaker is that I'm a real person and he's not. Also, I've got herpes."

Unlike the kids in the movie, Mueller's players are actually getting worse as the season wears on. At the rate they're going, they will finish in last place with a total of 0 victories.

"We suck," said 10-year-old Danny Gorseman. "At the beginning of the season we thought we might be pretty good, but then Mueller took over and we lost all hope. The guy doesn't even know half our names. He's a fucking idiot. What's worse, his language is rubbing off on us."

Fortunately the end is in sight for the beleaguered children, as the season wraps up next month.

"I'm going to miss these little rascals," Mueller said. "When I first got here I thought I was really going to hate it, but eventually the kids and I forged a bond. It's been a learning experience for all of us, even the parents. Sure, they may hate me now, but they'll all come crawling back when Hollywood decides to make a movie about me."

Astros Ownership Looking to Build Less Gay Ballpark

HOUSTON, TX—Astros owner Drayton McLane is urging city officials to approve funding for a new ballpark that is less gay than Minute Maid Park. "I was walking around the field just to clear my head, when all of a sudden it hit me: This place is totally gay," said McLane, who spent $265 million on the park. "I mean, what's with those cutesy arches and that ridiculous hill in center field? It's something a 10-year-old girl would've designed. Oh, and don't even get me started on the name. Minute Maid Park. We may as well have just named it the 'Tampax Pussy Palace.'"

THE BRUSHBACK GLOSSARY

SLAM DUNK: The act of depositing a ball through a basketball hoop at close range, usually while screaming "motherfucker."

Loser To Get Breaking Fantasy News E-Mailed To Him

OMAHA, NE—Barry Elderidge, 28-year-old loser, has signed up to get the latest fantasy news e-mailed to him by NFL.com. The service will provide Elderidge with up-to-the-minute news alerts about injuries, transactions, and predictions from around the league. "For a fantasy freak like me, this is like a dream come true," said Elderidge, a resident of Omaha, NE, and  participant in three different fantasy football leagues. "Now if one of my guys gets hurt or traded, or moves down the depth chart, I'm getting an e-mail notification almost instantaneously. It gives me a head start on the rest of the guys in my league, who have to get their news the old-fashioned way—by manually visiting the website." Elderidge tried replying to an e-mail alert last week when he was "really bored," but his reply was returned as undeliverable.

Tattooed, Cornrowed NBA Player Proud of Being Conformist

DETROIT, MI—Detroit Pistons rookie Darius Thompson, with cornrows in his hair and tattoos on his arms, is proud to be a conformist, sources reported Tuesday. The shooting guard from the University of Miami said he always wanted to be a conformist, and joining the NBA has finally made that dream come true. "I've always wanted to look exactly like everybody else," said Thompson, who occasionally wears a headband for no reason other than his insatiable desire to conform. "When I was at Miami, I was clean-cut and didn't have any tattoos. But when I joined the NBA, I got the official NBA makeover. It's like a rite of passage. Rigid conformity is what this league is all about. I'm just happy to be part of it."

THE BRUSHBACK REPORT

ALL THE SPORTS NEWS THAT'S UNFIT TO PRINT

Report: Some Professional Athletes May Not Be Adequately Fellated

WASHINGTON, DC—An alarming report released today by Columbia University indicated that some professional athletes may not be adequately fellated. Experts around the country are calling the underfellation of our nation's athletes the sports world's "dirty little secret."

"You won't hear people talking about this on *SportsCenter*," said Dr. Althea Hoffman, who spearheaded the study. "It's something that's been swept under the carpet, so a lot of people are going to be surprised by the sheer number of athletes who have slipped through the cracks here. It's hard to believe that something like this could happen in our country."

If true, the chilling report will be a major embarrassment for the sports world, and for the nation in general. The lavishing of oral favors on our sports stars is a ritual dating back decades to the dawn of the television age. In fact, many athletes report that if it weren't for oral sex, they never would've considered a career in sports.

"Everyone knows that jocks get crazy blow jobs all the time," said one high-profile NFL player. "In high school it was still sort of hard to get head, but I knew if I worked hard, practiced every day, and studied tape, that eventually I'd have all I could handle. And I have

not been disappointed. I can pretty much get it anytime I want, which makes sense because I can catch a football."

Though most athletes do still claim to be adequately fellated, the report has sparked a flurry of interest among fans and media. Many are wondering if the outrageous claims are true, and, if so, what effect underfellation will have on the national sports landscape.

"There are athletes out there, professional athletes, who are giving it their all—night in and night out—and all they ask is for a little head," said basketball analyst Bill Walton. "Are you telling me that we as a society can't give a little back to these men, these gladiators, who put their bodies on the line just to enter-

see FELLATIO, page 60

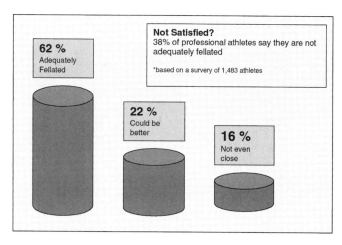

Not Satisfied?
38% of professional athletes say they are not adequately fellated

*based on a survery of 1,483 athletes

62 %
Adequately Fellated

22 %
Could be better

16 %
Not even close

> FELLATIO, continued from page 59

tain us? Come on, America. These dicks are not going to suck themselves."

NFL commissioner Paul Tagliabue admitted that pro-sports leagues must do more to ensure that their players are being adequately blown.

"We have to look in the mirror to address this problem. We all must be held accountable, as owners, commissioners, and GMs, to ensure that this problem is stamped out before it becomes an epidemic," Tagliabue told reporters yesterday. "George Bush did not wait for Saddam Hussein to attack the United States, and we will not wait for the lack of fellation to bring the sports world to its knees, so to speak."

Though Tagliabue seems sincere, some in the league feel the commissioner is just giving the problem lip service.

"Tagliabue is a hypocrite," said one league insider. "He knew about this problem five years ago, when the players union sent a memo to his office detailing a sharp drop-off in the volume of blow jobs. The front office scoffed at the memo back then, and now they're just trying to cover their tracks. Same can be said for the NBA, MLB, and the NHL. Well, not the NHL. Those toothless bastards weren't getting that much head in the first place."

The Brushback Presents
QUICK QUESTIONS WITH A REFORMED STEROID USER

BB: So what was it like to do steroids?

SU: It was awful. The worst time of my life.

BB: Really? What happened?

SU: I won the home run crown and became an international superstar.

BB: I see. What else happened?

SU: I married a model.

BB: That doesn't sound awful.

SU: No, on second thought, it was actually pretty cool.

Disembodied Voice in Iowa Cornfield Urges Farmer to Go On Shooting Spree

POSTVILLE, IA—It was a day just like any other day for Iowa farmer Ray Manzella. The 36-year-old Postville resident was tending to his cornfield and relaxing in the summer sunshine when a mysterious disembodied voice called out to him from above and implored him to "Go the distance."

At first Manzella believed it was his imagination, but after hearing the voice three days in a row, he knew it was for real.

"I kept hearing 'Go the distance,' but I couldn't figure out what it meant," said Manzella. "Did the voice want me to build a baseball field and summon the spirits of dead baseball players to my Iowa cornfield? No, I saw a vision, and it turns out the voice wanted me to go downtown to the farmers market and open fire on everyone."

Manzella described the vision as "extremely realistic and graphic."

"It was pretty clear right then what the disembodied voice wanted me to do," said Manzella. "I don't know why it wants me to go on a shooting spree, but I think I'm going to do it. After all, how many opportunities in life do you have to do something wild and irrational?"

Opening fire on the farmers market will surely lead to a long jail sentence and loss of his farm, but that's a price Manzella is willing to pay.

"All my life I've been following the rules and doing the right thing," said Manzella. "I've never taken any risks. Sure, we may lose the farm, but there are some things more important in life than material possessions. I'm going to throw caution to the wind and shoot up that market."

Complicating matters is John McDermott, Manzella's brother-in-law, who has tried repeatedly to talk some sense into him.

"I keep telling him not to go through with this insane plan," said an exasperated McDermott. "There is no such thing as disembodied voices. There is no such thing as these crazy visions. For a few minutes of fun, he's willing to risk everything. Next thing you know, he'll be building a baseball field in the goddamn cornfields."

ON THIS DAY...

In 1970, Curt Flood filed a lawsuit challenging baseball's reserve clause, paving the way for modern free agency. Send death threats to PO Box 4398, St Louis, MO.

Damon Stoudamire Swears Off Marijuana After Powerful After-School Special

PORTLAND, OR—Damon Stoudamire, point guard for the Portland Trail Blazers and noted pothead, has reportedly sworn off the drug for good. Teammates were shocked by the sudden turnaround, which Stoudamire attributed to a powerful after-school special called *Everybody's Doing It,* starring TV's Scott Baio.

"I always thought smoking pot was cool," Stoudamire began. "I used to do it with all my friends when I was growing up, and it just kept on going right into adulthood. That is, until I saw *Everybody's Doing It.* Talk about being scared straight. I'll never touch the stuff again."

Although it's been a few weeks since Stoudamire saw the film, he claims to remember it like it was just yesterday. One scene that still haunts him is when Baio, playing a pot-addicted character named Danny, goes on a fishing trip with his friends and, in a fit of marijuana-induced rage, strikes his friend James in the head with an oar, nearly killing him.

"Danny finally got his wake-up call, and so did I," said Stoudamire. "I could totally relate to that because I have a boat. What if I smoked too much reefer and bludgeoned my friend to death with an oar? That's the kind of stuff that keeps me awake at night."

Another scene that resonated with Stoudamire is when Danny becomes so desperate for pot that he robs a liquor store to get his fix.

"I got a lump in my throat watching that," said Stoudamire. "I can't tell you how many times I've craved pot so bad that I would've been capable of anything, even robbing a liquor store."

Stoudamire's friends reacted with relief and elation at the news that he had given up marijuana. Teammates Rasheed Wallace and Bonzi Wells sent him a flower basket and greeting card expressing their support.

"To be honest, I was real worried when I found out about Damon's pot habit," said Wells. "To think, someone on the Portland Trail Blazers was doing drugs. What an eye-opener! I just admire my friend for being able to overcome his demons."

Stoudamire has been arrested twice in the past year on marijuana-related charges. His addiction seemed to be getting worse instead of better. Fortunately for Stoudamire and the rest of the Trail Blazers, *Everybody's Doing It* made its television debut at just the right time.

"I now believe there's a light at the end of the tunnel," Stoudamire said. "I drew a lot of strength from Scott Baio and have turned my life around. Like young Danny, I'm no longer beating myself or my friends with the oar of drug addiction."

THE BRUSHBACK GLOSSARY

GREENS FEE: Fee that recreational golfers pay to drink, swear, urinate in the bushes, and shoot a 112.

Love Train Driver Charged With Operating Under the Influence

TAMPA, FL—Frank Masterson, driver of the Coors Lite Love Train, was arrested and charged with operating under the influence this weekend after ramming into a crowd of partygoers outside Raymond James Stadium in Tampa. The train was reportedly on its way inside the stadium, where it would provide a rush of cool, arctic air to the sweltering crowd inside. Unfortunately, things went horribly wrong.

"Oh my God, that was so scary," said Megan Whitten, 26, who was tailgating with friends when the Love Train burst onto the scene. "We were just standing around shooting the shit when all of a sudden we heard this loud whistling sound and we turned and saw the Love Train approaching. We started cheering and waving to it, but we noticed something was wrong. It wasn't slowing down. It was barreling toward us, and it sure looked to me like that driver was passed out."

Sure enough, Masterson was asleep at the wheel. Instead of veering right toward the stadium, he kept the train charging straight ahead at full speed.

"I got away because I got lucky," recalled 44-year-old Doug Kipling. "But others were not so lucky. There was this one guy who was standing on the roof of his van when the train came and rammed it. The dude went flying through the air and landed in a tree. The rest of us were just diving out of the way. The one

thing I remember, though, is how frigging cold it was. I had icicles hanging off my face. Now I'm sick as a dog. Thanks, Coors."

After plowing through dozens of parked cars, the Love Train slowed down and eventually stopped. An eerie silence filled the air as disoriented bystanders assessed the damage. With the disabled locomotive coughing and wheezing in front of them, the people did the only sensible thing.

"We looted the fucker," said Kipling. "The driver was either dead or passed out, and we weren't about to let that opportunity pass. Then we put on some music, any music, so we could get that insipid 'Love Train' song out of our heads. Then we got drunk and waited for the cops to come. When the driver woke up, he got out of the train and joined us! We ended up having a great time."

The Coors Brewing Company said they were "shocked" by Masterson's behavior and threatened to suspend him from his duties driving the Love Train. When reached for comment, Masterson said he was just doing his job. He blamed Coors for creating a corporate mentality that encourages drinking and debauchery.

"Of course I was drunk. I'm the driver of

see LOVE TRAIN, page 64

> LOVE TRAIN, continued from page 63

the Coors Lite Love Train. What did you expect me to be doing, drinking lattes and reading poetry?" Masterson said. "Now my bosses are telling me that I'm not representing the values of Coors. Are they crazy? I'm the embodiment of those values. Let's see, drinking in huge quantities, listening to bad music, hanging out with shallow people—for all that I'm surprised they haven't named me employee of the month."

Nike Orders Tsunami Survivors Back to Work

BEAVERTON, OR—In a faxed memo today to dozens of manufacturing plants in Southeast Asia, Nike executives informed tsunami survivors that "the party's over" and they will be expected to get back to work stitching Nike apparel. The memo was a devastating blow to the thousands of workers affected by the disaster, but officials insisted that they had no choice. "I know it's hard, but people here in the States need sneakers," said Gary Wolaston, Southeast Asia regional manager. "We're rolling out a lot of new products and they need to be manufactured and shipped pronto. Plus, most of these people have far surpassed their annual allotted sick time of one day. We feel we've been extremely charitable and understanding here. Come on, people. The party's over. Get back to work."

Offensive Lineman Successfully Evades Blitz

DALLAS, TX—An offensive lineman for the Dallas Cowboys successfully evaded blitzing defenders three times on Sunday. The lineman, left tackle Torrin Tucker, deftly stepped out of the way as marauding linebackers streaked past and hammered quarterback Drew Bledsoe. "Drew's gotta be more mobile," Tucker said after the game. "If he was like me, he would've had those defenders whizzing right by him." Tucker indicated that he was willing to give Bledsoe footwork tips in order to prevent another bruising day like Sunday.

Baseball Season Trimmed to 125 Games Following Amphetamine Ban

NEW YORK—Baseball's tough new steroid policy calls for a fifty-game penalty for a first-time offender and a lifetime ban after three positive tests. It also includes, for the first time, testing for amphetamines, or "greenies." As a result, the league has trimmed thirty-seven games off the schedule as a way to combat the players' sluggishness.

"For decades, players have relied on the energy-giving qualities of amphetamines to get them through the grueling baseball season," commissioner Bud Selig told reporters on Friday. "Now that we've banned the drugs, it's only right that we let them play fewer games. 162 games is simply too many for a player under the influence of nothing at all."

Though the recent scandal in baseball has revolved around steroids, some say that amphetamines are a more widespread problem. According to many insiders, greenies have been as much a part of baseball in the past fifty years as sunflower seeds and chewing tobacco.

"You're definitely going to see a wildly different game now," said one AL outfielder, who asked not to be identified. "Fans don't realize how much we all counted on those greenies. Ah, greenies. I sure will miss you. I can't tell you how many ground balls I beat out because my body was convulsing with so much energy that running at a normal pace would've caused me to get dizzy and vomit."

"I do have to hand it to the commissioner, though," he continued. "Shortening the season was the right thing to do for the players, fans, and the league. 162 games is an eternity. Now we can pace ourselves. I still can't get used to the idea, though. Baseball without amphetamines is like car racing without beer. It's like football without tailgating. It's like the WNBA without lesbian jokes. It's almost impossible to enjoy one without the other."

Former major league pitcher and current U.S. senator Jim Bunning played an integral role in the creation of baseball's new testing policy. He called the rule changes "a victory for baseball" and said fans should expect a radically different style of play in 2006.

"I think when people see how different the game is now, it will really hit home how much of an impact these drugs had," Bunning said. "For instance, you're probably not going to see any more bench-clearing brawls. You're not going to see as many home runs, either. So what's left for baseball fans? Bunting. Hold onto your hats, fans, because we are standing on the precipice of the golden age of small ball. Be careful what you wish for!"

DID Y?U KNOW

Recreational tennis players are generally less attractive than pro tennis players.

Kobe Accuser Signs Deal with Reebok

LOS ANGELES, CA—In response to Nike's new ad campaign featuring controversial Lakers star Kobe Bryant, who was acquitted of rape charges last year, Reebok has signed Bryant's accuser to an endorsement deal of her own. The move is a continuation of the decades-long war between the rival sneaker companies.

"This is a nice little signing for us," said Rob Pirsig, marketing director for Reebok. "Now that Nike has decided to dust off Kobe Bryant and give him his own line of sneakers, we have to make a move as well. Now that they've got Kobe, we have his accuser. Talk about a great rivalry. It's like Larry and Magic all over again."

Pirsig admitted that the signing was a direct response to Nike's new Kobe Bryant–themed ad campaign.

"When we saw that, we were pretty intimidated," Pirsig continued. "The ads have this whole 'I just beat a rape charge so don't mess with me' attitude. We knew we had to counter that with something, but what? That's when I got the idea. Let's sign the girl who accused him of rape! We're going to call her—and the new sneaker line—'The Accuser.' I really hope this will dispel the myth that Nike is the sleaziest shoe company out there."

The ad campaign surrounding "The Accuser 2K5" will focus on the young accuser and her brave battle against one of the most powerful athletes on the planet.

"We've got one ad that looks like one of those Japanese-style cartoons, and it shows The Accuser dunking a basketball right in

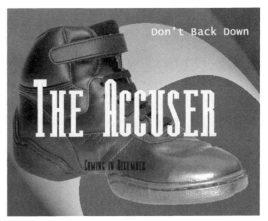

Don't Back Down

THE ACCUSER

COMING IN DECEMBER

"NOW THAT THEY'VE GOT KOBE, WE HAVE HIS ACCUSER. TALK ABOUT A GREAT RIVALRY. IT'S LIKE LARRY AND MAGIC ALL OVER AGAIN," SAID ROB PIRSIG.

Kobe Bryant's face," said Pirsig. "Then we've got this giant billboard going up in Times Square, and another one in downtown L.A. that's just a close-up of her face, all beaded up with sweat, glaring menacingly at the camera. Pretty powerful stuff, huh?"

Reebok's new ad campaign is being called tasteless by some in the industry, most notably executives from Nike, who are accusing their rival of exploiting a painful situation.

"They've got the Kobe accuser signed to an endorsement deal? Oh, that is shameless," said Nike vice president of marketing John Wexler. "Here's a girl who may or may not have been raped, who has been through a tragic and trying ordeal, and they're exploiting her image to sell sneakers? How do these people sleep at night?"

Seemingly unruffled by the competition, Nike is predicting that their new Kobe Bryant

see ACCUSER, page 67

> ACCUSER, continued from page 66

sneaker will outsell "The Accuser" by millions of units.

"Oh, we're going to crush those guys," Wexler said. "The Accuser? Give me a break. We've got the man himself here, Kobe Bryant.

Sure, he was accused of rape, but who among us hasn't been? If I had a dime for every woman who has accused me of rape, I'd have . . . well let's see here . . . carry the one . . . I'd have . . . two dollars and twenty cents."

Bossy JumboTron Demands Some Noise

PHOENIX, AZ—An incredibly bossy and rude Jumbo-Tron at Arizona's Bank One Ballpark loudly demanded some noise from the crowd during a day game between the Diamondbacks and the New York Mets. After an extended period of inadequate cheering, the JumboTron displayed, in giant block letters, the demand "LET'S MAKE SOME NOISE, PEOPLE!" accompanied by a booming voice. When the fans failed to respond, the JumboTron repeated its demand, only louder and with larger letters. "LET'S MAKE SOME NOISE! I CAN'T HEAR YOU!!! I WANNA HERE SOME FUCKING NOISE!!" The frightened crowd responded with a half-hearted cheer, temporarily silencing the overbearing JumboTron. Afterward, many vowed not to return to the ballpark until the JumboTron learned to control its temper.

Midnight Basketball League Great Place to Buy Crack

CHICAGO, IL—Chicago's midnight basketball league is a great way for inner-city youths to stay out of trouble and build character through athletic competition. It's also a great place to buy crack, say Chicago-area junkies. "Wow, just think, the entire drug supply of Chicago brought together under one roof," said Eli "Poppy" McCay, local crack smoker. "Look, there's Joe Joe, Lil' D, Alamoe, my man G-Kronic—the whole gang's here. All I got to do is ask one of them guys at halftime for a couple of rocks. The mayor is right. This *is* a great place for inner-city kids to come and hang out."

Under Armour Guy Switches to Decaf

ATLANTA, GA—Big E, spokesman for Under Armour apparel, has switched to decaffeinated coffee in an attempt to curb his violent outbursts and short temper. The switch has worked wonders for the muscle-bound athlete. "As you know, I've had quite a short fuse in the past and have been prone to some pretty scary outbursts," said Big E while relaxing at his home in Los Angeles. "I've bullied my friends, my fellow weight lifters, and pretty much anyone who wasn't wearing Under Armour formfitting Lycra workout apparel. Well, my wife decided I should try decaf in the morning instead of the straight black coffee I've been drinking. And you know what? It's worked wonders for me. I'm still very much concerned about this house and whether or not my colleagues will protect it, but I'm much more laid back about the whole thing. I'd like them to protect the house, but only if they want to."

All-Black College Inexplicably Has Bad Basketball Team

ATLANTA, GA—Howard University, a large, predominantly African American college, inexplicably has a terrible basketball team. The Howard University Bisons have wallowed in anonymity for years, unable to compete with high-profile Division I teams even though their student body consists almost entirely of black people. "When I heard we were playing Howard University, I thought, 'Uh-oh, that's the all-black school,'" said Dan Giminski, center for Norfolk State University, which played the Bisons earlier this month. "But they turned out to be really bad for some reason. I was surprised. I just figured with all those black people to choose from, they could put together a pretty good team. That just goes to show you how meaningless those racial stereotypes are." Other black universities, such as Tuskegee University, Morris College, and Dillard University are helping to shatter ignorant stereotypes by boasting similarly inept basketball teams.

NFL Collapses After Nation Suddenly Gets Its Priorities Straight

NEW YORK—The National Football League, once the most popular professional sports league in the nation, collapsed last week after Americans suddenly, and without warning, got their priorities straight. Season ticket purchases came to a screeching halt, merchandise sales have fallen off the map, and fantasy football leagues have been almost totally eliminated in what officials are referring to as "Black Monday."

"It's like people suddenly realized that sports are meaningless, and their growing obsession with them is unhealthy and even weird," said Dr. Richard McNeil, sociologist. "What we are looking at is a complete rearranging of the nation's priorities. Something happened to snap people out of their reverie. Perhaps it was the rapidly approaching apocalypse."

The collapse of the NFL happened in less than a week, shocking the football community, which had been banking on the nation's insatiable thirst for everything football for years to come.

Said former NFL commissioner Paul Tagliabue: "I . . . I . . . don't know what to say. How could this happen? Everything was going normal and then . . . poof. It was gone. Don't people care about their favorite players anymore? Their favorite team? The hottest trade rumors? Fantasy leagues? The NFL Network? *Madden 2K5?* Has the world gone completely mad?"

While experts are perplexed at the remarkable chain of events leading to the collapse of the NFL, fans say that the change was perfectly logical and that it was "a long time coming."

Rebecca Thomas of Islip, NY, a die-hard Giants fan, says her revelation came while reading *The New York Times* for the first time in three years.

"Usually football season is my time of year," said Thomas. "I used to spend half my workday surfing the Web, reading about my favorite players, and memorizing their stats. But that's over now. I just found out we're at war in this place called Iraq. I was, like, 'Whoa, holy shit! A war?' Who knew? I guess that's what my son was talking about when he said he was going to fight in Iraq."

Even some members of the media admitted to having a change of heart about the importance of sports. Trey Wingo, ESPN anchor, said his "epiphany" came during the taping of a routine segment of *SportsCenter.*

"I was just sitting there mindlessly reading the TelePrompTer, talking about Ricky Williams for the 50 millionth time, when all of a sudden it hit me: This is a big fucking waste of time," said Wingo. "Yesterday I was reporting on fucking Web gems and Greg Maddux's three hundredth stupid win, and then I was talking about the Dolphins running back problems. Why? Why? It's all a

> "I JUST FOUND OUT WE'RE AT WAR IN THIS PLACE CALLED IRAQ. I WAS LIKE, 'WHOA, HOLY SHIT! A WAR?' WHO KNEW? I GUESS THAT'S WHAT MY SON WAS TALKING ABOUT WHEN HE SAID HE WAS GOING TO FIGHT IN IRAQ," SAID REBECCA THOMAS.

see PRIORITIES, page 70

> PRIORITIES, continued from page 69

façade. It's all a lie, goddamn it. It's all going to come crashing down. I just hope I can still get my severance package."

The fantasy football industry has experienced perhaps the largest drop-off of any industry other than the NFL itself. Enrollment in rotisserie leagues has dropped to an all-time low, with many participants wondering if there is, in fact, more to life than pretending to be an NFL general manager.

"What the hell have I been doing all these years?" asked Fred Dolby, 47. "What's next, fantasy-fantasy football, where you pretend to be a fantasy football team owner? I'm done with all of this. I'm turning over a new leaf. I just hope that my bookie doesn't commit suicide."

Unfortunately for Dolby, his bookie probably did commit suicide. As news of Black Monday spread across the nation, over three thousand bookies were reported to have taken their own lives. Experts say it is only a matter of time before all sports betting ceases to exist, potentially grinding the U.S. economy to a halt.

Republicans Try to Block Blacks From Voting in SportsNation Opinion Poll

WASHINGTON, DC—Civil rights groups are complaining that the Republican Party is trying to block black voters from taking part in the latest SportsNation opinion poll. Hundreds of blacks were apparently harassed, threatened, and intimidated via e-mail as they tried to cast their votes for Sunday's top NFL performer. "Just as I was about to cast my vote, I received an IM [instant message] from someone named Karl Rove," said Ronald Hart, 37, of Chula Vista, CA. "He said that if I had any outstanding warrants and tried to vote in this opinion poll, I would be arrested immediately and my children would be taken away from me. Talk about racist. I went and voted anyway, because I'm an American and I have a right to vote for my top NFL performer of the week without fear of reprisal. Black power!"

Hockey Surpassed in Popularity by Air Hockey

TORONTO, CANADA—Just over a month into the regular season, the National Hockey League is still struggling to regain its fan base. Things have gotten so bad, in fact, that traditional hockey has been surpassed in popularity by air hockey. Experts say the reasons are clear. "Air hockey kicks ass in so many ways," said Jack Lechtein, president of Air Hockey America, the largest air hockey league in the country. "It's one-on-one, it's fast-moving, it's extremely intense, and it's still very much a blue-collar sport, unlike the NHL. Also, we weren't stupid enough to put a franchise in Nashville."

Bush Vows to Prosecute "Criminal" Who Leaked Palmeiro's Test Results

CRAWFORD, TX—The fallout from the Rafael Palmeiro case continued yesterday when President Bush, speaking from his ranch in Texas, vowed to prosecute the "criminal" who leaked Palmeiro's steroid test results to the media.

Bush has taken a personal interest in the scandal, as he and Rafael Palmeiro have a friendship dating back to their days with the Texas Rangers.

"Whoever committed this heinous crime should be brought to justice immediately," Bush told reporters at his ranch. "Anybody who leaks confidential and damaging information has no right to walk among us. Major League Baseball must get its house in order. If I ran the country like this, I'd be the laughingstock of the world."

The commissioner's office has vowed to look into the leak, which violates the guidelines of the steroid testing policy. However, a cursory investigation may not be enough for the White House.

"The president is urging Major League Baseball to do the honorable thing," said White House spokesman Scott McClellan.

"Stop hiding behind the so-called 'investigation.' The nation will not sit idly by while this spineless, crooked, bigmouthed leak suspect remains free. To quote the president: 'Liberty cannot be preserved without general knowledge among people.' That was President John Adams, of course."

According to some high-ranking baseball officials, the league is searching for a way to deal with the leak crisis without outing the person responsible. However, it is exactly that kind of blind loyalty that infuriates President Bush, who places truth and justice above personal favoritism.

"This is just not sitting well with the president," said Greg Mitchell, political analyst from MSNBC. "Anyone who knows Bush knows that he values transparency and personal accountability over cronyism. What baseball is doing right now reeks of a major institutional cover-up. You might be able to get away with that with another president in office, but not George W. Bush. He's like a pit bull. He'll lunge at the truth, gobble it up, and then shit it out at the feet of the American people."

Steinbrenner Fires Scoreboard Operator After Lopsided Loss

Brutal Assault and Battery Nets 15-Yard Penalty

Arizona Cardinals Accidentally Left Off 2004 Schedule

"I CAN ONLY IMAGINE WHAT WAS GOING THROUGH THEIR HEADS WHEN THEY DIED. PERHAPS THEY WERE REGRETTING HIDING IN MY SHRUBS AND MASTURBATING," SAID ANNA KOURNIKOVA.

Fire In Anna Kournikova's Shrubs Kills Seven

BEVERLY HILLS, CA—A fire at Anna Kournikova's Beverly Hills mansion took the lives of seven people yesterday. The blaze started in the shrubs underneath the tennis star's bedroom window and engulfed the men who were crouching there. Kournikova, who was sleeping at the time, expressed her condolences to the victims of the tragic fire.

"I wish to extend my sympathy to the families of those men who were crouching in my bushes when the fire started," Kournikova said. "I can only imagine what was going through their heads when they died. Perhaps they were regretting hiding in my shrubs and masturbating."

Fire officials say the fire probably started when one of the men attempted to extinguish a cigarette among the dry leaves and twigs surrounding the house.

"I always tell those guys to be careful with their cigarettes," said Kournikova. "Some of them smoke like chimneys, and I knew that eventually we would have a tragedy on our hands. That's why I put the 'No Smoking' sign out there."

Doug Crosby, Beverly Hills fire chief,

see MASTURBATING, page 74

> MASTURBATING, continued from page 73

described the scene as "grisly" and said the last few moments of the men's lives were probably spent frantically trying to pull their pants up.

"We've pieced it all together, and the way I see it, the seven men were engulfed in flames pretty quick. Five of them died with their pants around their ankles, so you have to believe that hindered their ability to flee. It's just terrible that a routine stalking could turn into such a tragedy. That could've been me in there. That could've been my son. I guess the Lord works in mysterious ways," Crosby said.

City officials are asking how the tragedy could have occurred, and how a similar incident can be prevented in the future.

"This is clearly a terrible oversight by fire safety officials," said Beverly Hills mayor Tom Levyn. "Miss Kournikova's shrubs should be subject to the same stringent regulations as any other public gathering spot. Also, where were the glowing exit signs?"

The legal ramifications of the fire could be severe. Families of the victims want to know how something like this could happen, especially at such a high-profile meeting place.

Fire and security officials both indicated that they would launch a full investigation into the matter. They would also survey the rest of Kournikova's property for potential trouble spots.

"We've got a lot of work to do here," said Fire Chief Manning. "We've got to comb the grounds of this place and make sure any areas generally used for stalking and peeping are safe. We also may have to cut down that big palm tree outside her bathroom window. As of now there are nine people in that tree with binoculars, digital cameras, and Kleenex. There are no safety regulations in place there, and those palm trees could go up in flames in no time."

He added: "If these guys are so bent on whacking off to Anna, they should just buy a calendar like the rest of us."

Golf Announcer Whispers He's Having a Heart Attack

HOYLAKE, ENGLAND—Golf announcer Richard Siskel had a heart attack Sunday while doing commentary for the British Open golf tournament. Unfortunately, he had a difficult time communicating the urgency of the situation to his partner in the polite whisper that is required of PGA commentators. "I'm having a heart attack," Siskel whispered discreetly while Ernie Els lined up a crucial putt. "My chest is constricting and I can't breathe. Call a priest. Please. Hurry." His partner, Phil Ogden, was unable to distinguish Siskel's words and focused intently on Els's putt while Siskel fell to the ground and blacked out. "Whoa! Great putt!" he exclaimed as Els sank a ten-footer for a birdie. "That's the kind of play that just might win this tournament for Ernie. Wouldn't you agree, Richard? Richard?"

Referee Forced to Sit Through Fox Promos Before Viewing Replay

PHOENIX, AZ—Referee Ed Hoculi became enraged on Sunday when he was forced to watch promotional advertisements for *My Big Fat Obnoxious Boss* and *Nanny 911* before viewing a crucial replay during the Giants-Cardinals game. The Fox network defended the airing of the promos, claiming that it was all part of an aggressive campaign to publicize their new fall lineup.

"Let's not rush to judgment here," Fox producer Sandy Weil told a group of reporters yesterday. "You've seen *My Big Fat Obnoxious Fiancé*, right? Well, *My Big Fat Obnoxious Boss* throws the whole premise on its ear. You won't believe what these Ivy League 'smarty pants' will do to get a job. I would think that Mr. Hoculi, if he had seen the shows, would understand why we're so desperate to get the word out."

Fox's explanation did not sit well with Hoculi, who maintains that the network has gone too far this time.

"It is wholly unacceptable to be force-fed TV promos while I'm trying to do my job," said Hoculi. "I've got a crowd of sixty thousand people sitting here waiting for me to review the play and make a decision. But does Fox care? No. All they care about is self-promotion. Well, I say they're shooting themselves in the foot with all these promos. The shows look horrible. If I were Fox, I'd be burying those ads in a WNBA telecast or something."

What made the situation even worse for Hoculi was the complexity of the play being reviewed. Giants coach Tom Coughlin was challenging whether an Arizona receiver caught a ball in bounds. It was a painfully close play that required a slow and deliberate review, and the advertisements delayed the game even longer.

"We always try to make a conscious effort to review plays as quickly as possible, so as not to ruin the flow of the game," Hoculi said. "So by the time I got to the actual review, I was already a good minute behind. I will say this, though. That nanny looks like a carpet muncher. There, I said it. Somebody had to."

Fox executives said they had no plans to curb their television promos during sporting events. According to Weil, advertising during football and baseball games is at a premium because of the popularity of both sports.

"Anytime you have the opportunity to plug your own shows during some sports broadcast, you jump at it," Weil said. "At some point we may consider airing an entire episode of one of our reality shows in the corner of the screen during a game. That's one step closer to forcing people to watch it, and two steps closer to actually making a show they'd want to watch on their own."

ON THIS DAY...

In 1943, to promote diversity, Major League Baseball opened its doors to players who were not wife-beaters.

Every White Person in America Secretly Rooting For Gonzaga

"THEY WERE LIKE A WHOLE TEAM OF LARRY BIRDS," SAID DAN PHELPS.

SPOKANE, WA—According to a recent survey, every white person in America is secretly rooting for the Gonzaga Bulldogs, a predominantly white NCAA basketball team from Washington. In the past few years the 'Dogs have overcome tremendous odds to become a nationally ranked team. Their surprising success has earned them a devoted following that includes every white person in America.

"There are a lot of closet Gonzaga fans out there," said Dr. Cheryl Batch, a sociologist who has been researching the phenomenon since 2003. "Many of them care very little about NCAA basketball, but they still have a soft spot in their heart for the Bulldogs. It may seem racist, but it's actually just human nature. We tend to root for the people we can most easily relate to, and the nation's whites apparently have an easy time relating to shaggy-haired hippie kids from the Northwest."

In 1999, Gonzaga rose to national prominence when it came out of nowhere to make the "Elite 8" in the NCAA basketball tournament. It was during that season that many white Americans got their first glimpse of the Bulldogs.

"I remember watching *SportsCenter* and seeing this team full of white guys with this crazy name, Gonzaga, and they were beating the crap out of the rest of the teams," said Boston resident Dan Phelps, a Gonzaga fan. "Even though I knew nothing about college hoops, I was intrigued. They were like a whole team of Larry Birds."

One of the NBA's all-time greats, John Stockton, played for the Gonzaga Bulldogs. His decorated career put the school on the map and also encouraged other young white athletes to follow in his footsteps. Stockton can speak firsthand about the unique appeal of the 'Zags.

"Gonzaga has always been kind of a Cinderella team, an underdog," said Stockton. "I think that's why people can relate to us so well. And let's face it, the fact that we're a bunch of white dudes doesn't hurt. I know a lot of white people out there who are secretly praying for Gonzaga to win a championship. It would just be kind of cool for a change, you know? It would be like a black hockey team

see 'ZAGS, page 77

> 'ZAGS, continued from page 76

winning the Stanley Cup or an English-speaking team winning the World Series."

The 'Zags's best player this year is junior Adam Morrison, who was just named West Coast Conference Player of the Week. Morrison says that every white person in the country is a Gonzaga fan on some level.

"Obviously we have a lot of fans out there," he said. "I know they're pretty excited about us right now. I guess it's just hard to believe that a bunch of white kids can be so good. I can't explain it myself. Maybe it's the fact that we're such great team players. Maybe it's the fact that we have a great coach in Mark Few. Or maybe, just maybe, it's because we do actually have a couple black kids on the team."

Stoner Too Tired to Play Video Game

COLUMBUS, OH—Local stoner Doug Rothstein, 32, said he was too tired yesterday to play a game of *Madden 2005,* marking the first time in history that a person was too lethargic to sit on a reclining chair and move his thumbs around. Rothstein's room-mate, Kyle Sutton, called the incident "a new low." "This is pretty bad, even for him," said Sutton, 25. "I smoke pot myself, and I understand what it's like to feel all sluggish and tired, but I'm always in the mood to play a little *Madden,* no matter what. I can't imagine a stoned person being too tired to partake in an activity that is tailor-made for stoned people who are too tired to do anything. He's setting a new standard for laziness. I think he's about one more hit from slipping into a coma."

Phish Performs Mind-Bending, Thirty-Seven-Minute Version of National Anthem Before Basketball Game

BURLINGTON, VT—The popular jamband Phish performed an epic, mind-bending version of "The Star Spangled Banner" before a sold-out crowd at Saturday's University of Vermont basketball game. The performance began with an ambient, spacey intro, which morphed into the opening lyrics. The first part of the song was sung in a straightforward manner but was followed by a genre-hopping, twenty-minute, improvisational odyssey that included bits of jazz, blues, funk, and calypso. The rest of the lyrics were sung over a multilayered tapestry of sound effects and swishing cymbals, culminating with a dramatic, drawn-out ending. The crowd was appreciative, but the delay caused players to tighten up, resulting in a groin injury to star center Taylor Coppenrath.

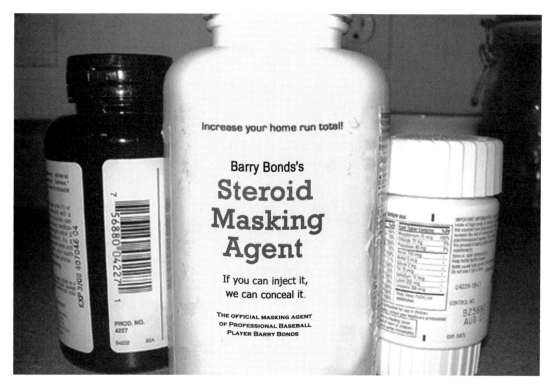

Increase your home run total!

Barry Bonds's
Steroid Masking Agent

If you can inject it,
we can conceal it.

THE OFFICIAL MASKING AGENT
OF PROFESSIONAL BASEBALL
PLAYER BARRY BONDS

Bonds Raises Suspicion by Launching Own Line of Masking Agents

SAN FRANCISCO, CA—The cloud of suspicion around Barry Bonds grew even larger today after the slugger announced he was launching his own line of designer steroid-masking agents. The new line, dubbed "The Barry Bonds Collection," will be available for purchase on his website.

"Hmm . . . this is an awfully ominous sign," said ESPN's Pedro Gomez. "He must know a lot about masking agents if he's launching his own line. In fact, one of the more expensive ones says 'Guaranteed to mask the steroids in your bloodstream during Major League Baseball drug tests.' That's not very discreet. It's almost like he wants to get caught. And I've always wanted to be the one to catch him. So consider this an exclusive: Bonds is on steroids. Woohoo! I'm a real reporter."

In spite of this venture, Bonds continues to deny using steroids. He says his new line of products is nothing more than a business.

"Hey, I would never use these things myself because I don't do steroids," he said. "I just wanted to offer some help to players who do steroids and need something to cover it up. These new masking agents are inexpensive, easy to use, and perfectly safe. I just sold a truckload to Sammy Sosa yesterday. Today

see BONDS, page 79

> BONDS, continued from page 78

he was back for another truckload. I heard that when the doctors gave him his urine test, they couldn't even find the urine."

Major League Baseball officials said they are aware of the situation and monitoring it closely. However, they have no plans to take disciplinary action against Bonds.

"Of course we're aware of the situation," said MLB spokesman Rich Levin. "We are monitoring it every day just like we've been doing all along. There's nothing we can do about it. He's never tested positive and we've never actually seen him injecting them. You might think this is the smoking gun, but it's not. We've never found a smoking gun. Well, there was that one time when a security guard found an actual smoking gun in his locker along with some bloodstained clothing, but that had nothing to do with steroids."

The new masking agents have been selling like hotcakes. Sources say that over three thousand orders were filled the first day alone, though no major league ballplayer has admitted to purchasing them. In fact, the players union immediately condemned Bonds for offering his product line.

Despite the controversy, Bonds has no plans to stop selling his designer masking agents.

"Stop selling them? Why? I'm doing something perfectly legal," he said. "Just because I'm selling masking agents doesn't mean I take [steroids] myself, although I must say that my most expensive masking agent, 'The Eliminator,' does do a great job of masking THG. Oh shit. I bet someone's going to take that quote out of context now and use it to portray me as some kind of steroid abuser, right? You guys have no shame at all."

Bush Outraged at Condition of Superdome Luxury Boxes

NEW ORLEANS, LA—President Bush took a tour of the storm-ravaged city of New Orleans yesterday, a week after catastrophic Hurricane Katrina made landfall. One of his first stops was the Superdome. The facility, used as a shelter for hurricane survivors, is in a state of ruin, covered in trash and human excrement. But what outraged the president most was the "abhorrent" condition of the Superdome's luxury boxes. "I've been all around this city, but the one thing that will stick in my mind is the horrific condition of those beautiful and expensive corporate luxury boxes," Bush said at a press conference at Louis Armstrong Airport. "These boxes are owned and used by some of our nation's finest corporations, and they were littered with paper cups and discarded food wrappers. What a shocking lack of respect shown by the evacuees. I demand a full investigation."

ESPN Urges Rest of WNBA to Come Out of Closet

BRISTOL, CT—When Sheryl Swoopes came out of the closet in a recent issue of *ESPN The Magazine,* the public's response was overwhelmingly warm and positive. Now ESPN is urging the rest of the WNBA to follow suit, so that every player in the league can be free of the shackles of secrecy and be profiled in *ESPN The Magazine.*

"It's so great and heartwarming that Sheryl was able to come out of the closet in our magazine," said *ESPN The Magazine* editor Kenny McAlister. "It's such a beautiful story of courage and perseverance. Now I think the rest of the WNBA should follow Sheryl's lead. Come on, ladies. We all know you're a bunch of muff-divers. Let's hear your stories."

Many WNBA players insist that they are not gay and have no plans ever to "come out of the closet." The ones who are gay criticized ESPN for its over-the-top coverage of the Swoopes story, saying it actually discouraged them from following in her footsteps.

"I've thought about coming out of the closet, but after seeing that story, forget it," said one player who asked not to be identified. "I want to be treated like a normal person if I come out, not like some freak of nature. I'm sure the rest of the lesbians in the league would agree with me. Oh, and we're not all lesbians, thank you very much. It's just a stereotype. That's like saying that all guys who listen to the Dave Matthews Band are gay. Okay, bad example."

One player, Phoenix's Diana Taurasi, said she supports Swoopes's decision to come out and would support any teammates who did the same thing. However, she said it's up to the individual to decide, not the media.

> "COME ON, LADIES. WE ALL KNOW YOU'RE A BUNCH OF MUFF-DIVERS. LET'S HEAR YOUR STORIES," SAID KENNY MCALISTER.

"If people are gay and want to come out, I'm all for it," said Taurasi. "We should treat them just like we treat anybody else. But I don't think we should be pressuring anybody to do anything. People's sexual orientation is their own business. ESPN likes to pose as an advocate for gay people, but they're just trying to sell magazines. They don't really care about gay people. If they did, they wouldn't be so harsh in their coverage of Alex Rodriguez."

It remains to be seen if Swoopes's recent admission inspires any of her peers to follow suit. One thing is for certain, though. If they do, *ESPN The Magazine* will be there to document their heartwarming stories of triumph over adversity.

THE BRUSHBACK GLOSSARY

SLEEPER TEAM: A team predicted to surprise everyone and win it all, though it's not much of a surprise if the team has already been designated as a team that could surprise everyone and win it all.

Yankee Fans Will Be Asked to Shower Before Entering New Stadium

Bench Coach Studies Clipboard in Attempt to Look Busy

Mel Kiper Totally Forgets About Draft

Referee Apologizes in Advance for Horrible Call

LOS ANGELES, CA—In an unusual move during last Sunday's Spurs–Lakers game at the Staples Center, referee Joe Crawford apologized in advance to Tim Duncan for a horrible call he was about to make. The incident occurred during a pivotal stretch in the fourth quarter, when the Spurs were trying to close the gap. "I'm sorry, Tim. I know you got all ball, but I haven't made one terrible call today and I think I'm due," said Crawford. "So I'm about to call you for a bullshit foul. Here goes." Duncan was upset about the call, but credited Crawford for his honesty.

Kyle Boller Regrets Selecting Self in Fantasy Football Draft

BALTIMORE, MD—After his team's demoralizing loss to the New England Patriots and a terrible year in general, Ravens quarterback Kyle Boller said he regrets selecting himself in this year's fantasy football draft. "Having a lousy year is bad enough," said Boller. "But this just compounds matters. I didn't get so much as one lousy point in the last three weeks of the season. It's hard to believe. I thought I got a bargain when I fell to the third round in the draft, but I guess I was wrong." The Boller family fantasy football league consists of Kyle, his two brothers-in-law, his uncle Ray, and his friend Gregg, all of whom passed on Boller in the first two rounds of the draft.

LeBron James Hands Firstborn Over to Nike

CLEVELAND, OH—In accordance with the contract he signed in 2003, LeBron James handed his firstborn child over to Nike yesterday. The unnamed infant was immediately whisked away to Nike headquarters in Beaverton, OR, where it will be raised by the Nike Corporation. "We have received infant LJ-17 and have placed it in the care of our marketing executives," read a press release issued by Nike. "They will be the child's legal guardians until he is old enough to legally appear in television commercials and promote the goods and services provided by the Nike Corporation. The baby, like its father, will have the Nike logo branded into its backside in accordance with copyright laws. All of LeBron's future babies will be utilized in the same manner."

Royals Trade Mike Sweeney Just to Get Their Name in the Paper

KANSAS CITY, MO—The Kansas City Royals pulled off a blockbuster trade on Saturday that caught the attention of everyone in the league. The team traded its best player, first baseman Mike Sweeney, to the Anaheim Angels for a minor league prospect and some cash. Though the move made very little sense for the Royals, it did get the team's name mentioned in the sporting press.

"Look! Look! There we are!" cried GM Allard Baird as he pointed to a *USA Today* article describing the trade. "See? It's right here: 'Royals Make Bonehead Trade.' That's us. We got our name in the paper. Yes! Where's the phone? I gotta call my wife. She's gonna totally freak."

Afterward, Baird was thrilled to see his team mentioned on ESPN.com, CNNSI.com, MLB.com, and even *SportsCenter*. He spent the day fielding phone calls from excited family and friends.

"Pretty much everybody I know has called me today," said Baird. "They all want to tell me they saw the Royals mentioned on *SportsCenter* or read about it somewhere on the Internet. I think this trade is really going to put the Royals on the map. Now everyone in America knows that, yes, we do have a Major League Baseball team here in Kansas City."

Baird and the Royals have been following

see ROYALS, page 84

"I THINK THIS TRADE IS REALLY GOING TO PUT THE ROYALS ON THE MAP. NOW EVERYONE IN AMERICA KNOWS THAT, YES, WE DO HAVE A MAJOR LEAGUE BASEBALL TEAM HERE IN KANSAS CITY," SAID GM ALLARD BAIRD.

> ROYALS, continued from page 83

the winter meetings closely this year. With teams like the Red Sox, Yankees, and Diamondbacks dominating the press coverage at the winter meetings, it was Baird's idea to trade Sweeney, one of the cornerstones of the team, in order to generate some buzz.

"Every time I turn on the TV or pick up a newspaper, I'm always hearing about some other team," said Baird. "I'm just damn tired of being on the outside looking in. We are a card-carrying member of Major League Baseball and we will not sit here and be ignored, at least not until the season starts."

Even though the Royals are enjoying some extensive publicity, the biggest beneficiary of the trade appears to be the Anaheim Angels. The Angels received a top-notch player for a prospect that most scouts never expect to play beyond Double A.

Angels GM Bill Stoneman insisted, however, that it was a good deal for both sides.

"I wouldn't say this was a lopsided trade. I think that's unfair to the Royals and to the prospect we gave up," said Stoneman. "The prospect, second baseman Julian Tarasco, was one of the top players in our system until he got in that car accident. All in all, I'd say the uh . . . um . . . the . . . ah, fuck, what was their name again? The Royals! That's it. The Royals have acquired a pretty fine baseball player."

The Royals will probably face some heat for trading away their best player, but for now the team is going to enjoy its brief time in the spotlight.

"The repercussions of this move might be pretty bad, especially since we got so little in return," said Baird. "But right now there's nothing you can do to wipe this smile off my face. The Kansas City Royals on the front page of USA Today's sports section. Right there in black and white. The Kansas City–Fucking-Royals. They even mentioned me personally in paragraph two where it says 'GM Allard Baird approved the reckless and wrongheaded trade, and should probably have his head examined.' Yes! Thank you very much. Guess who's getting laid tonight?"

Chinese Authorities to Lift Ban on Smiling for 2008 Olympics

BEIJING, CHINA—Hu Jintao, president of China, announced plans to lift the country's ban on smiling during the 2008 Olympics in Beijing. The stunning announcement underscored Jintao's efforts to soften the image of the world's largest communist nation. "From the start of the 2008 Olympics to the closing ceremonies, all people of China will be allowed to smile freely and without fear of repercussion," Jintao said during a press conference Tuesday. "This is to show the world that China is a friendly, warm nation of happy citizens." Jintao added that after closing ceremonies, any citizen caught smiling would be shot, in accordance with traditional Chinese law.

FEMA Mistakenly Descends on Miami Hurricanes Game

TALLAHASSEE, FL—In another embarrassing mishap for the embattled organization, the Federal Emergency Management Agency (FEMA) descended in full force on Monday's NCAA football game between the Florida State Seminoles and the Miami Hurricanes. FEMA head Michael Brown received word of a hurricane in Tallahassee and immediately ordered the deployment of dozens of rescue workers and emergency food drops, costing the federal government a total of $5.3 million.

Unfortunately, many of the rescue workers could not reach the disaster area, Doak Campbell Stadium, because they were stuck in traffic.

"I can tell you right now that we have emergency medical, food, and water supplies headed to the area right now," Brown said. "I wish we could get there faster, but you must understand this is a logistical nightmare. There are thousands of people lined up in their automobiles waiting to get to the disaster area, many with painted faces and large quantities of alcohol. This new, dangerous breed of 'superlooters' is hampering our rescue operations."

Witnesses in the area reported "mass confusion" as FEMA attempted to rescue people who did not want to be rescued in an area that did not appear to be affected by a hurricane. In fact, Fox News correspondent Geraldo Rivera, on location in the stadium parking lot, reported that nothing was going on but an innocent football game.

"Death. Destruction. Disease," he began. "Swarms of fire ants, poisonous snakes, widespread looting, and the hopelessness of a city destroyed, its inhabitants left to wander the streets like postapocalyptic desert marauders. These things would all be happening if this was a hurricane, but it's actually just a football game. Boring!"

Fans who attended the game repeatedly informed the FEMA rescuers that "Hurricanes" was simply the name of a college football team and that there was no actual hurricane. Still the rescuers would not be deterred.

"We were hanging out in the parking lot tailgating and these guys in helicopters were hovering over us the whole time," said Katie Doyle, 19, a Florida State student who attended the game with friends. "They kept dropping these big baskets down to us and telling us to get in. When we refused, they tried to force us. One of them actually took my friend Sarah. She was kicking and screaming the whole time, but they wouldn't let her go. I haven't heard from her since."

Afterward, Brown defended the agency's actions, saying they were simply acting out of "an abundance of caution."

"Look, this agency has been under fire lately, and we just wanted to err on the side of caution," Brown told Katie Couric on *The Today Show*. "We heard 'hurricane' and we immediately mobilized. The good news is, it wasn't a totally wasted trip. We actually saved a kid who drank too much. We airlifted him from the parking lot. Turns out he was about to hook up with the nastiest girl on campus and we swooped in just in time. So at least there's one ultracatastrophe that we were able to prevent."

> "LOOK, THIS AGENCY HAS BEEN UNDER FIRE LATELY, AND WE JUST WANTED TO ERR ON THE SIDE OF CAUTION."

Scores of Cubs Fans Killed in Tragic Bandwagon Crash

CHICAGO, IL — Body parts and debris littered Waveland Avenue in Chicago after a tragic bandwagon crash took the lives of scores of Cubs fans Friday night. Survivors were airlifted to a nearby hospital as city officials tried to piece together what happened.

"Oh my God, the carnage!" cried officer Paul Linderman as he surveyed the scene. "I've never seen anything like it. All these poor Cubs fans killed just because they chose to jump on that bandwagon. That's why I always stay away from those things. They're really not that dependable."

One survivor told the harrowing story of the doomed bandwagon:

"It happened around the sixth inning of the Cubs-Marlins game. We were listening to the broadcast on the radio. The Marlins had just scored their seventh run when all of a sudden the bandwagon started to smell funny," said Richard Hinman of Oak Park. "It was that awful smell you get when the radiator is leaking. Then right before the game ended 11-1, the whole damn bandwagon pretty much self-destructed, taking a lot of innocent lives with it. Who would've thought the Cubs bandwagon would be so dangerous and destructive?"

With the addition of all-star shortstop Nomar Garciaparra at the beginning of the season, Cubs fans have been riding a tidal wave of optimism this year. But that optimism started to wane in recent weeks, and the team's downward spiral finally came to a head with the bloody wreck yesterday afternoon.

"Geez, I'm real sorry to hear that all those folks got hurt," said pitcher Mark Prior. "I'd be lying if I said I didn't see this coming, though. You could hear the wheels squeaking on that thing weeks ago. A lot of people were whispering that it wasn't that sturdy and something terrible was going to happen, just like last year. This should be a lesson to all Cubs fans. Next time the wheels start falling off, bail out as fast as you can. Never, ever get on a Cubs bandwagon. You're taking your life into your own hands."

At Chicago's Northwestern Memorial Hospital, beds are scarce and the sound of tortured screams echoes down the hallway. But many witnesses maintain that those who died in the crash were the lucky ones. For the survivors must live with the nightmarish memories of a great ride turned tragic.

> THOSE WHO DIED IN THE CRASH WERE THE LUCKY ONES. FOR THE SURVIVORS MUST LIVE WITH THE NIGHTMARISH MEMORIES OF A GREAT RIDE TURNED TRAGIC.

"Why? Why? Why?" cried one young woman, her legs mangled beyond recognition. "Why can't we get any clutch hitting? Why is our pitching staff suddenly mediocre? Why did Nomar get hurt again? Why did we even get Nomar, the cursed bastard?"

Across the hall another young man cursed himself for failing to heed the advice of his father and grandfather.

"My father told me never to get on that thing," he said. "My grandfather did too. But did I listen? No, I was too arrogant. I thought I was immortal. I thought it couldn't happen to me. This should be a lesson to everyone who has faith in the Cubs. Faith should be reserved for religious deities, not baseball teams owned by giant media conglomerates."

Defender Can't Stop Laughing at Latrell Sprewell's Hair

OAKLAND, CA—The Warriors' Troy Murphy had a difficult time defending Latrell Sprewell during Monday night's game against the Timberwolves. Though Sprewell is a quick, crafty offensive player, the main reason for Murphy's struggle was his inability to stop laughing at his opponent's hair.

"Holy shit, have you seen that guy's hair?" Murphy asked reporters after the game. "Man, I couldn't keep a straight face the entire game. How am I supposed to defend somebody like that?"

Although many in the league find Sprewell's hairstyle utterly hilarious, the joke's apparently lost on him.

"What's so funny? Why's everyone laughing at me?" asked Sprewell at a postgame press conference. "For your information, I have to put my hair in pigtails in order to pre-

vent my braids from dangling in my eyes while I'm playing."

Sprewell's scoring has been up lately, and many around the league are crediting his hair, which has become a distraction for opposing players. Murphy found out firsthand just how distracting it can be and is warning other defenders to try to block it out.

"I know it's hard to do, but don't look at his face. Defend from the neck down," advised Murphy. "That's how you can contain Spre'. The minute you look up, you're gonna see his pigtails bouncing around like a schoolgirl and it's going to set you off."

While adding to his defenders' difficulty guarding him, Sprewell's hairstyle often gets in the way of their ability to take him seri-

see SPREWELL, page 88

> SPREWELL, continued from page 87

ously. Last week, during a fight between the Nuggets' Nene Hilario and Minnesota's Michael Olowokandi, Sprewell engaged in some bitter trash-talking with the Denver crowd. The glowering, barking Sprewell might have been an intimidating figure if not for the two tufts of hair springing playfully from the sides of his head.

"Fuck you, motherfucker!" shouted Sprewell to the Pepsi Center crowd. "That's right, bitch, I'm talkin' to you. Suck my dick! What'd you say, motherfucker? Huh? What's so funny? Am I missing something?"

"Hey, look! Pippi Longstocking is swearing at us!" yelled one fan seated courtside. "Oooo, please don't hurt us, Pippi! Quick, someone give me a beer so I can throw it on this son of a bitch. I'd pay anything to see him charging into the stands with those stupid pigtails flopping around."

Meanwhile, Billy Hunter, head of the NBA players union, defended Sprewell's freedom of expression and called charges that his hair is a distraction "outrageous."

"This is America. People can wear their hair however they want," said Hunter. "Latrell Sprewell is an individual, and so are all these gentlemen who wish to wear their hair in braids and pigtails. If you ask me, I think Latrell is trying to be a role model for all the young schoolgirls out there. Girls, if you work hard, study, behave yourselves, and get good grades, you, too, can be an NBA star. Although if you're working hard and studying, then you probably have loftier goals than to emulate Latrell Sprewell."

Football Player Proud of American Flag Nasal Strip

JACKSONVILLE, FL—Jay Pollard, offensive tackle for the Jacksonville Jaguars, is proud to express his patriotism through his American flag nasal strip. The inch-long sliver of nylon is his way of paying respect to the men and women who fight for our freedoms. "It's just my way of saying 'thanks,'" said Pollard, his patriotic nasal strip expanding and contracting with each breath. "People say football players are heroes, but we're not. The soldiers are the real heroes, and this nasal strip is a small token of my appreciation." Pollard pointed out that he also wears a stars-and-stripes mouthpiece as another way to remind himself of the sacrifices our armed forces make every day.

Pat Summerall Predicts Oilers Will Win This Year's Super Bowl

BRISTOL, CT—Pat Summerall, 74-year-old football commentator, has predicted that the Houston Oilers will win the 2005 Superbowl. The venerable icon also predicted that Warren Moon would win the MVP and that nothing could stop Jerry Glanville and his men from their quest to win the Lombardi Trophy. Summerall made his prediction to Chris Berman during a taping of ESPN's *Sunday NFL Countdown.*

"I'll tell ya, Chris, it looks like the Oilers' year this year," Summerall said, after Berman asked for his Super Bowl prediction. "Jerry Glanville has got his boys all revved up, and Warren Moon will silence all those critics who say blacks shouldn't play quarterback."

Baffled by Summerall's inexplicable retreat into the past, Berman attempted to clarify his question to Summerall, stressing that he meant the 2005 Super Bowl.

"That's right. I heard you. 2005," said Summerall. "And I'll stand by my pick. It's the Oilers all the way. They're going to dethrone Montana and the 49ers once and for all."

Berman, becoming increasingly flustered, then tried to steer the conversation back to that night's Ravens versus Falcons contest.

"OK, I see you're going with the Oilers. Well, that's fine, but can you tell me who you think will win tonight's game?" he asked, trying in vain to cover up Summerall's embarrassing gaffe. "It's a good matchup tonight between a couple of teams with intriguing young quarterbacks. What's your take?"

"Baltimore has to rely heavily on its defense since its offense is a little weak," said Summerall. "But that shouldn't be a problem with Cal Ripken patrolling the middle of the field. Atlanta's going to have a hard time getting anything through the hole tonight, that's for sure. If I had to make a prediction for tonight's game, it would be Cowboys by a touchdown."

"Cal Ripken Jr., of course, is the sensational shortstop for the Baltimore Orioles," replied Berman, sweating profusely. "A fine, um . . . really good shortstop who might have been a great football player if he'd ever played football. Very interesting, to make the connection between the Ravens' strong defense up the middle and one of the strongest defensive players in Baltimore sports history. And now we go to Chris Mortensen, God willing."

After his appearance on *Sunday NFL Countdown,* Summerall made a guest appearance on Fox's *Best Damn Sports Show Period,* where he made another wild prediction: San Francisco's Ronnie Lott will take this year's defensive rookie of the year honors.

THE BRUSHBACK GLOSSARY

LONG JUMP: Olympic event in which an athlete jumps as far as he can. That's it. That's the whole event.

WNBA Players Give Up Trying to Be Sexy

NEW YORK, NY—After months of trying to present themselves as attractive, sexually desirable entertainers, WNBA players are refocusing their energies on playing basketball, bringing the league's embarrassing marketing strategy to its long overdue conclusion.

"Whew. I'm glad that's finally over," said WNBA rookie sensation Diana Taurasi. "I understand the theory behind it—that we're trying to appeal to a demographic outside of lesbians and our relatives—but it was just a bad idea. We're just not that sexy. Some of us are cute in a tomboyish kind of way, but let's face it, we're not the cast of *Melrose Place*. We're just a bunch of jocks."

Taurasi is being heralded as the savior of the WNBA. She's personable, cute, and extremely talented. The league wants her to be the female version of LeBron James, but even Taurasi has her limits.

"I'm happy to promote the league any way I can," she said. "I travel all over the country trying to attract fans to the game. But I'm not really interested in posing in a goddamn strapless evening gown with my boobs taped up and my face covered in makeup. I'm sure America would much rather watch us execute a perfect pick-and-roll than see us dress in slutty little dresses."

WNBA president Val Ackerman said the league chose to abandon the new ad campaign after viewing some of the finished spots on television.

"Okay, I can admit when I'm wrong," she said. "These chicks don't have a sexy bone in their bodies. Those ads have so many shadows, strobe lights, and quick edits that you can hardly see any of the girls anyway. I guess that shows you what kind of product we have here. Any league that has to resort to jamming Diana Taurasi into a rubber miniskirt doesn't have much else to offer."

WNBA officials held a brainstorming session in Orlando last week in an effort to come up with new promotional ideas.

"Well, we don't have much to work with here, but someone did make an interesting suggestion," she said Linda Godfrey, director of marketing for the WNBA. "We could do an ad campaign highlighting the players' great penmanship. Have you seen Sue Bird's cursive? Wow, it's elegant. And the way Lisa Leslie writes her 'G's' in that big, looping circular style is simply exquisite. And Tamika Catchings writes like a seventeenth-century British scholar. So that's something to think about. God, this is a depressing job."

THE BRUSHBACK GLOSSARY

SEAT LICENSING FEE: A fee that franchises charge for the right to purchase season tickets. Also referred to as "extortion."

Kobe Bryant to Resume Cheating On His Wife

LOS ANGELES, CA — Kobe Bryant announced through his agent today that he would resume cheating on his wife now that the rape charges have receded into the past. The Lakers star said he was relieved to be able to sleep around again.

"It's been a long, dark journey for me and my family," said Bryant. "When this all happened, I had no idea that it would last this long or be this painful. I have made great sacrifices for my wife, Vanessa, including the gift of fidelity for the duration of this difficult period. Now that period is over and I feel like I owe it to myself to resume cheating on my wife. She is in complete agreement, of course. What other choice does she have?"

When Bryant was first arrested for sexual assault in July 2003, he immediately came forward to pronounce his innocence. Though he admitted to committing adultery, he and his defense team insisted that the sex was consensual. After a long and grueling year of conflicting stories, controversial decisions, and media hysteria, the charges were dropped. Though a civil trial still looms, Bryant can rest easy knowing he's a free man and his long, personal nightmare is over.

ESPN basketball analyst Jim Gray credited Bryant's selflessness and discipline with helping him endure twelve months of marital fidelity.

"You can only imagine what Kobe was going through all this time," said Gray during an interview on *SportsCenter*. "Here's a man who can get laid just walking down the street, and he had to stay loyal to his wife for all those cold, dark months. I don't know what happened in that hotel room in Eagle, Colorado, and frankly, I don't care. Why does every encounter have to be consensual, anyway? It's like living in a goddamn police state."

With the start of the NBA season rapidly approaching, the opportunity for Bryant to commit adultery will only increase. Most NBA superstars are deluged with offers for sex everywhere they go. Bryant said he intends to take "full advantage" of each and every opportunity he gets.

"Oh my God, I'm going to get so much pussy next year I won't even be able to stand up," Bryant said. "I'm tired of sacrificing all the time. I'm tired of putting my wife's needs before my own. I give and I give and I give some more, and what do I get in return? Nothing but unconditional support, loyalty, and love. Big deal. I can get that from Lakers GM Mitch Kupchak."

? DID YOU KNOW

Ty Cobb once beat a man within an inch of his life for stepping on his toe.

Cash-Strapped Devil Rays to Eliminate Shortstop Position

Terrorist Suggests Building New Washington Ballpark Near Airport

Underage Girls Evacuated From Denver Prior to NBA All-Star Weekend

Insomniac Cured by Little League Game

Impatient Hiker Saws Arm Off After Being Trapped Under Rock 10 Minutes

Gritty, Hardworking Underdogs Lose Tenth Straight

Man Sheds Tears of Joy After Completing Iron Man Triathlon Video Game

"THE RUNNING, THE BIKING, THE SWIMMING, AND THAT BONUS ROUND WHERE YOU GET CHASED BY ALLIGATORS. MAN, WHAT A RIDE."

BRIDGEPORT, CT—Matthew Karp of Philadelphia, PA, was emotionally spent last night after finally completing the fabled *Iron Man 2K4* video game. Karp shed tears of joy as he slumped exhausted on the couch.

"Oh my God, this is such a great day," said a winded Karp. "It's been such a long road, there were times when I didn't think I would make it. The running, the biking, the swimming, and that bonus round where you get chased by alligators. Man, what a ride."

Karp, 25, started playing the game at 10 a.m. at his friend Kenji's apartment. He was determined to finish the grueling Iron Man Triathlon by the end of the day. Kenji didn't believe it was possible.

"I just laughed at him. That's the Iron Man competition," he said. "It's not for the faint of heart. But he was confident and so determined. He would not be denied."

By the end of the day Karp's thumbs were swollen and sore, his eyes were bloodshot, and he had a pounding headache—all the result of a grueling marathon that would test the will of any video-gamer.

"I just set aside my fears and went for it," says Karp. "Sometimes in life you just have to believe in yourself and know you can get the job done. A lot of people would've gotten discouraged the first time they drowned, but not me. I kept hitting 'quit' and then starting over."

Although he made it look easy, it was anything but. Karp recalls moments when he truly thought he was finished and was running on nothing but guts and heart.

"Toward the end when you're running and the commandos are shooting at you, it really gets hairy. You go through all this stuff, then you get to the end, and they start shooting at you! I swear, it was enough to make me wanna quit. But something kept me going. I'm not sure what it is, but I have plenty of it."

Immediately after finishing the game, Karp called family members to tell them the good news. The first person to hear was his mother, Freddi.

"Oh, he was all excited about it. I'm just tickled for him," said Freddi from her home in Baltimore. "He works so hard at those games. I haven't heard him this excited since he finished *Jak and Daxter*. He was crying about that, too. But this is more exciting. The Iron Man competition? I never thought my son would finish the Iron Man competition."

As a result of Karp's fantastic accomplishment, he had to call in sick to his job at Equinox Communications, where he works as a data processor.

"This is my third time calling in the past month," said Karp. "I already have a written warning against me, so I might be fired this time. But you know what? It was worth it. How many people in this life get to say they completed *Iron Man 2K4*? This is something I can tell my grandkids about, even though I'll probably never have grandkids."

Man Achieves Dream of Running Onto Field and Getting Pummeled by Security

SAN FRANCISCO, CA—Hank Pattell, 28, of Berkeley, CA, finally achieved his life-long dream of running onto the field during a baseball game and being pummeled by security guards. During the third inning of Saturday's Giants-Padres game at SBC Park, Pattell left his bleacher seat and heroically charged into the outfield, where he was set upon by six security guards, who viciously beat him within an inch of his life. "Whoa, that was awesome!" exclaimed Pattell from his hospital bed, where he is recovering from a broken fibula, four broken ribs, and fractured vertebrae. "I bet everyone in America was cheering for me as I defied security and ran out there onto the field. I'm a hero! And the experience would not have been complete without the obligatory ass-kicking from security. They did a great job, and I'm sure I'll regain movement in my arms and legs someday, despite what the doctors say."

French Cycling Fans Looking for New Cyclist to Spit On

FROMENTINE, FRANCE—The announcement of Lance Armstrong's retirement has left a void in the hearts of France's cycling fans. Without the legendary American competing in the race, who will they boo, heckle, and spit on? "Oh, Lance, we will miss you," said Jean-Paul Garin, avid cycling fan who has been a spectator at the last ten Tours. "Who will amaze us with his record-breaking performances? Who will overcome seemingly insurmountable odds to win race after race? Who will be the subject of rampant steroid speculation and our rabid anti-Americanism? In short, who will we spit on?" Tyler Hamilton, Armstrong's teammate, is said to be the most likely candidate to replace him. Starting in 2006, he will ride with a protective shield over his face.

THE BRUSHBACK REPORT

ALL THE SPORTS NEWS THAT'S UNFIT TO PRINT

The Brushback's Exclusive Interview with LeBron James

When *The Brushback* first approached Lebron James for an interview, we were predictably and justifiably kneed in the groin by a security guard. However, after going through the proper channels (sending a handwritten letter and some chocolates to the marketing firm that represents James' team of agents) and waiting the standard two years, we were awarded a ten-minute sit-down with the king. During those ten minutes, we shared some laughs, heard some revelations (he likes video games!) and were condescended to several times. It was all worthwhile, though, as you will see in this exclusive Brushback interview with Lebron James.

BB: LeBron, let me start off by asking you this: What makes you so awesome?

LeBron: Good question. There are a lot of things that America loves about me. There's a

see LEBRON, page 97

> LEBRON, continued from page 96

lot of things I love about myself. But I guess if I had to pick one thing, it would be my amazing wealth.

BB: That's fascinating. Now I want to talk about your relationship with Nike. You signed a $100 million contract with them while you were still in high school. Do you think you got a fair deal, or do you think they took advantage of you because you were so young?

LeBron: I think it's fair, for the most part. It was pretty reasonable for a high school kid, I guess. The funny thing about the shoe business is that those shoes cost just pennies to make. They pay foreign laborers next to nothing to stitch them together.

BB: So why's that funny?

LeBron: [laughs] I don't know, man. I just think it's funny.

BB: Couldn't agree more. When you were a kid growing up, did you have any idea that you would someday leave the slums of Akron—and all those dirty, dirty people—to achieve superstardom?

LeBron: Yeah, right around the age of 12 I felt there was something special about me. There was this, I don't know, this light around me. I just knew that eventually, if I worked hard enough, I'd be able to get out of the ghetto and start hanging out with Jewish people.

BB: Like agents, CEOs, people like that?

LeBron: Yeah, exactly. People who have my best interests in mind, and nobody else's.

BB: Well, what I'd like to ask you now—what I want you to describe to me—is a typical day in the life of LeBron James. What's it like to be you?

LeBron: Well, let's see . . . first I wake up in the morning and I tell myself, "I'm going to be the best me I can be today." Then I summon my assistant to prop me up in bed and put my slippers on my feet.

BB: Interesting.

LeBron: Thank you. Anyway, I eat breakfast, and then I watch a little *SportsCenter* to see which of my dunks made the highlights. Believe it or not, many of them don't. There are nights when I'm not featured at all.

BB: It seems odd that you wouldn't be in every single highlight. Is that frustrating for you?

LeBron: It can be, but you just deal with it. I don't want to make a big stink about it.

BB: A lot of athletes don't have that kind of humility. So what do you do next, LeBron?

LeBron: After breakfast? I play video games.

BB: Really? See, that's something that I think would surprise a lot of people—a young male in the 18 to 35 demographic playing video games. That's very unique.

LeBron: [laughs] Yes, a lot of people are like, "Wow, video games? Holy cow." But it's all good. I just like to play basketball because it really does improve my court vision. Often I play against myself just to experience the sheer terror that my opponents feel when they face me.

BB: Okay, so we know you play video games. Tell us something else about yourself that would surprise everyone. What's one thing that people don't know about LeBron James that would make them go, "Wow, I had no idea."

LeBron: Okay, well, I guess I can let you in on a little secret: I drive a Cadillac Escalade.

see LEBRON, page 98

> LEBRON, continued from page 97

BB: You drive a high-priced luxury SUV? You? LeBron James?

LeBron: Yeah, I have for a while. I know a lot of people think "NBA player" and then think "small, reasonably priced sedan." But for me, I just need something bigger than that. The only problem is they keep running out of gas. I've gone through five Escalades in the past two months. Goddamn gas guzzlers.

BB: Um, LeBron, you don't need to buy a new one every time it runs out of gas. You can just get more gas.

LeBron: What the hell are you talking about?

BB: Nothing. Who am I to tell you your business? Let's just move along. I'd like to play a little game. It's called "word association." I say a word, and you say the first word that pops into your head.

LeBron: I'm not following you.

BB: Just play it by ear. It's easy. Ready? Here's the first word: Prodigy.

LeBron: Prodigy . . . Okay, lets see. First word that pops into my head. Well, the first word that popped into my head was "pickle," because I just ate a sub, and I can still sort of taste the pickles. Is that acceptable?

BB: Yes, but from now on, try to stick to the first word that pops into your head that relates to the word I say. Now, let's try again. Ready? "Jordan."

LeBron: Pickle.

BB: Okay, here's another: "Legacy."

LeBron: Lawn mower.

BB: "Championship."

LeBron: Legacy.

BB: "Happiness."

LeBron: Chair.

BB: "God."

LeBron: Chair.

BB: You already said that.

LeBron: I know, but I can't get it out of my head because we're both sitting in chairs.

BB: I understand. This game can be tricky like that.

LeBron: Are you patronizing me?

BB: Yes.

LeBron: Good.

BB: Let's switch gears again. Where does LeBron see himself being in ten years?

LeBron: That's a tough one. I don't know. I suppose I'll be a wealthy superstar basketball player, a corporate pitchman, a dad, possibly a husband, but whatever I am, I will be much, much better than everyone else—including you. Especially you.

BB: So true, so true. Well, thanks for joining me, LeBron. May I shake your hand?

LeBron: Shake my assistant's hand.

BB: Of course. Thank you so much.

ON THIS DAY...

In 1913, Emily Davison threw herself under the hoofs of King George's horse at the Epson Derby. Historians say Davison was protesting on behalf of women's rights, but she was probably just on the rag or something.

49ers Not Mentioned in Recap of 49ers-Bears Game

Mike Vanderjagt Unaware How Close He Is to Getting His Ass Kicked

Entire Special Olympics to Be Included in Special Olympics Blooper Video

Athlete Gives Back to Community to Avoid Going to Jail

LOS ANGELES, CA—Darius McKinney, reserve forward for the LA Clippers, spends his weekends reading to blind schoolchildren at a school in Irvine, CA. The blind children have become as much a part of his life as basketball, ever since a judge sentenced him to community service for his role in a nightclub brawl almost a month ago.

"It was either read to the kids or go to jail for ninety days," said McKinney. "I thought about it long and hard, but in the end I decided to do the charity work. Giving back to the community is so very rewarding, especially since there's no danger of being stabbed with a shiv or raped in the shower."

The children at the Lentz Academy for the Blind hang on McKinney's every word as he reads from *The Little Engine That Could* and *Clifford the Big Red Dog* while serving out his sentence for spitting on a waitress and bludgeoning a bartender with a pool stick.

"Seeing the look on the kids' faces—that's what makes this all worthwhile," said McKinney. "You can make them so happy just by reading them a little story and spending some time with them. When my community service is up in sixty-seven days, thirteen hours, and thirty-two minutes, I sure will

"THIS EXPERIENCE HAS BEEN SO REWARDING THAT I'M ALMOST GLAD I SPIT ON THAT WOMAN," SAID DARIUS MCKINNEY.

miss it. In fact, this experience has been so rewarding that I'm almost glad I spit on that woman."

A teacher at the academy, Kim Robbins, has personally asked McKinney to return on a regular basis after his community service obligations are fulfilled. She said he was very receptive to the idea.

"I asked him to keep coming out of the goodness of his heart," said Robbins. "He was actually quite thrilled with the idea. So much so that he fell to the ground laughing. So you see, this community service is bringing him joy, too."

Despite Miss Robbins' optimism, McKinney is said to be counting the minutes until his time is up.

"Every day I put an 'X' on the calendar, marking the days until I am free of this community service," said McKinney. "It's not like I hate it or anything. It's just that I have better things to do with my time. Does it beat jail time? Absolutely. Does it beat sitting in my luxury apartment playing Playstation? Fuck no. It's time to teach these kids a valuable lesson: Life is unfair, people are mean, and professional athletes are pricks. Class dismissed."

DID YOU KNOW

On December 25, 1978, Major League Baseball celebrated Christmas.

Make-A-Wish Foundation Asked to Punch Barry Bonds in the Nuts

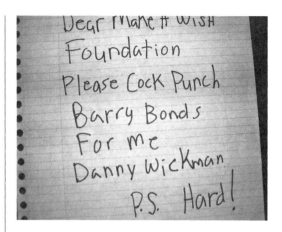

AMES, IA—Members of the Make-A-Wish Foundation struggled to come up with a response to a dying 9-year-old boy's request that they punch slugger Barry Bonds in the nuts repeatedly. The boy, Danny Wickman of Ames, IA, hates Bonds and wants desperately to see him in debilitating pain. The director of the foundation said that it was the first such request he had ever received.

"That's a first. Obviously the kid really hates Barry Bonds, as a lot of people do, but I don't know if we can comply with his request," said Charles Hopkinton, managing director of Make-A-Wish. "We'll have to call Barry and see if he's okay with it. What really strikes me, though, is the fact that he [Danny] isn't even interested in doing it himself. He's happy just to watch someone else do it. Now that's hatred."

Hopkinton first met Wickman during a visit to a children's hospital and eventually offered him a wish on behalf of the foundation. After mulling it over, Danny decided it would be most satisfying to watch his least favorite ballplayer get punched in the nuts.

"I kept asking him if he was sure," said Hopkinton. "And he kept saying 'yes.' I offered him all kinds of other stuff, but he was adamant. Danny insists he can only die peacefully once he has seen Bonds doubled over in pain."

Hopkinton has been trying to come up with a way to present the idea to Bonds. He does not expect the slugger to agree to have his testicles punched, but he may agree to make an appearance with young Danny, at which point they could ambush him.

"That's the only solution I can come up with right now," said Hopkinton. "As bad as it may sound, we might have to trick him into showing up and then just sneak in a few quick cock-punches so Danny can get his wish. After that, we'd probably have to run like hell, but this is a kid's dying wish. We can't say no. And frankly, we don't want to."

The director's biggest concern, he said, is Bonds' willingness to show up at all, even for a brief handshake and autograph session. The famous slugger has a reputation for being ornery and extremely private, even when it comes to cute, dying children.

"I know this guy doesn't do autographs and has a track record of turning down charity causes," said Hopkinton. "I know because one time I asked him to send a sick kid a signed eight-by-ten and he said no. Can you imagine that? Then I told him that he could just have his secretary sign it and send it out, and the kid wouldn't even know any better. He said, 'Nah, she's too busy.' Then I asked him to just turn his head slightly and look in the direction of the young boy, who was sitting behind the dugout. He just said, 'Nah. Got a sore neck.' That's why, if we can pull this off, I'll be the first in line to give him a good kick."

Sucker NFL Player to Attend Training Camp

DETROIT, MI—In the modern NFL, holding out of training camp is as common as a screen pass or a zone defense. Yes, training camp is "mandatory," but that doesn't stop anyone with a lousy contract and a good agent from staying home. Well, almost anyone. There is still 1 sucker who insists on showing up for camp every year, despite the fact that his contract is not worth the paper it's printed on. That player? Linebacker Earl Williams of the Detroit Lions.

"Earl is a great guy. He shows up to play every year and he never complains," said Lions GM Matt Millen. "That's the kind of player that I love. It doesn't matter how much money he's making or how bad we shit on him during contract negotiations. He still comes to camp, and you know why? Because he's a pussy."

In 2003, Williams was the recipient of a 6-year deal from the Lions worth $4.5 million. He received no signing bonus and the contract is loaded with incentives that he may never reach. What's more, the team will most likely cut him after the 2006 season to clear room under the salary cap. While most players would try hard to get a payday before being cut, Williams is a stubborn throwback.

"I'm not going to skip training camp just because I'm not happy with my contract," he said. "That's not what I'm about. I signed the contract and I will honor it, even though the team has no obligation to honor it themselves. Hell, they can rip it up and throw it in the trash if they want. But I'm not going to complain. I have no right whatsoever to demand fair treatment from my employer."

One factor that may be working against Williams is his decision to work without an agent. That approach has endeared him to owners across the league.

"He has no agent! None whatsoever! Oh man, I love that," said one NFC owner, laughing hysterically. "These guys walk into negotiations with this clueless look on their face. You give them a cup of coffee and hand them a contract that would insult a Malaysian sweatshop worker, and then watch them sign on the dotted line. Then they report to training camp right on time every year and work themselves nearly to death while you and your cronies sit up in a luxury box and smoke cigars. Oh, and here's the punch line: If they do hold out of camp, *they* get vilified for it. As a ruthless billionaire, you can't ask for much more than that."

> "IT DOESN'T MATTER HOW MUCH MONEY HE'S MAKING OR HOW BAD WE SHIT ON HIM DURING CONTRACT NEGOTIATIONS. HE STILL COMES TO CAMP, AND YOU KNOW WHY? BECAUSE HE'S A PUSSY," SAID GM MATT MILLEN.

THE BRUSHBACK GLOSSARY

HANDICAP: The number assigned to golfers that indicates how much they've lied about their scores.

PETA Demands Marv Albert Remove Dead Animal from His Head

NEW YORK, NY—People for the Ethical Treatment of Animals (PETA) is at it again. The radical animal rights group is now targeting TNT basketball analyst Marv Albert for wearing a dead animal on his head during NBA broadcasts.

"What kind of message is that sending to kids, that it's okay to ruthlessly murder animals for your own personal use?" asked PETA president Ingrid Newkirk. "This is really a despicable display of animal cruelty and degradation. And worse yet, it doesn't even look good. Be bald and be proud, Marv! And don't drag the animal kingdom down into your pathetic vanity."

For the past three nights, Newkirk and her PETA cronies have been picketing outside Continental Airlines Arena, where Albert is doing commentary for the Knicks-Nets series.

The protest was largely peaceful until Sunday afternoon, when Albert attempted to make his way through the throng of people and one overzealous woman attempted to pull the animal carcass off Albert's head.

PETA is known for its aggressive pro–animal rights stance, but the latest crusade has drawn ridicule from the general public, as most people believe that Albert has a right to wear whatever he wants on his head.

"Hey, that's his business. If he wants to wear a skunk carcass on his head, who are we to judge?" asked Gil Vernon of Long Island,

"I HAVE A RIGHT AS AN AMERICAN TO WEAR A DECEASED MEMBER OF THE RODENT FAMILY ON MY SKULL FOR THE PURPOSES OF FOLLICLE ENHANCEMENT," SAID MARV ALBERT.

who attended Game 1 at Madison Square Garden. "It's not like he killed the thing. It was already dead. At least now it's going to good use. Well, not good use exactly, but use nonetheless."

There are several stories going around about the origin of the hairpiece, but Albert is not revealing how and where he acquired it.

"I have a right as an American to wear a deceased member of the rodent family on my skull for the purposes of follicle enhancement," Albert told reporters after the game. "I'm not about to remove it now because this animal rights group thinks I've done something wrong."

PETA is facing an uphill battle, as there are currently no laws that prohibit the wearing of animal carcasses on the head.

Darryl Strawberry Fondly Recalls Battle with Drug Addiction

LOS ANGELES, CA—Darryl Strawberry once had it all. The former baseball star was one of the premier sluggers of his era, winning rookie of the year honors in 1983 and a World Series in 1986. In his prime he was the toast of Manhattan, frequenting the city's famous hot spots with his teammates, cavorting with beautiful groupies, drinking excessively, and ingesting huge amounts of high-quality cocaine.

Almost ten years later Strawberry is drug-free and an active member of the Without Walls International Church. He spends most of his time attending mass, performing charity work, and fondly recalling his days of booze, drugs, and hookers.

"Boy, those were days," said Strawberry, a warm smile on his face. "Especially '86. Man, '86 was the year. We won 108 games, we were the talk of the town, and all we did was take drugs and get laid. Don't get me wrong. Drugs are a terrible, terrible thing, but there is something to be said for using a rolled up hundred-dollar bill to snort lines off a stripper's stomach."

Strawberry often travels to elementary schools to educate children on the dangers of drug abuse. Sometimes, when he is speaking to a classroom, his voice drifts off and he becomes lost in reverie.

Maria Gonzalez, a teacher at Miami's Dade County Elementary School, recalls the day when Strawberry addressed her class: "He was great, for the most part. But when he was telling all his so-called horror stories he was smiling. At one point he was like, 'And when I was at my lowest point, I'd go to

> "I OFTEN WARN MY OWN CHILDREN ABOUT THE PERILS OF DRUG AND ALCOHOL ABUSE, BUT FRANKLY, I'D GIVE MY LEFT NUT TO GO BACK TO THOSE DAYS," SAID RAY KNIGHT.

Scores and pick two of the most beautiful strippers, buy some really amazing coke from one of the bouncers, go to a penthouse in the Four Seasons, and just party all night.' Then he paused for a moment and stared off into space with this little grin on his face. I don't blame him, really. That does sound like fun."

Though none of Strawberry's former teammates experienced the same crippling addiction he did, many of them shared his affinity for decadence and debauchery.

"He was the life of the party all right," said former teammate Ray Knight, now a broadcaster for ESPN. "Whenever we needed something, he got it. Whenever we were looking for something to do, Darryl was the one with the ideas and the connections. I often warn my own children about the perils of drug and alcohol abuse, but frankly, I'd give my left nut to go back to those days."

Today, Strawberry is on his way to a church-sponsored youth conference in Los Angeles. He will once again stand before a group of teens and speak honestly about his transgressions. He's looking forward to the opportunity, but said that "total honesty" is not always the best policy.

"Let's face it. If we were all totally honest with kids about drugs, they'd be running out and trying them immediately," said Strawberry. "I mean, I'm not about to get up there and say 'Yeah, smoking Acapulco gold and drinking champagne in a hot tub is a terrible nightmare.' They'd laugh in my face. I have to skip over that stuff and tell them about the aftereffects. You know, like finding Jesus. Now that's a drag."

Dream Job Winner Given Coloring Book to Keep Him Busy

BRISTOL, CT—When Mike Hall was chosen as winner of the ESPN reality show *Dream Job,* he expected his life to change drastically. He was prepared for long hours, hard work, and national exposure on the popular show *SportsCenter.*

Instead, the 21-year-old Hall has been given odd jobs around the office to earn his salary. Whether it's getting coffee for Stuart Scott, waxing Dan Patrick's Bentley, or running errands for Linda Cohen, Hall has proved himself a hard worker who is eager to please.

"Mike has been a great addition to the ESPN staff. We're thrilled to have him on board," said producer Carol Silver. "He'll be getting a chance to shine on television before long, but right now we just have to keep him out of the way. That's why we gave him that great *Frosty the Snowman* coloring book. It might be a little out of season, but it should keep him busy for a while."

Though most television viewers believed Hall would be a regular on *SportsCenter* following *Dream Job,* Silver insists that was not the case.

"*Dream Job* was designed to get ratings. It's not like we were strapped for anchors," she said. "Mike's going to be a good sportscaster someday, but for now we just need to keep him out of the way. *Hey, Hall! I said half and half, not milk! Get your ass back to Krispy Kreme!* Anyway, he's a nice kid."

Hall's family and friends, who expected him to be the next Dan Patrick, claim they have not heard from him since he moved to Bristol for his new job.

"Every time I call his cell phone, that Carol Silver woman answers," said Melanie Hall, Mike's mom. "She keeps telling me he's 'indisposed' and that he'll call back."

As for Hall, he will continue to pay his dues in hopes of becoming a part of *SportsCenter*'s all-star cast. For now his main focus is on doing odd jobs and coloring.

"Ah, fuck me, I colored out of the lines again," said a frustrated Hall. "Damn it. Why do they have to make Frosty's buttons so small? I tell you, this has been a real challenge. It sort of reminds me of the first *Karate Kid* movie, when Mr. Miyagi is having Daniel wax his car and paint his fence and stuff, and Daniel can't understand what's going on. Well, before you know it, Daniel can do all these great karate moves. That's how I feel about this whole process. Maybe all this coloring and running errands is supposed to be a way for me to develop the proper fundamentals to be a real ESPN anchor."

Long Home Run Causes Chris Berman's Head to Explode

HOUSTON, TX—Friends and family of ESPN broadcaster Chris Berman expressed sadness Tuesday night when a tape measure home run off the bat of Barry Bonds caused the popular sportscaster's head to explode. The incident occurred during the home run derby in Houston, where Berman was providing commentary for the event.

Joe Morgan, who co-anchored the event with Berman, admitted that he saw the tragedy coming a mile away.

"Well, Chris was just very excited over all the home runs being hit, and I kept warning him to calm down," said Morgan. "Every time a ball flew out of the park, he would scream and yell and act like he'd never seen a home run before. I kept saying, 'Hey, Chris, it's only a home run. We see them all the time. It's not the frigging moon landing.' "

Morgan then described the moment when Berman's head swelled to twice its normal size and exploded all over the set like a dropped watermelon.

"I think it was right around Barry Bonds' seventh dinger. Chris's head got really, really red like it was ready to burst, and I told him to calm down, but he didn't listen. Then number seven soared over the left-field wall and Chris yelled, 'BANG! THERE IT IS! NUMBER 7! CAN YOU BELIEVE IT? HOLY F——.' And that was it. I heard a sound like a balloon popping and the next thing I knew I was covered in blood, guts, and brain matter. At least he went out doing what he loved best—overreacting."

> "AT LEAST HE WENT OUT DOING WHAT HE LOVED BEST—OVERREACTING," SAID JOE MORGAN.

After the explosion, chaos ensued. Players and members of the media gathered around the table, frantically using their cell phones to call 9-1-1. Bonds insisted his at-bat continue, but security personnel put a halt to the proceedings to let the ambulance through.

"There were people everywhere wondering what the hell had happened," said ambulance driver Terry Meinholz. "Everyone was screaming and yelling, women and children were crying. It was all we could do to make our way through the mob to get to the victim. The only person who looked relaxed was Joe Morgan. He was standing off to the side calmly wiping the brain matter off his suit. The guy's never shown an emotion in his life. He's like the anti-Berman."

Players who witnessed the incident offered condolences to the Berman family and shared some of their memories of the venerable sports icon.

The Phillies' Jim Thome fondly remembered Berman as a "big, fat blob of hyperbole."

"That guy would call a home run like he'd never seen a home run before in his life," said Thome. "I mean, we're living in the age of the power hitters. We're living in a time when home runs are as routine as fly balls and groundouts. Not to mention Minute Maid Park is about the size of my backyard. He should be ashamed of himself, that self-aggrandizing, showboat ham. Oh . . . was this supposed to be a fond remembrance? Um . . . he wore a lot of stylish suits."

Mike Krzyzewski Turns to American Express Card for Comfort

DURHAM, NC—Devastated by his team's recent loss to Michigan State, Duke coach Mike Krzyzewski turned to his American Express Platinum card for comfort. The grieving coach gently caressed the smooth plastic surface before using it to purchase a brand-new Lincoln Navigator.

"Players come and go, victories and defeats pile up, but one thing that remains constant is my American Express Platinum card with unlimited spending," said Krzyzewski while driving his new Navigator through the streets of Durham. "It has all the qualities I would want in a player: It's loyal, dependable, efficient, and intelligent. The only difference is the card won't go on to become a moderately effective, chronically injured NBA player."

Aside from loyalty, the Amex card offers many more intangibles that basketball players cannot, including guaranteed success and poise in the clutch.

"When I go to make a purchase with my card, I know it's going to come through for me," said Krzyzewski. "It never lets me down, and I can always count on it not to go out and shoot 4 for 14 in a goddamn TOURNAMENT GAME AGAINST A LESSER OPPONENT! Thank you very much, J. J. Redick."

After the crushing loss to Michigan State, Coach K addressed his team in the locker room and gave them a heartfelt speech about the importance of team play, persistence, and American Express's zero percent APR for the first six months.

"Kids, whether you win these games or lose them, the important thing is that you grow as a person," said an emotional Krzyzewski as his players sat in rapt attention. "Take American Express, for example. These guys offer 5 percent cash back on all purchases, frequent flier mileage, and a plethora of great gift ideas. Do they have to? No. They could easily sit on their hands and count their money, but instead they choose to go that extra mile for the consumer, and that's why I say, 'My life, my card.' "

NASCAR Diversity Committee Tries to Look Busy

DAYTONA BEACH, FL—NASCAR's Diversity Committee held some kind of meeting at their Daytona Beach headquarters yesterday in an attempt to look busy. The meeting, headed by director Tish Sheets, took place in a conference room at a long table with a tray of bagels and cream cheese placed directly in the center. Afterward, Sheets said the committee was "extremely busy." "We've got a lot going on right now," she said. "We're working on lots of initiatives to do some stuff about diversity issues. We spent a lot of time in that meeting eating bagels, drinking coffee, and discussing, you know, initiatives. We're busy, okay? Jesus, do I come to your work and ask what you've been doing all day?"

93 Percent of U.S. Opinions Football-Related

NHL Labor Meeting Devolves into All-Out Brawl

Batter Talked Out of Suicide Squeeze

"THANK GOD WE LIVE IN A COUNTRY WHERE A WOMAN HAS THE RIGHT TO CHOOSE. I DON'T WANT MY FIRST GRANDSON TO BE BORN WITH TATTOOS," SAYS BUSH.

Bush Turns Pro-Choice After Daughter Impregnated by Ricky Davis

WASHINGTON, DC—President Bush was forced to reconsider his stance on abortion Friday when he learned that his daughter Jenna had been impregnated by NBA star Ricky Davis. Bush immediately suggested that his daughter have the pregnancy terminated.

"My fellow Americans, now is the time for us to be flexible, understanding, and tolerant," Bush said in his weekly radio address. "Sure, it's good to be resolute and hold firm to your convictions, but we must also be adaptable to different circumstances. For instance, there are certain situations when safe, professional abortions should not only be legal, but encouraged. Remember, it's only a fetus, not an actual baby."

First daughter Jenna Bush apparently met Davis at a Houston nightclub after a Celtics-Rockets preseason game last October. Bush, a huge basketball fan, allowed Davis to buy her a drink. Later, Davis and the first daughter were seen together on the dance floor. Afterward they went to Davis's hotel room, where the two allegedly had sex.

see PRO-CHOICE, page 110

> PRO-CHOICE, continued from page 109

Davis recounted the incident in an interview on *Best Damn Sports Show Period*.

"Yeah, yeah I got it on with the president's daughter," said Davis amid roars of approval from the crowd. "She's a nice girl. We met up at this club and we hooked up and went back to my room. We talked for a while, then I put in that new R. Kelly CD and went to town. Man, that bitch can suck the label off a bottle of gin. I'm just glad the Secret Service didn't shoot me. I kept seeing red laser dots on my chest while we were in the club."

The Secret Service agents assigned to protect Ms. Bush were taken to task by the president for failing to prevent the one-night stand. However, the agents defended their actions, insisting that it's not their job to interfere with her social life.

"We saw her leaving with Mr. Davis. We even stood outside the hotel room while they were in there," said Lawrence Petty, one of the agents assigned to protect Miss Bush. "What am I supposed to do, physically restrain her? I'm not her mother. If he was trying to kill her we would've stopped him.

But he was only having sex with her, which in this case is probably worse."

A month later, Jenna went to the hospital with stomach pains and discovered she was pregnant. When the president learned who the father was, he wasted no time in making his decision.

"Abort it. Abort it immediately," he was reported to have said to his daughter. "Call a doctor. We can have it done privately. It's very simple and it's safe. It won't hurt a bit. Thank God we live in a country where a woman has the right to choose. I don't want my first grandson to be born with tattoos."

Publicly, Bush was much more diplomatic about his daughter's pregnancy. He praised Davis as a "nice young man" but said that Jenna is not ready to be a mom just yet.

"I have nothing but respect for Mr. Davis and his unparalleled dunking ability," Bush began, "but, simply put, my daughter is still quite young and not ready to be a mother. I do believe in my soul that it is wrong to terminate a pregnancy, so it is with a heavy heart that I authorize this medical procedure—but not that heavy, since I've already been re-elected."

Poor Service Disrupts Cingular Call to the Bullpen

LOS ANGELES, CA—Dodgers manager Jim Tracy expressed frustration yesterday when his Cingular call to the bullpen was disrupted by Cingular's poor service. Tracy was attempting to call for a reliever, but his promotional MLB cell phone went dead before he could make the switch. "I really wanted to get [Eric] Gagne warmed up before the 9th, so I gave them a call on this stupid phone," said Tracy, holding up the cellular phone that was provided as an alternative to the old-fashioned bullpen phone. "I got [bullpen coach] Tony Cloninger on the phone, but just as I was about to give him the green light, the damn thing went dead. Every time I try to use it, it goes dead. Don't they have cell phone towers in Los Angeles?" Tracy then referred to the monthly plan as his "Cingular blows" plan.

Tragic Death of Teammate Fails to Put Things in Perspective

INDIANAPOLIS, IN — When Rod Macklin of the Triple A Indianapolis Indians was killed in a car accident on August 5, many thought it would throw the team into a tailspin as they struggled to deal with the stunning loss. However, a funny thing happened to the Indians after Macklin's death: absolutely nothing.

"Rod's death really put nothing at all in perspective," said manager Ed North. "We still feel like the game of baseball is really important, despite the fact that one of our players lost his life in a tragic accident. Yep, our perspective is exactly the same."

After hearing the news, North did not reflect on the importance of spending time with his loved ones, nor did he gain a greater appreciation of all that he has. His players didn't, either.

Even at the funeral, North confessed to thinking mostly about baseball.

"That funeral really made me stop and think. As the body was being lowered into the ground, all I could think about was how the hell I was going to replace his bat in the lineup. Then as we were singing 'Amazing Grace,' I was wondering who I should start in right field. Man, these unexpected deaths can create a glut of roster problems."

Macklin's teammates were shocked when they heard the news about their friend's death. But after a few hours the shock wore off, and there is no discernible difference in the players' attitudes or perspectives.

Aaron Ford, Indians first baseman, said that he would miss his friend but conceded that "shit happens."

"I guess it's sad that I won't have him to play cards with on the team bus," he said. "He was a nice guy and we had some fun times together. But there are more important things to focus on right now, like winning some ball games. We can't be worried about some dead guy. Life is for the living."

"This has not made me stop and reflect on all the blessings that I have," said catcher Rich Coady. "It certainly hasn't made me question the importance of sports or anything like that. And if anyone thinks that I went home and hugged my wife and kids after I heard the news, they couldn't be more wrong. Why would I do that? They didn't die. They're still alive and well and bleeding me for every penny I have."

Immediately after Macklin's funeral, the team placed all his belongings in a cardboard box and shipped them via regular ground mail to the family along with a bouquet of flowers and a condolence card. No special ceremonies or gestures are planned to honor the memory of Macklin, and the players will not be wearing black armbands for the remainder of the season. The team also declined to hold a moment of silence before the game immediately after Macklin was killed.

"A moment of silence? Why? We're a baseball team, not a goddamn congregation," said North. "Oh, and please don't ask if the team is going to rally around the memory of our fallen comrade and play inspired ball. I think we all know the answer to that question."

> "AS THE BODY WAS BEING LOWERED INTO THE GROUND, ALL I COULD THINK ABOUT WAS HOW THE HELL I WAS GOING TO REPLACE HIS BAT IN THE LINEUP," SAID ED NORTH.

Sportswriter Can't Stop Ranking Things

BRISTOL, CT—An ESPN.com sportswriter was diagnosed with obsessive compulsive disorder recently after confessing to an insatiable need to rank anything and everything. The writer, Jeff Merron, reportedly had a nervous breakdown after spending five straight hours trying to compile a Top 10 list of his all-time greatest pairs of socks. He was granted a leave of absence by ESPN.

"I thought I was going crazy," Merron said from his room at the Bristol Hospital psychiatric ward. "Everywhere I went I would rank things I came across. At first it was fun to rank great ballplayers or notable games for my column. But the compulsion started to seep into everything I did. I started to unravel last month when I took to compiling extensive rankings of every car I saw on my way to work. I got into six accidents."

Merron began compiling Top 10 lists at the behest of his ESPN.com editors. The media's increasing desire to place every play, player, and game into historical context has reached a fever pitch, and the demand on sportswriters has never been greater.

"Putting every single random occurrence into some kind of neat, numerical order has become a national obsession," said ESPN editor Jim Lemoine. "Sadly, this can be really trying for our writers. Jeff's case is extreme. I'd say he is probably one of the top three mentally fucked sportswriters of his generation—and that's saying a lot."

Jim Caple, senior writer for ESPN.com, sympathized with Merron and called for an ease on ranking and list making.

"This is a wake-up call for all of us," Caple said. "Any sportswriter out there who thinks it can't happen to them is in denial. I personally spend half my day maniacally labeling and categorizing things that really don't need to be labeled or categorized. It's really just a waste of time. Incessant ranking is probably the #1 problem facing sportswriters today, ahead of 2) obesity, and 3) body odor."

Although Lemoine sympathizes with his colleague, he and many others think the virtues of frantic categorization far outweigh the negative effects.

"Sure, what happened to Jeff is too bad, but prior to the dawn of the Internet there were thousands and thousands of facts, figures, and players that went tragically unranked," he said. "Nobody had any idea who the biggest Super Bowl goat of all time was, or which left-handed Latino catcher was the best at blocking wild pitches during day games, or who the Top 10 protective face mask–wearing rebounders in NBA history were. As scary as it sounds, all that information was just floating around out there, untethered, with nobody to organize it. A few sportswriters may go crazy now and then as a result, but we should all just be thankful that we live in the new, golden age of sports trivia categorization."

DID Y?U KNOW

Only seven pro golfers in history have had ugly wives.

Mysterious E-Mailer Informs Bud Selig Hot Teen Sluts are Waiting for Him

MILWAUKEE, WI—Bud Selig was confused and excited Friday afternoon when he received an e-mail informing him that a group of hot teen sluts was waiting for him at an undisclosed location. The subject line of the mysterious e-mail read "Hot teen slutz R waiting 4 U now!" and the body of the letter included several photos of what appeared to be hot teen sluts depicted in various suggestive poses. Selig attempted to respond to the e-mail, but was unsuccessful.

"I sent a response asking for more details, like who these girls are and where I could meet them," said Selig. "Unfortunately, the e-mail was returned, saying it was an 'unknown address.' I hope there wasn't some kind of e-mail malfunction. It sure would be a shame to miss out on an opportunity like this just because of some weird technical problem. I mean, how many chances do you get to bang hot teen sluts?"

Adding to the confusion was the mysterious, coded message embedded at the bottom of the e-mail: "congeal facilitate barter headstrong acquiesce obtuse thinking middle guarantee xvnswrjunwno."

"What could that possibly mean?" asked an exasperated Selig. "What are these people trying to communicate to me? If I'm able to decipher it, the hot teen sluts are mine. If not, it's back to my right hand and a box of Kleenex."

Selig ruled out the possibility of a prank since the e-mail provided actual photos of the girls who are waiting for him.

"When I first received the e-mail, I thought it could be some kind of practical joke or something," said Selig. "But then when I opened it up, I realized it was completely credible. There they were, right in front of me: a group of hot teen sluts, exactly as they were described in the subject line. Today's women sure are bold. In my day if you wanted to bang a hot teen slut you had to take her out for a root beer float and slip her a roofie."

In addition to questioning their motives, Selig is also wondering how the teen sluts and their collaborators were able to acquire his private e-mail address.

"Somehow these people got my personal e-mail address," said Selig. "I've thought this out extensively and there are only two ways they could have figured it out. Either they contacted somebody who knows me and is familiar with my address, or they know me themselves."

To complicate matters, Selig was the recipient of another mystery e-mail just yesterday. This one was not sexual in nature. Instead it offered him "the lowest mortgage rates in years."

"Wow, first hot teen sluts, now extremely low mortgage rates," said Selig. "This is all very overwhelming. Obviously I am being contacted by some secret benefactor or something. You know, all my life I've tried to treat people with respect, kindness, and generosity, and now all those things are paying off. Teen sluts, low mortgage rates—what's next, somebody offering to magically enlarge my penis?"

> THE SUBJECT LINE OF THE MYSTERIOUS E-MAIL READ "HOT TEEN SLUTZ R WAITING 4 U NOW!"

Slimmed-Down Ichiro Raises Suspicions at Mariners Camp

PEORIA, AZ—2004 batting champ Ichiro raised some eyebrows this week when he strolled into Mariners training camp 30 pounds lighter than last season. Though he attributed the weight loss to an off-season diet, some members of the media were openly skeptical.

"It's sad to say, but in this day and age, you really have to question anyone who sheds that much weight in the off-season," said ESPN's Jayson Stark. "One can't help but think those 8 home runs he hit last year were aided by some illegal supplements. And those bunts— did you ever notice how they used to pop off his bat? Like they were being shot out of a cannon. It just proves what I've been saying all along: Japanese people are not to be trusted."

Ichiro's off-season "dieting" has trimmed his weight down to approximately 85 pounds. He told reporters that he lost the weight in order to improve his speed and flexibility. He also pointed out that he was nowhere near the league lead in home runs last year.

"If I was doing steroids last year, they weren't helping," said Ichiro. "I broke the single season record for singles, remember? But at the end of the season, I was feeling a bit bloated. I was up to 115 pounds and it was starting to affect my speed. Now I can run to first base like a gazelle provided there is no breeze to blow me into the stands like a discarded paper plate."

Ichiro's teammates have come out in his support, saying that he's innocent until proven guilty. However, some opposing players were uncertain of his explanation and wondered whether the emaciated right-fielder was hiding something.

"He certainly has some explaining to do," said A's third baseman Eric Chavez. "Here's a guy who was around 115, 120 last year, and now he comes in weighing 85? Oh, and baseball just approved a tougher steroid policy, too. You're going to tell me that's a coincidence? I don't think so. It makes me so mad. Just think: To hit my 29 home runs last year, all I needed was a handful of amphetamines and a corked bat."

Sportswriter Awarded Pulitzer for "Basket-Brawl" Pun

BRISTOL, CT—ESPN.com staff writer Don Barber was awarded the Pulitzer Prize on Monday for coming up with the amazing and groundbreaking pun "basket-brawl" to describe the Pistons-Pacers melee Friday night. Though the Pulitzer Prize is normally awarded during the month of May, officials arranged a special ceremony to honor Barber for his contribution to world literature. "Mr. Barber is an innovator and a master of the English language," said Lee C. Bollinger, president of Columbia University, where the ceremony is held. "What he did was take the word 'basketball' and modify it so the word 'brawl' replaced 'ball.' The resulting word, 'basket-brawl,' is not only clever and original, it also aptly describes the incident at the Palace Friday night. Bravo, Mr. Barber. The English language has been enriched by your creativity."

Date Not Impressed by Wiffle Ball Comeback Story

"I CAN'T FIGURE OUT CHICKS ANYMORE. I GIVE UP."

FT. MYERS, FL—Kate Sullivan, 27, was forced to endure a lengthy Wiffle ball comeback story Saturday night during dinner. Her date, Steven Halstrom, recounted how he and a friend shocked their opponents by overcoming a staggering 10-run deficit in only three innings. Surprisingly, Sullivan looked bored.

"I don't know why she was being so snobby about it," said the 29-year-old Halstrom. "I know it's only a Wiffle ball game, but on a first date you want to impress the girl. I thought she'd like to know that I have the heart of a champion and never quit. Qualities like that have gone out of fashion, I guess."

According to Halstrom, the date was going "a little slowly" when he decided to break out the Wiffle ball story.

"She didn't have much to say. She was extremely quiet and shy," said Halstrom. "So I thought she'd appreciate hearing about how me and my friend Tim came back from a seemingly insurmountable 10 runs behind to beat Eric and Kyle. I thought it was pretty impressive, but what do I know? I can't figure out chicks anymore. I give up."

Sullivan disagreed with Halstrom's version of events. While she admitted being bored by his Wiffle ball story, she denied being "quiet and shy."

"Quiet and shy? He said I was quiet and shy? Well, I guess that's his side of the story," she said. "The truth is, I had plenty to say but he wasn't a very good listener. I told him about my job at the hospital and he just nod- ded without even looking up from his salad. Then I told him a little bit about my family, and he just nodded and said, 'Cool.' Then he starts talking about his little Wiffle ball game, and I'm supposed to get all excited about it? I mean, it's nice that he won the game and everything, but I would be more impressed if he had a job. Plus, everyone knows runs are easy to come by in Wiffle ball."

Unfortunately for Halstrom, Sullivan insisted that there would be no second date.

"Look, he's a nice guy and all, but I'm just not interested," she said. "Why would he bust that story out on a first date when we could've talked about so many different things? And why would he keep going on and on when I was clearly bored? I don't know, maybe if he was just slightly attractive physically I could overlook all this stuff."

Even though his chances at a second date seem bleak, Halstrom said he has no regrets. He said that he will gladly talk about his Wiffle ball prowess on future dates, until he finds someone who can appreciate his courage and determination.

"A lot of girls would love a guy who has a never-say-die attitude and busts his butt until the final out is recorded, so I'm not really concerned," he said. "Perhaps I just need to modify my approach to first dates. Maybe I should wait awhile before I start bragging about my exploits. I don't want to come across as being arrogant."

Red Sox, Yankees Feel Obligated to Fight

NEW YORK, NY—Players from the Red Sox and Yankees acknowledged today that they will probably fight each other during their upcoming series at Yankee Stadium. Though the teams would rather concentrate on playing baseball than engaging in a brawl, they do feel an obligation to meet the expectations of the fans and media.

"I guess we'll probably have to have some kind of incident," said Red Sox catcher Jason Varitek, sighing. "The TV crews will all be there, everyone will be watching back home, the fans will be inebriated. Plus, the Fox peo-

ple have really been putting the pressure on us. They're hoping we can fight near the backstop right in front of that big *American Idol* sign."

In recent years the Red Sox–Yankees rivalry has reached new levels. Each season brings a new chapter, complete with heroes, villains, and high drama. Under the glare of the spotlight, the pressure builds to do something memorable.

"Oh boy, here we go, another damn series against the Red Sox," said Yankees shortstop Derek Jeter. "I suppose something 'monumental' and 'historic' is going to happen. For me and a lot of the other guys it gets boring, but the media never gets sick of it. So I guess it's time for another epic battle. Wake me when it's over."

Jeter's teammate Bernie Williams says the

see FIGHT, page 117

> FIGHT, continued from page 116

pressure to appease the masses will push the players to instigate fights whenever the opportunity arises.

"You can bet we'll fight the first chance we get," said Williams. "It's not like we want to, but deep down we are all entertainers. Us not fighting would be like Lynyrd Skynyrd not doing 'Freebird.' So next time we play each other, I'll have my game face on. You know, the one that looks like I'm sitting at the kitchen table and reading the back of a cereal box."

The media is doing its part to ensure the two teams have the proper motivation for their next brawl. The Fox network has already finished its trailer for the big matchup, which will be aired dozens of times over the next few weeks and once again during the pregame show. The trailer will feature slow-motion shots of classic Sox-Yankees fights with this voice-over by Joe Buck:

"The Empire. The Jedi. Two fierce rivals square off in an all-out, no-holds-barred smackdown that will leave both teams bloodied, but only one team defeated. Who will be this year's hero? Who will be this year's villain? Will somebody be killed? Yes, hopefully, if there's any justice in this world."

With so much pressure to fight, managers on both teams are having a hard time focusing their players on the game itself. In fact, both managers said they'd be happy when the series is over and they can return to the business of playing baseball.

"I used to look forward to these series with the Red Sox, but not anymore," said Yankees skipper Joe Torre. "I've even got the Fox people telling me to get involved in the fighting. They say it would be 'momentous' and 'historic' if I body-slammed Terry Francona and maybe stomped on his testicles. It would be 'just another chapter in this century-long blood feud.' Whatever. If I want to stomp on some guy's testicles, I'll go to one of Jeter's S&M parties."

MasterCard Voice-Over Guy to Be Executed in Pay-Per-View Special

LOS ANGELES, CA—John Wallace, the voice behind MasterCard's "Priceless" ad campaign, will be executed on a pay-per-view special to be aired October 11. The long-awaited execution will put a stop to the incessant commercials while silencing forever Wallace's irritating, smug little voice. "If there's one thing every American has in common, it's our undying hatred for those MasterCard commercials," said Richard Tomkins of Tomkins Entertainment, the event's organizer. "That's why people are lining up to experience the visceral thrill of seeing the voice behind those commercials placed in front of a firing squad. Bring the whole family. Popcorn: $5. Soda: $3. Pay-per-view cost: $49.95. Seeing the MasterCard voice-over guy executed on live TV: Priceless."

Allen Iverson Not So Tough-Looking in Khakis, Loafers

PHILADELPHIA, PA—The NBA instituted a new dress code for its players this week in an attempt to soften the league's image. Instead of gold chains, baggy jeans, and do-rags, players will be forced to dress in "business casual" attire. The dress code is already having an impact, as some of the NBA's most intimidating players, like the 76ers' Allen Iverson, now look like total pussies before and after games.

"I look so goddamn gay right now," Iverson said to reporters as he was walking off the team bus Tuesday for a game against the Knicks. "Look at these pants. Khakis? I never in my life thought I'd be wearing khakis. I didn't even know what the word meant until last week. And these shoes suck. If I knew I was going to have to dress like this, I would've stuck to my original career path of being a mutual funds trader."

Iverson also knows that he is no longer intimidating to older white people.

"One thing I'm already missing is the frightened glances I used to get from white people when I walked by. You could tell they were really intimidated when I had my sideways hat, my oversized gold chains, my knee-length Julius Erving retro-shirt, and of course, my tattoos. Now all you can see is the one on my neck, and it's partially covered by my shirt collar so it actually looks like I have some hideous skin disease."

The dress code applies to all players and must be worn during public appearances, interviews, and games if the player is injured and not wearing his uniform. Any player who violates the dress code will be fined. Some, like Denver's Marcus Camby, are willing to pay the fine if it means dressing how they want.

"They can fine me. I don't really care," said a defiant Camby. "They can't be telling us how to dress. We're grown men here. That would be like an accountant or banker being sent home from work because he's wearing jeans, a bandana, and a 50 Cent shirt. It's ridiculous. That would never happen. We should be held to the same standards as everyone else."

The idea for the dress code originated with commissioner David Stern, who wants the NBA to be more like the NFL, in which players must wear suits and ties when they travel in public with their teams. He scoffed at the suggestion that he was trying to distance the league from hip-hop culture and style.

"It's not about hip-hop. It's just about carrying yourself in a dignified and professional manner," said Stern. "These players are representing the league and their team every time they go out in public. They're making millions of dollars. They should be able to afford a few nice suits. And for those players who disagree with the dress code, well, maybe it's time to grow up. Nobody gives a shit about your collection of retro-jerseys."

Stern did admit, however, that some of the players look "damn funny" in their new duds.

"Okay, I admit that some of the guys don't exactly look comfortable in their new attire," he said. "Take Steve Nash, for example. He normally dresses like he's going to a Pearl Jam concert. Now he sort of looks like some generic temp worker in an office. And how about Allen Iverson? Holy shit, I used to run and hide when he came around, now I have to stifle a laugh. He looks less comfortable in that suit than I would in a pair of ass-less leather pants. And I can tell you from experience that those things chafe like crazy."

Disciplinarian Parcells Kills Two Rookies with Bare Hands

College Basketball Player Declares for Draft After Hitting Uncontested Layup

Starving Iraqi War Orphans Inspired by New Adidas Ad

Little Leaguer Charges Into Stands After Being Called "Belly Itcher"

INDIANAPOLIS, IN—A melee broke out between players and fans at a Little League World Series game Saturday in Indianapolis. According to witnesses, the fight started when Owensboro, KY, player Kevin Paxon, 11, charged into the stands after a heckler referred to him as a "belly itcher." He was followed by several teammates, and the ensuing brawl resulted in five arrests.

A fan seated nearby described the events that led to the incident.

"Kevin [Paxon] was pitching, and he got pulled from the game because he wasn't doing so well," said Anne McCowan, 37, who was seated on the first base line. "As he was walking back to the dugout, this group of kids, they couldn't have been more than 8 years old, started chanting, 'We want a pitcher, not a belly itcher.' Well, that just rubbed Kevin the wrong way. He threw his glove on the ground, climbed over the wall, and went after them."

Paxon managed to punch one of the young-sters before being swarmed by a group of spectators. That's when his teammates came to his aid.

"After Kevin punched that one little kid, everything went kind of nuts," said McCowan. "A bunch of people grabbed him and started hitting him, and then four or five of his teammates jumped into the crowd and joined the fray. One of them picked up a folding chair and threw it. Fans have gotten out of control. I can see criticizing someone's game, but calling him a 'belly itcher'? That's personal."

Paxon, in a statement released to the press, apologized for the incident, calling it "unfortunate."

"This is an embarrassing and unfortunate incident, and I apologize to anyone I may have hurt or offended," the statement read. "It's just too bad people can't come to the game and enjoy themselves without verbally abusing the players, especially with small children in the vicinity—like me."

Tom Gordon Referred to as "Uncle Tom" by Nephew

NEW YORK—Yankees reliever Tom Gordon was shocked and offended when his nephew Jason referred to him as "Uncle Tom" during a family dinner on Sunday. Gordon reprimanded young Jason and demanded an apology. "Apologize to me now, young man!" Gordon snapped to the confused 6-year-old. "That is a disrespectful term that brings back memories of slavery and discrimination. I don't know where you learned that, but I have a mind to wash your little mouth out with soap. Now apologize!" "I'm sorry! I'm sorry!" cried Jason, his eyes welling up with tears. "I just wanted you to pass the salt. Can I have it now? Please? Thank you. Now pass the butter. And fill up my drink . . . more . . . more . . . okay, that's good. Jesus, you *are* an Uncle Tom."

THE BRUSHBACK REPORT

Texans Defense Wishes It Could Face Texans Offense

HOUSTON, TX—The Houston Texans defense did not fare well on Sunday, allowing 34 points to the Titans and recording no sacks against Steve McNair. This was a sharp contrast to the Titans defense, which sacked Texans QB David Carr seven times and allowed only 20 points. After the game, Houston defenders confessed to being jealous, saying they wish they could face their own offense.

"It's not really fair that all these other defenses get to pad their stats against our offense," said defensive back Demarcus Faggins, who had a team-high ten tackles against the Titans. "Every week it's the same thing. They get to tee off on our QB, while their QB gets to stand in the pocket and throw touchdown passes all day. I wish just once we could go up against our offense. I bet that would really get us back on track."

As the Titans wreaked havoc with the Houston offensive line, the Houston defense watched from the sidelines in awe.

"Whoa, did you see that sack that [Titans linebacker] Keith Bulluck got? Holy shit," said Faggins. "That was awesome. He got into the backfield without even getting touched. Then he picked up David, twirled him around over

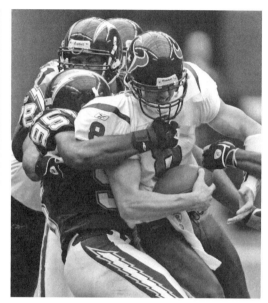

"I JUST WISH I HAD MORE TIME TO FIND THAT OPEN MAN. USUALLY I HAVE ENOUGH TIME TO DO A THREE-STEP DROP AND THEN LET OUT A BLOOD-CURDLING SHRIEK AS I'M ENGULFED BY DEFENDERS," SAID DAVID CARR.

his head, and body-slammed him while our offensive linemen stood there and watched. I wish that was me out there. I would tear that pussy in half like a rag doll."

Carr himself admitted that the team is offensively challenged, but refused to point fingers, saying that everybody needs to step up their game.

see DEFENSE, page 122

> DEFENSE, continued from page 121

"Hey it's been rough for us for a long time," Carr said. "Ever since I was drafted we've had problems on offense. Obviously we need to do a better job of protecting me, but I also need to do a better job of finding the open man. I just wish I had more time to find that open man. Usually I have enough time to do a three-step drop and then let out a blood-curdling shriek as I'm engulfed by defenders."

Since the Texans offense gets most of the blame for the team's failures, the defense's shortcomings often go overlooked. They rank 13th in the AFC, and there are a few offensive players on the Houston roster who would love to get a crack at their own defense.

"I'm sure they would love to face us on offense, but we wouldn't mind lining up against them on defense, either," said receiver Andre Johnson. "It would be a welcome respite from all those fast, strong, aggressive defenses that can actually penetrate an offensive line. I'd probably be able to get open and catch some passes, and David would have a little room to breathe. I wonder who would win if we went full contact, head-to-head, starting offense versus starting defense. Hmmm . . . hard to tell. With our coaching staff, we'd probably both lose."

Stephen A. Smith Interview with Michael Irvin Shatters Studio Windows

NEW YORK—A one-on-one interview between Stephen A. Smith and Michael Irvin on ESPN's *Quite Frankly* went horribly wrong yesterday when several windows shattered during the segment. Sources say that the breakage was caused by the sheer volume of Smith and Irvin's voices. "SO YOU'RE SAYING TO ME THAT TERRELL OWENS WAS RIGHT TO HOLD OUT. IS THAT WHAT YOU'RE SAYING?" bellowed Smith. To which Irvin replied "YEAH. AS A WIDE RECEIVER IN THIS LEAGUE, YOU GOT TO TAKE CARE OF YOURSELF AND YOUR FAMILY. THIS IS A BUSINESS. YOU GOT TO MAKE SURE YOU GET PAID. IT'S—HEY, WHAT'S THAT NOISE? THE WINDOWS ARE SHATTERING! TAKE COVER!" Next week, producers plan to put masking tape over the windows for Smith's interview with columnist Woody Paige.

Scott Boras Demands $35 Million to Rescue Drowning Child

EAST HAMPTON, NY—Scott Boras, well-known sports agent, has long been known as a tough negotiator. That reputation was bolstered yesterday when he demanded $35 million to rescue a small child drowning in the ocean near Boras's home in East Hampton.

The child, 8-year-old Danny Keelan, was swimming at a private beach when he was caught in the undertow and dragged away. As he flailed and cried for help, Boras relaxed nearby on the deck of his luxury yacht.

"My grandson was swimming around when all of a sudden he was caught in a riptide and dragged out to sea," said Ethel Keelan, the boy's grandmother. "I didn't know what to do. I saw that man on his yacht, reading a book like there was nothing going on. When I asked for his help, he said, 'You want me to save a drowning child? Hmmm . . . that kind of thing will run you around $35 million.' I tried to negotiate with him, but he was unwavering. I've never seen anyone so stubborn, greedy, and heartless in my life. What is he, a sports agent?"

Keelan said she was struck by Boras's casual demeanor and dogged self-interest.

> "HE EVEN HAD CONTRACTS ON HAND. HE JUST WHITED OUT 'THIRD BASEMAN' AND ADDED 'DROWNING CHILD,'" SAID ETHEL KEELAN.

"I thought for sure that [Boras] would help, but he really wanted that money. He said I could give him $10 million up front and sign a written guarantee to deliver the rest within a week. He even had contracts on hand. He just whited out 'third baseman' and added 'drowning child.'"

In the end, a deal was not struck. Fortunately, a fishing boat came by and plucked young Danny out of the water before he drowned.

For his part, Boras explained that he was just exercising good business sense and prudent negotiating.

"Look, am I supposed to interrupt my day, and rescue this kid for nothing?" he asked. "I can't believe she would call me greedy when she was the one who was willing to let her grandson drown just to save a few bucks. When you say '35 million' it sounds like a lot of money, but this is a human life we're talking about here. In my opinion, she ought to be arrested for child neglect."

While Boras's actions have been deemed despicable by some, Major League Baseball players are flocking to him in record numbers. His aggressive, tough-nosed tactics, on display yet again in yesterday's run-in with the Keelans, have made his clients some of the most highly paid in the game.

"He refused to save a drowning child because his grandmother wouldn't pay him $35 million?" asked Red Sox pitcher Derek Lowe, who is scheduled to be a free agent at the end of the year. "That's sick. It's cruel. It's inhuman. He has absolutely no sense of decency or restraint. Anyone have his number?"

The Brushback Presents...
Team Curses You Probably Didn't Know About

Curse of the Caesar Salad

CLEVELAND INDIANS: On December 3, 1949, a man in Cleveland, OH, ordered a Caesar salad from a popular restaurant. When it arrived, he noticed the lettuce was wilted and ordered it sent back to the kitchen. The Cleveland Indians haven't won a World Series since.

Curse of the *Curse of the Jade Scorpion*

ARIZONA DIAMONDBACKS: Woody Allen's *The Curse of the Jade Scorpion* was released in 2001. The Arizona Diamondbacks haven't won a World Series since.

Curse of the Shitty Front Office

KANSAS CITY ROYALS: The Kansas City Royals have a horrible front office and will never win a goddamn thing, period.

Curse of the Kid Who Couldn't Get Aubrey Huff's Autograph

TAMPA BAY DEVIL RAYS: On June 19, 1998, a 10-year-old boy named Timmy stopped first baseman Aubrey Huff on his way into the clubhouse and asked for his autograph. Huff politely declined, explaining that he was late for practice. The Devil Rays haven't finished higher than 4th place since.

Curse of the Never-Returned Library Book

DETROIT TIGERS: In the summer of 1984, Tigers infielder Lou Whitaker borrowed the book *Ball Four* from the Detroit Public Library. Two weeks later he received a letter from the library urging him to return the book, which he disregarded. His shameless hubris threw the Tigers into a tailspin from which they have not yet recovered.

DID YOU KNOW

Hockey is the only sport in which ice skating is not considered gay.

Female College Athlete Receiving No Free Cars From Alumni

COLUMBUS, OH— Tiffany Mann, point guard for the Ohio State women's college hoops team, has received no free cars from alumni despite the fact that she is the team's leading scorer and rebounder. She hasn't received any special assistance in the classroom, either,  nor has she been awarded a part-time job in which she doesn't have to actually do anything. Mann believes that these slights are a result of sexism among corrupt school officials.

"These crooked alumni are not just crooked—they're also sexist," said Mann after scoring 30 points in her team's victory against Georgetown. "I go to the same school as Maurice Clarett, yet I'm not getting any of the benefits he got. I give and I give and I give to this school, and just once I would like someone to hand me the keys to a new Ford Explorer. But I haven't gotten anything. I guess the Title IX gender equity law doesn't cover SUVs."

Mann recounted an incident in which she approached an alumnus of the school looking for "a little something." She was turned away immediately, a stark reminder of the inequities that still exist in the college ranks today.

"I ran into this alum at a party, this guy named Frank," she began. "Everyone knows him as one of the richest and sleaziest boosters there is. So I was chatting with him, and I just casually brought up my Honda. I told him it was running really bad and that I could use something more dependable to get me around, wink wink. You know what he said to me? He referred me to an auto mechanic, but he wouldn't give me the guy's phone number because he said it would be improper."

On a separate occasion Mann sought "extra help" from her biology professor to ensure that she would pass the class. The professor happily obliged, but not in the way Mann had hoped.

"I was failing this class miserably, but I figured they would let me slide anyway because I'm a big-shot athlete," said Mann. "So I asked my professor to help me out. I said, 'Gee, I hope I don't fail this class. It could really jeopardize my basketball eligibility.' Then I gently elbowed him in the side to let him know what I was getting at. He just said, 'Stop elbowing me,' and then told me to report to his office for tutelage every day for the next two weeks."

Women's rights activists are demanding that female college athletes be given the same illegal benefits as their male counterparts.

"The actions of university boosters around the nation with regard to female athletes are shameful and degrading," said Martha Burke, president of the National Council of Women's Organizations. "We must do more to ensure that they are doing their job of handing out money, cars, and other favors to ALL athletes, not just the males. It will be a great day when a female hoops prospect is fawned over by slobbering alumni the same way that male athletes are. Women can be just as crooked and dishonest as men if they are just given the opportunity."

The Brushback Presents:

QUICK QUESTIONS WITH A COLLEGE BASKETBALL FAN

BB: Hello, college basketball fan. Today is a very tough day. I'm sure you heard about the horrible earthquake in Japan.

BF: Yes, I have. That's hilarious. What a bunch of losers. Lo-sers! Lo-sers! Lo-sers!

BB: Gee, isn't that a little inappropriate?

BF: No. I have a right to say whatever I want to say. By the way, what's up with your left arm?

BB: I don't have one. I lost it in the war.

BF: Ha Ha! Arm loser! Look at him, he's got no arm! No-Arm! No-Arm! No-Arm!

BB: Don't you have any shame?

BF: Nope.

Sales Lackluster for New *Brokeback Mountain* Video Game

LOS ANGELES, CA—Officials from Electronic Arts (EA) say they are baffled by the lackluster sales for their latest video game, *Brokeback Mountain: The Cowboy Diaries*. As of its release two weeks ago, the game has sold a paltry 3,000 copies, forcing EA to rethink its strategy for targeting the 18 to 35 male demographic. "I don't get it. People love cowboys, right? This is the ultimate cowboy game," said Dan Mattrick, EA Sports vice president. "You can ride on the range, herd cattle, shoot people—heck you might even fall in love with another cowboy. This is a deep, multilayered game with endless possibilities. I guess I'm out of touch with our target demographic. Now I'm starting to second-guess our latest video game project, *How Stella Got Her Groove Back 2K7.*"

Bush Loses White House Spelling Bee

WASHINGTON, DC — George W. Bush, 43rd president of the United States, lost the White House spelling bee this weekend, marking the third year in a row the commander in chief failed to capture the title. The spelling bee, performed annually at the White House as a good-natured competition between members of the administration, was won by National Security Adviser Condoleezza Rice. President Bush failed to make it out of the first round, getting derailed by the word "cantankerous."

"Cantankerous?" Bush asked after Secretary of Education Roderick Paige read the word from an index card. "Cantankerous? Is that even a real word? Is he making that up?"

After Paige assured him that it was real, Bush made a feeble attempt to spell it properly.

"K-A-N . . . No, wait a minute," said Bush as he closed his eyes and tried to enunciate each syllable, as he was taught in grade school. "C-A-N-T-A-N-K-O-R-U-S. Cantankerous. Is that right? No? This whole competition is stupid and dumb anyway. I don't even want to win it."

Bush then stormed off, leaving the remaining members of his Cabinet to compete for the title.

In an attempt to defend the president's childish behavior, Attorney General John Ashcroft explained that Bush was frustrated about being knocked out of the first round for the third year in a row.

"I feel sorry for the guy," said Ashcroft, who was disqualified after refusing to spell the word "vulva." "He really committed himself this year to winning the competition. He had Laura drill him on some words using index cards, and he was up all night doing it, but then 'cantankerous' came up and that was it."

Ashcroft noted that last year's spelling bee ended in a similar fashion, with the president suffering a humiliating defeat.

"Mr. Paige made the colossal mistake of asking the president to spell 'nuclear.' We all know about the president's problems with that word, and it was a little inconsiderate of Rod to embarrass him like that," said Ashcroft.

Several Cabinet members noted that Bush has come a long way with his spelling, but the latest defeat indicates that he still has a long way to go to catch up to the level of the nation's elementary school students.

> "LET'S JUST LEAVE THE SPELLING TO OTHER PEOPLE, AND THE PRESIDENT-ING TO ME," SAID BUSH.

"The guy has worked so hard, you have to give him credit for that much," said one White House source, speaking anonymously. "He's really come a long way, believe me. Guy couldn't even tie his own shoes when he came into office."

Some have criticized Bush for his lack of intelligence, claiming that the leader of the free world should be a person of keen mind and razor-sharp intellect. But the president defended himself today.

"It's a disappointment to lose that spelling bee, but I've got other priorities to focus on," said Bush. "So let's just leave the spelling to other people, and the president-ing to me. Oh, and by the way, Saddam Hussein was a vicious and cruel man. Dare I say he was 'cantankerous'? See? I looked it up after I misspelled it!"

The president added that next year's White House spelling bee will go on as planned. "Next year is my year, baby. I already started studying for it. I even had index cards in my lap while I was listening to the 9/11 Commission."

Die-Hard Yankee Fan Psyched to Have Lou Gehrig's Disease

WHITE PLAINS, NY—Carl Keane, a die-hard Yankee fan for over twenty years, was reportedly "psyched" upon being diagnosed with amyotrophic lateral sclerosis (ALS), otherwise known as Lou Gehrig's disease. The 29-year-old tax accountant from White Plains learned of his ailment earlier this month after several weeks of persistent muscle stiffness and chronic fatigue.

"Wow, of all the maladies to be afflicted with, Lou Gehrig's disease is definitely on the top of my list," said Keane, speaking slowly and deliberately. "I know the life expectancy isn't long, but to be in the company of Lou Gehrig means more than having my health. Now I feel like a true Yankee."

He added: "You know, a lot of people say I got a bad break. But today, I consider myself the luckiest man on the face of the earth."

Keane has been a fan of the Bronx Bombers since he attended his first game at the age of 8. The highlight of his career as Yankee superfan came when he took a tour of The Stadium and visited historic Monument Park, where he was able to touch the monuments of several Yankee legends, including his favorite, Lou Gehrig.

"I remember that day like it was yesterday. It was my sixteenth birthday, and my dad got me a Yankee Stadium tour," said Keane. "I walked through Monument Park feeling like I was walking amongst the ghosts of baseball past. Then I got to Gehrig's statue and I stood in front of it while my dad took a picture. I love old Lou, so getting ALS is an honor,

"YOU KNOW, A LOT OF PEOPLE SAY I GOT A BAD BREAK. BUT TODAY, I CONSIDER MYSELF THE LUCKIEST MAN ON THE FACE OF THE EARTH," SAID CARL KEANE.

despite the crippling muscle atrophy and loss of motor skills."

Now that he has the world-famous disease, Keane is the envy of his friends and neighbors. He constantly entertains visitors, who want to know what it's like to suffer from the same disease as the Iron Horse.

"Me and Keane are the two biggest Yankee fans in the world, man," said lifelong friend Jay Bentley, 30. "We've been to dozens of games, we've met Jeter, O'Neill, and Bernie Williams. We have every piece of Yankee merchandise and memorabilia you can imagine. But now Carl has the ultimate piece of Yankee merchandise: Lou Gehrig's disease. Lucky bastard. I'm just surprised that Steinbrenner hasn't trademarked the name yet and forced Carl to pay up. Obviously the guy has a bigger heart than people think."

see LOU GEHRIG, page 129

> LOU GEHRIG, continued from page 128

Keane even has his funeral planned out. He said he wants to "go out like a Yankee," and has given his family explicit orders to carry out after his death.

"Well, I would love Ronan Tynan to sing the national anthem at my funeral," said Keane. "And I also would like it to be held at Yankee Stadium in front of a crowd of A-list Hollywood celebrities. Then I would like my ashes scattered over the field so I can be another Yankee Stadium ghost. Is that all too much to ask? I don't think so. Not for a true Yankee like myself."

349th *Cold Case* Promo Sends Man Over the Edge

ROCHESTER, NY—Local football fan Jim "Jimbo" Laramie of Rochester was sent over the edge during CBS's broadcast of the Colts-Patriots game on Sunday after the network aired its record-breaking 349th trailer for the series *Cold Case*. "That's it. If I see one more of these damn promos I'm going to kill someone," Laramie noted as CBS reminded him for the umpteenth time that *Cold Case* would air that night on CBS as part of a stellar lineup that also included *60 Minutes* and *CSI: Miami*. "Seriously, if I hear that voice-over again and see that pasty-faced bitch one more time, I'm taking that rifle and going nuts." Laramie's rage caused him to pick up his hunting rifle and embark on a shooting spree that left four dead. CBS officials had no comment except to say that next week's *Cold Case* will feature a stunning twist that will leave you breathless.

Departure of Kurt Warner Enables Rams to Start Cursing Again

ST. LOUIS, MO—The departure of veteran quarterback Kurt Warner has had a ripple effect on the Rams organization. In addition to opening the door for Marc Bulger to be the team's starting quarterback, Warner's exit has had a noticeable effect in the locker room, where Rams players and coaches are now able to curse again without fear of reprisal.

"Fuck, fuck, fuck-ety fuck fuck!" shouted Mike Martz as he walked into his office yesterday morning. "Fuck, shit, piss, bitch, ass-hole! Ahhh, that feels good. Sorry, I just have to do that every once in a while now that Kurt's gone. Do you know how hard it is to run a football team without profanity? It's hard—especially when you have a defense like this."

Soon after joining the Rams, the deeply religious Warner declared that he did not use foul language and did not wish to be in the presence of foul language in the locker room or on the field. Warner's teammates obliged during his tenure, but most were relieved to discover that he had signed with another team.

"When I heard Kurt was gone, I was like,

> "FUCK, FUCK, FUCK-ETY FUCK FUCK!" SHOUTED MIKE MARTZ AS HE WALKED INTO HIS OFFICE YESTERDAY MORNING.

'Fuck, shit, bitch, motherfucker!' " said running back Marshall Faulk. "It's funny because I've never really been that much of a curser. I guess you don't appreciate something until it's gone, because now I'm cursing my fucking balls off."

Faulk isn't the only Rams player reveling in his freedom to use naughty words. All through the locker room, profanities are flying through the air like footballs.

"Shit, fuck, I twisted my ankle today," said wideout Torry Holt, limping around in a towel. "Oh fuck me, it really frigging hurts. Goddamn it! I guess I'm just going to have to keep swearing until it gets better. Fuck!"

Members of the media have also noticed the change in the Rams locker room since the departure of Warner.

"Wow, what a difference a year makes," said Lisa Steward of the *St. Louis Post-Dispatch*. "When Kurt was here, everyone was on their best behavior. Now, it's the polar opposite. It's like being in a room with a bunch of sailors. It's not bad, although I didn't appreciate Mike Martz calling me a cunt the other day."

Another reporter from the *Post-Dispatch* claimed to have been sexually harassed by a Rams player early this season. Oddly enough, she claimed to have been relieved after the incident.

"One of their guys, I won't say his name, came over and grabbed my ass as I was standing around waiting for an interview," she said. "I was angry at first, but then I was strangely relieved. Being in an NFL locker room with no sexual harassment is a little jarring, a little disorienting. It's like being in a baseball locker room without, well . . . without sexual harassment."

Palmeiro: Steroid Policy Unfair to Players Who Do Steroids

BALTIMORE, MD—One day after being suspended for steroid use, Orioles slugger Rafael Palmeiro had some harsh words for baseball's new testing policy.

"The Major League Baseball steroid policy is the height of hypocrisy," Palmeiro said at a press conference Monday. "It claims to be unbiased, yet it targets one small group of players and nobody else. As a steroid user, I certainly feel that this new 'zero tolerance' policy has slapped a bull's-eye right on my back.

"You know, back in the fifties there was this thing called 'the Red scare,'" Palmeiro continued. "Everyone was accusing everyone else of being a communist. The thing is, most of the people weren't communists at all. They were just being targeted as part of a witch hunt. The steroid controversy is nothing like that, of course. We actually are doing steroids. Still, it's an interesting story."

Palmeiro's lawyer, Allan Rothstein, announced that he will file a complaint on behalf of his client alleging bias and discrimination.

"This is a calculated and systematic targeting of individuals in the league who use performance-enhancing drugs," said Rothstein. "Clearly Major League Baseball is threatened by these players and has decided to eradicate them from the league. It's downright fascist, if you ask me. What's next? Are they going to round them all up and send them to a concentration camp? We need to make this policy fair. Steroid users have as much right to be in the league as anyone else."

The league has responded to Palmeiro's charges with a mixture of confusion and anger. Bob Dupuy, president of Major League Baseball, reiterated that the policy is sup-

"IT'S DOWNRIGHT FASCIST, IF YOU ASK ME. WHAT'S NEXT? ARE THEY GOING TO ROUND THEM ALL UP AND SEND THEM TO A CONCENTRATION CAMP?"

posed to catch steroid users and that Palmeiro was in the wrong for using steroids in the first place.

Despite the league's strong words, Palmeiro insists that he will soldier on against the unfair steroid testing policy.

"Believe me, all that tough talk is not going to scare me away," he said. "I always stand up for what I believe in, and I won't be treated like a second class citizen just because I inject performance-enhancing drugs into my body. I have given my heart and soul to baseball, for nothing more than the love of the game and tens of millions of dollars. And this is the thanks I get?"

White Guy Inexplicably Named Karim Garcia

NEW YORK, NY—Baseball fans, players, and members of the media expressed shock upon discovering that Karim Garcia, right-fielder for the New York Yankees, is actually white. "No, he's not white. No way," said Ron Molligan, Yankees fan. "Karim Garcia? Wow. That's a new one." Even players had a hard time putting the name with the face. "I didn't know who he was," said Torii Hunter of the Minnesota Twins. "I read that they picked up some guy named Karim Garcia, but I just didn't make the connection. This guy looks like a truck driver from Topeka, not a Mexican." Sources close to Garcia say he has no plans to change his name to help alleviate the confusion.

Anonymous Source Inducts Peter Gammons Into Hall of Fame

COOPERSTOWN, NY—Peter Gammons, noted baseball writer and television personality, was inducted into the Hall of Fame on Sunday in an emotional ceremony in Cooperstown. Prior to his speech, Gammons was formally inducted by an anonymous MLB source. "Today we honor Peter Gammons, a legend who has been covering baseball brilliantly since the early seventies," the source reported. "His love for the game and enthusiasm for his work are second to none. His name is synonymous with baseball, and it is my humble honor to induct him into the Baseball Hall of Fame. Peter, welcome home." Afterward, the source reported that the Orioles may make a run at Johnny Damon next year.

Fan Boycotts High Beer Prices for One Inning

PHILADELPHIA, PA—Philadelphia Phillies fan Jake Lipowski took a stand yesterday against high concession prices by boycotting Citizens Bank Park draft beer. Lipowski's boycott lasted through the top half of the first inning.

"Eight dollars for a cup of Bud Light? That's like an 800 percent profit," Lipowski exclaimed. "That's ridiculous. You know what? I'm not even going to buy one. I'm not drinking. Sure, I love beer, but you have to draw the line somewhere. You have to have some standards."

Following the top of the first, Lipowski backed off his protest and purchased a 22-ounce jumbo draft beer for $8.50, saying that he had "proved his point" and felt no need to belabor it.

Hockey Players Back to Being Blue-Collar Again

TORONTO, CANADA—Hockey purists were delighted to learn about the new NHL collective bargaining agreement (CBA), which heavily favored the owners. With a 24 percent reduction in player salaries combined with a rigid salary cap, hockey players have now returned to their gritty, blue-collar roots. Union head Bob Goodenow boasted about the NHL's hip, new "retro" look.

"This is the hockey that you and I grew up with," Goodenow said in a press conference announcing the new CBA. "Our players are once again the lowest-paid of any professional sports league in America, including soccer. We're a blue-collar league, a bunch of Joe Lunchpails. And the owners? They're still stinking rich. All is right with the world again."

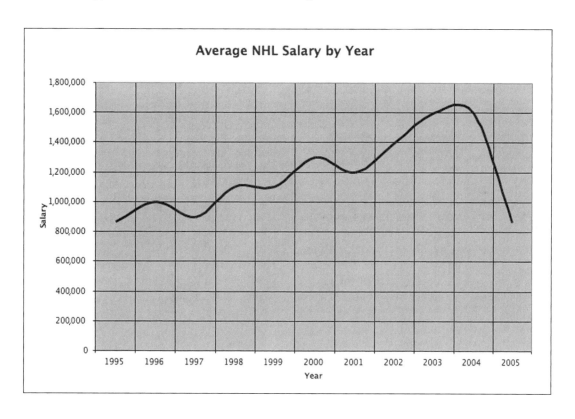

White NBA Player Not Physically Gifted, But Really Has a Head for the Game

DENVER, CO—Kyle Wohlers, backup center for the Denver Nuggets, may not be the fastest or the strongest person on the court, but he makes up for it with his instincts. While the white Wohlers is not physically gifted, he really has a head for the game.

"This white player is going to add a lot of depth to our bench," says Kiki Vandeweghe, Nuggets GM. "Yeah, he's not flashy. You won't see him do any 360 dunks or anything. He's just a grinder who sees the court really well, has a great understanding of the game, and relies on his smarts to make plays. Sort of like John Stockton."

Wohlers is a 7-footer whom the Nuggets hope will help beef up their interior defense. His footwork is average, his hands are decent, and he's good at getting himself in a position where he can do some damage under the basket.

Wohlers is also an excellent free throw shooter and has a nice short-range jumper. He's a real team player, often choosing to dish it off to his teammates in lieu of taking the shot himself. It's that kind of selfless play that's earned him the respect of his teammates.

"Oh yeah, Mark's great," says teammate Marcus Camby. "He never tries to do anything stupid and shoot the ball himself. His job is to get under the net, grab the ball, hand it off, and step out of the way. He reminds me a little of that Scot Pollard guy from Sacramento. I don't know why. Just something about him."

Wohlers says he prides himself on being ready to play every day and being the hardest worker on the team. Not a trash-talker, Wohlers has a respect for the game that's missing in many of today's stars.

"I guess I'm kind of a throwback," says Wohlers. "A throwback to the days where a layup was just as good as a slam dunk, and teamwork was more important than selling athletic sneakers. I would've fit in a lot better back then because, well . . . because those guys were all, you know . . . they were all white. There. I said it, okay?"

DID YOU KNOW

Bowling is the only sport that won't get you laid no matter how good you are at it.

Raiders Fan Insists On Taking Driver's License Photo in Full Pirate Ensemble

PETA: Fishing Video Games Linked to Violence Against Fish

Ivy Leaguer Dunked On

Player Vows Never to Hustle Again After Hamstring Injury

LOS ANGELES, CA—After being sidelined by a painful hamstring injury, Dodgers utility infielder Kevin Schultz has vowed never to hustle again.

"Well, that seals it. I'm never hustling again. Never," said a visibly frustrated Schultz. "I've already alerted my coaches and teammates. Hustling is for losers. Look at me. I'm sitting here not contributing at all. I'm totally useless. Next time I'm going to jog down the line and save myself the trouble. Who gives a shit if I get thrown out?"

Schultz has been struggling for playing time all season. Now that he has injured his hamstring in a misguided attempt to beat out a throw, Schultz's entire season is in jeopardy.

"That's the second time that's happened in his career," said teammate Shawn Green. "Some people never learn, you know? It's just a sign of the times, I guess. People are always in such a hurry these days."

Coach Jim Tracy is said to be pleased with his infielder's hard-nosed style of play, though he admits Schultz is lacking in common sense.

"Schultzie is a good kid and he plays hard," said Tracy. "But I don't understand his weird fixation with hustling. Jesus, kid, relax. What's the worst that can happen? Are you going to drop dead if you don't get to first? I don't think so. Worst-case scenario, you get thrown out and the team loses. We're going to get paid anyway, so calm down."

In order to address the growing problem of hamstring injuries, the Dodgers are being proactive. Tracy has called for his players to attend a mandatory seminar explaining the proper technique for running down the base paths and fielding batted balls.

Schultz is one player who need not attend the seminar. He knows better than anyone the perils of hustling and has made up his mind never to do it again.

"I'll never, ever hustle again. That's a promise," he said. "I've learned my lesson. I agree with Jim, though, that hustling is something that's learned at a young age. If we don't stop drilling into these kids' heads how important it is to 'try your hardest' and 'respect the game' we're going to end up with half the damn team on the DL. It's just irresponsible. Kids, don't ever hustle. If you do, you could end up like me. If you don't, you could end up like Manny Ramirez. Now, which would *you* prefer?"

DID YOU KNOW

Monument Park is the area of Yankee Stadium where they keep the corpses of former Yankee greats.

Paparazzi Stalks Diana Taurasi Just to Be Nice

PHOENIX, AZ—With the popularity of the WNBA sagging, the league's players aren't in high demand by the tabloids and sporting press. Even its biggest star, Diana Taurasi, is a relative unknown. But that hasn't stopped the paparazzi from relentlessly stalking the former UConn star, if only because they wish to be nice.

"I've been following Diana around since she was drafted by the Phoenix Suns or Mercury or whatever," said Ralph Jamison, 52, a freelance photographer. "She seems like a nice girl. It's wrong that she gets so little attention in the press. I know the WNBA is kind of a joke, but as a member of the paparazzi, I feel it's my duty to stalk her anyway. I wouldn't want to hurt her feelings by not doing so."

Jamison is not the only member of the paparazzi to stalk Taurasi. Several cameramen can be seen following the WNBA star wherever she goes, snapping pictures and

see TAURASI, page 138

> TAURASI, continued from page 137

shouting her name. The gracious Taurasi always stops to chat and pose for pictures.

"She's such a sweetheart. She's very polite and engaging, and never shouts at us," said Barry Mathewson, photographer for the *National Enquirer*. "I'm sure that she expected a large contingent of photographers to swarm her when she came to the league, so we didn't want to let her down. Oh shit, here she comes. Miss Taurasi! Miss Taurasi! One moment of your time . . . please! Miss Taurasi!"

The humble, personable star understands that fame goes hand in hand with being a member of the hugely popular WNBA.

"Oh, you know, I just take it all in stride," Taurasi said, smiling graciously. "I know a lot of people hate the paparazzi, but they're just doing their job. If you're going to go into professional women's basketball, you'd better understand that everybody's going to want a piece of you. If they feel the need to crouch in my bushes, that's cool. They can even come in my house if they want. I'll leave the door open."

With the paparazzi relentlessly pursuing her, Taurasi is growing accustomed to life in the glare of the spotlight. She insists that it doesn't bother her, although there are days when it can be a little too much.

"Like I said, when you're in the WNBA, it's to be expected," she said. "I wouldn't have signed up for this if I wasn't prepared to have every aspect of my life under public scrutiny. It's tough sometimes, but I wouldn't trade it for anything in the world. I'm a WNBA basketball player. This is who I am."

Knicks Cheerleaders Now Just Quietly Weeping

NEW YORK, NY—The New York Knicks cheerleading squad, beaten down by years of defeat and heartache, have gone from cheering wildly to silently weeping during the team's home games. Despite numerous pleas from management, the group cannot seem to muster the enthusiasm to wave pom-poms and chant slogans. "Oh, who cares anyway? It's not like anyone even comes to the games," said Tatia Williams, Knicks cheerleader since 1998. "It used to be fun, but now it's like, 'What's the point?'" Renee Mace, 31, has been with the team for ten years, but she may have finally reached the end of her rope. "I can't take it anymore. I can't pretend to be happy anymore. I can't plaster this stupid fake smile on my face like everything is all hunky-dory. It's time for me to move on to another line of work." Mace reportedly is planning to pursue her childhood dream of being a stripper.

Needy Families Turn Down Free Turkeys From Miami Dolphins

MIAMI, FL—The Miami Dolphins were embarrassed yesterday when dozens of needy families rejected their offer of free Thanksgiving turkeys. The annual turkey giveaway is normally a big hit among poor families in the Miami area, but the Dolphins' awful performance this year has alienated them from fans.

"No thanks. I can't bring myself to meet those guys, shake their hands, and thank them for their charity," said Will Meggete, 42, who lives with his two children in a Buick station wagon. "It's a nice gesture, but have you seen the way they've been playing this year? Ugh. The last thing I need right now is to be face-to-face with those guys. I might be poor and destitute, but I still have my pride."

Meggete admitted that his children are starving, but still refused to accept free food from the Dolphins.

"Yes, I know, it tugs at my heartstrings to see my children begging for morsels of nourishment," he said, "but as a father, you must teach them to have self-respect and dignity. If we went to that soup kitchen and received a turkey, we would've been fed for a day, sure. But if you teach children to avoid the 2004 Miami Dolphins, you feed them for a lifetime."

Dolphins players were shocked and saddened by the small turnout for this year's turkey giveaway. Only twenty-five people came, and most of them were expecting to see the Miami Heat.

"Where the hell is Shaq?" asked one disgruntled homeless man, staring at a row of Dolphins players holding turkeys. "Where's Dwyane Wade? I thought someone said the Heat was gonna be here. You don't look like the Heat. You look like the Dolphins. You're Jason Taylor, and you're Travis Minor, and you, you over there, you're A. J. Feeley. You want me to take a turkey from A. J. Fucking Feeley? He'd probably fumble it on the hand-off."

After several hours the NFL players realized they would never get rid of the turkeys if they stuck around trying to give them out, and thus decided to leave. As the Dolphins' bus pulled away, Suzanne Welsch, director of the Helping Hand soup kitchen, placed a sign on the window indicating that the Dolphins had left but there were still dozens of turkeys available. Within minutes the soup kitchen was packed with needy, appreciative families.

ON THIS DAY...

In 776 B.C., the first ever Olympic Games were held, with only one event: a race called "the stadion." Snowboarding would be added three years later, when snow was discovered.

Nation Increasingly Uncomfortable Around Gary Sheffield

"HANGING AROUND WITH GARY IS LIKE WALKING ON EGGSHELLS," SAID ONE VETERAN PLAYER. "YOU NEVER KNOW WHAT'S GOING TO SET HIM OFF."

NEW YORK, NY—According to a recent study, Americans are feeling increasingly uncomfortable around Yankees outfielder Gary Sheffield. From his teammates to the media to the general public, most people prefer to avoid any contact with the high-strung, grumpy slugger.

"Yeah, that guy freaks me out a little," said one Yankee player. "He's so on edge. I think the last time I talked to him was when I asked him to sign a baseball for my nephew. He agreed to sign it, but later I looked at the autograph and it said, 'To Kyle: You have no idea what it's like to be a black man in America.—Gary Sheffield.' "

One veteran player said that he felt "awkward and self-conscious" around Sheffield. "Hanging around with Gary is like walking on eggshells," he said. "You never know what's going to set him off. He needs to lighten up a little, maybe smoke a joint or something. Not that I'm implying that all black people smoke pot or anything."

Members of the media have the most difficult time dealing with Sheffield. He has very little respect for sportswriters and isn't afraid to say it. Ironically, that very attitude has made him one of the most sought-after interviews in baseball.

"Interviewing Gary is great, because you never know what he's going to come out with," said *Sports Illustrated*'s Tom Verducci, who interviewed Sheffield in a recent issue.

"He's so intense and honest that he'll say anything that pops into his head. As a reporter, you can't ask for much more than that. But as a person, it does get a little weird. He hates the media so much it's disturbing. I just have to keep reminding myself that we are the media, and he has every reason to hate us."

Members of the general public, too, have reported feeling uncomfortable around Sheffield.

"I was at the airport once, riding in the elevator, and who walked in but Gary Sheffield

see SHEFFIELD, page 141

> SHEFFIELD, continued from page 140

of the New York Yankees," said Sidney Fleming of Queens, NY. "My first thought was to shake his hand and try to get an autograph, but I stopped myself because I know about his reputation. So I just stood there with my hands in my pockets. Then I took them out because I didn't want to seem racist, you know, like I was protecting my wallet because there was a black guy in there with me. Then I reminded myself that there *was* a black guy in there with me, so I put my hands back in my pockets."

As for Sheffield, he understands all too well what it's like to be uncomfortable in the company of others.

"Let me tell you about being uncomfortable," said Sheffield. "Uncomfortable is walking into a ballpark and looking into the stands and seeing nothing but white faces around you. You have no idea what it's like until you've walked in my skin—or at least done that thing C. Thomas Howell did in *Soul Man*, where he painted his face black and went around acting like he was black. To this day, C. Thomas Howell is the only white person I've ever respected."

Defender Refuses to Tackle Brett Favre Out of Respect for Everything He's Accomplished

GREEN BAY, WI—Minnesota defender Corey Chavous admitted that he purposely allowed Brett Favre to score during Sunday's game out of respect for everything he has accomplished in his career. Chavous was standing at the goal line as Favre scampered toward him on a sneak, and politely stepped aside to let the legend score another touchdown. "Yeah, I let him score," said Chavous, whose team went on to lose 34-31. "I was getting ready to tackle him, and all of a sudden I looked at his face and thought about all the things that he has accomplished during his remarkable career. I thought about how much adversity he has overcome, and how he gives it everything he has day in and day out. Allowing him to score that touchdown was the least I could do. Here's to you, Brett Favre."

Player Confused By Term 'Invaluable'

ST. PAUL, MN—Minnesota Twins center-fielder Lew Ford was confused Saturday when Ron Gardenhire told a reporter that he was "invaluable." Ford was uncertain about whether the term meant "really valuable" or "not valuable at all." "Coach said I was 'invaluable,' but I'm not quite sure what he means," said Ford. "At first I was excited, but then when I thought about it I got a little concerned. If common grammar and syntax rules are applied, 'invaluable' should mean that I'm not valuable. Then again, if you look at the context it was used in, clearly the coach was trying to pay me a compliment. Looks like I have to brush up on my grammar skills. Wait . . . no I don't. I'm a professional ballplayer."

Report: Legless Athletes Less Likely to Get Shoe Contracts

BALTIMORE, MD—Disabled athletes have made great strides in recent years. But despite all the gains, some major obstacles still remain. According to a report released yesterday by the Association of Sports Medicine (ASM), legless athletes are statistically much less likely to get shoe contracts than athletes with legs.

"This is quite disturbing," said Philip Mecklenburg, director of the ASM. "There clearly is a trend in athletics toward giving shoe contracts to athletes who actually have feet. The rest of them are left out in the cold. This kind of exclusion only promotes ignorance and should not be tolerated. This is the twenty-first century, for God's sake."

The study examined all major shoe contracts given out in the past ten years. Nike, Reebok, and Adidas have been the main providers for these endorsement pacts, and all seem determined to sign only those players that have legs upon which to wear the shoe.

"Its clear as day," Mecklenburg continued. "Tracy McGrady, Kobe Bryant, LeBron James, Carmelo Anthony, Paul Pierce, the list goes on. We researched for months to see the one quality these men had in common, and our conclusion was irrefutable. They all have legs."

Mecklenburg also polled hundreds of legless

see LEGLESS, page 143

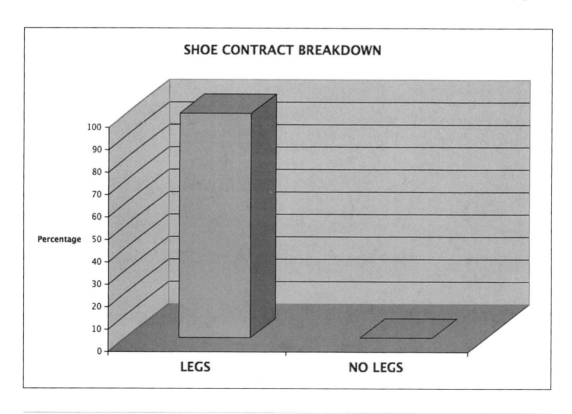

SHOE CONTRACT BREAKDOWN

> LEGLESS, continued from page 142

athletes to determine if any had been contacted by a sneaker company for an endorsement deal. Not one of them had.

"I've made huge strides . . . no pun intended . . . overcoming every obstacle in my way," said Don Angelo, a wheelchair basketball star. "When I lost my legs, I thought my life was over, but I continued to persevere. Now look at me. I'm an established wheelchair basketball player. Sure, I have no feet or legs, but is that any reason to be denied a shoe contract?"

When reached for comment, Nike CEO Phil Knight defended his company's actions. He pointed out that Nike has sponsored several wheelchair marathons, races, and basketball games. However, signing a legless person to a shoe contract has been deemed "impractical."

"We have a lot of respect for legless athletes, believe me," said Knight. "However, since they don't have any feet, a shoe contract really doesn't work for us. It's bad business, plus it's just not feasible. Where are we going to put the shoes, on their hands?"

The responses of sneaker companies have not satisfied Mecklenburg or his legless friends. Discrimination is discrimination, whether it is racial, sexual, or otherwise.

"Ah, all the excuses those fat cats make are so predictable," said Mecklenburg. "We've heard it all before, haven't we? 'Oh, they have no feet. Where are we going to put the shoes?' Come on, guys. You can do better than that. Get creative. You made LeBron James the second coming of Christ before he even stepped on a court. Surely you can put a shoe on a stump and make it look good."

Sudanese Refugees Inspired by How Much Allen Iverson Has Been Through

NORTH DARFUR, SUDAN—A group of Sudanese refugees expressed amazement yesterday at how much 76ers star Allen Iverson has been through in his basketball career. Iverson has had to endure multiple coaching changes, pressure from fans and media, and the burden of carrying a moderately talented team on his back throughout his tenure in Philadelphia. His ability to overcome adversity has been an inspiration to the refugees in the North Darfur region. "Allen Iverson has much heart and we admire that greatly," said Miriam Bakhid Idriss, a woman whose entire family was slaughtered in the genocide in Sudan. "His career has had so many ups and downs, yet still he comes to play every single day. He leaves everything on the court, too, and sacrifices his body for the good of the team. If he retires without a world championship, that will be one of the great tragedies of our time."

Baseball Purists Call for Players to Go Back to Doing Coke

NEW YORK, NY—The Major League Baseball steroid scandal has tarnished the game's image and alienated some of its oldest fans. With the integrity of baseball in serious doubt, purists are calling for a return to simpler times: the golden age of the late 1970s and '80s, when Major League Baseball was in the grip of a widespread cocaine epidemic.

"In my day the players didn't need any steroids to help them hit home runs," said Dick Vernon, hitting coach for the Pittsburgh Pirates from 1976 through 1981. "Guys spent more time working on their swings than on their physiques. And everyone, from the batboy to the star center fielder, was on coke. I guess there's just no room in today's sophisticated, cynical game for some good, old-fashioned nose candy."

Steve Howe, a former major league pitcher who was suspended seven times for cocaine use, supports the league's strict new steroid policy. He is also calling on the union to educate players about possible alternatives to performance enhancers.

"I think as part of the new program, players should be encouraged to try other drugs, like coke or speed," Howe said during a recent interview with the *New York Post*. "It's only fair to let them know their other options. It's not all about hitting more home runs. For instance, cocaine will not increase your muscle mass, but it will convince you that you're an interesting person and that people enjoy hearing you talk. In other words, it'll turn you into Curt Schilling."

But cocaine is not the only drug missing from major league clubhouses these days. The use of marijuana, alcohol, and cigarettes is on the decline as well.

"COCAINE WILL NOT INCREASE YOUR MUSCLE MASS, BUT IT WILL CONVINCE YOU THAT YOU'RE AN INTERESTING PERSON AND THAT PEOPLE ENJOY HEARING YOU TALK. IN OTHER WORDS, IT'LL TURN YOU INTO CURT SCHILLING," SAID STEVE HOWE.

"You don't see too much of that stuff anymore. It's gone out of fashion," said Cards manager Tony LaRussa. "Players today are much more interested in consuming protein shakes and health food. It seems their only vices these days, if you can call them that, are taking steroids and soliciting underage prostitutes."

Baseball may never see a return to its glory days of rampant cocaine and alcohol abuse. Still, old-timers would like to see some of today's stars give cocaine a chance.

"Don't knock it till you try it," said Howe. "Some of today's players would probably benefit from a couple 8-balls if they would just grow a pair and try it. Take Rafael Palmeiro for instance. A few quick lines could give him the self-confidence he needs to beat that impotence problem. And if he's still impotent, at least he'd have a decent excuse."

Ray Lewis Makes Dramatic, Game-Saving Tackle in New Nestlé Crunch Commercial

BALTIMORE, MD—Ray Lewis has done it again. The multitalented linebacker made a dramatic game-saving tackle as time was winding down to restore his team's Super Bowl victory. Only this time, it wasn't in a game situation, but a brand-new commercial for Nestlé Buncha Crunch caramel chocolate bars.

"He made that hit like only Ray can," said Gordon McLean, Nestlé CEO. "He is such an intense, high-level competitor with an unparalleled feel for the game. His tough, rugged, in-your-face attitude goes perfect with the crunchy crisped rice and smooth Nestlé chocolate of our new Buncha Crunch bars."

The exciting new ad features Lewis lining up at his linebacker position wearing a nondescript purple-and-black uniform, while the opposing quarterback barks out the signals. The ball is snapped and the back slashes through the line of scrimmage and into the secondary, when he is leveled by Lewis. A split second later, Lewis springs up from the ground, pounds his chest, and roars, "When I need that extra edge for a goal line stand, I turn to the new Nestlé Buncha Crunch bar. It's got chocolate, crisped rice, and smooth, creamy caramel. Me and my dawgs eat two each before the game, and so should you. Why? Because I said so!"

see LEWIS, page 146

> LEWIS, continued from page 145

From athletic apparel to sports drinks, Ray Lewis has carved a place for himself in the lucrative field of product endorsement and has become one of America's most coveted pitchmen. After last weekend's heartbreaking loss to archival Eddie George and his team, the Tennessee Titans, Lewis immediately contacted his agent and let him know he was available.

"He told me he was bored and wanted to get out of the house," said his agent, Roosevelt Barnes. "He also said he was really pissed off and wanted to hit somebody. I took that into consideration when working out the deal with Nestlé. I told them that Ray would refuse to do any commercial that didn't involve him laying the lumber to some poor, unsuspecting quarterback or running back. Did you see the hit he put on that guy? That actor looked like he was hit by a truck."

The runningback, Donald Cohen, claims that Lewis took the commercial "way too seriously" and that he actually sustained an injury during one of the takes.

"We had to do twelve takes and this asshole really laid into me every time," said Cohen from his hospital bed. "The director distinctly told him to go easy on me and lay me down softly. He said that they could add sound effects to give the impression that it was a bone-crunching hit. But Ray didn't give a shit. He drilled me into the ground over and over again. One time he even called me 'Eddie.' Fucking weirdo."

Vincente Borghese, director of the ad, agrees that Lewis got a bit carried away during the shooting.

"Ray is a great guy to work with," said Borghese. "He's just a little intense, that's all. He really gets into his role, sort of like Marlon Brando in *Apocalypse Now*, only much, much scarier. Sometimes it's hard to deal with, but that's the price you pay. The gangster-thug-murderer image is perfect for our new Buncha Crunch bars."

Firstborn's College Education Depending On River Card

LAS VEGAS, NV—Jon Karlin silently prayed for good luck yesterday as he waited for a Binion's Casino dealer to show him the "river card," or the final card, in a hand of Texas Hold 'Em. The card was particularly meaningful to Karlin since he had just pushed his firstborn son's college education fund into the middle of the table. Witnesses reported seeing Karlin sweating and shaking as the dealer reached for the card. "It's just like it is on TV," said one witness, who was part of a crowd of onlookers watching the game. "This Ron guy went all-in because he had a pair of 9s. Then it turned out another guy at the table had a pair of 10s. So then the Ron guy had to pray the river card was a nine so he could get 3 of a kind. Turned out the river card was a 6. The guy was crying uncontrollably. I think I may give this Texas Hold 'Em thing a try."

Owens Has Eagles Right Where He Wants Them Now

PHILADELPHIA, PA—Days after arguing with his head coach, being thrown out of training camp, and publicly berating his teammates, receiver Terrell Owens has the Philadelphia Eagles right where he wants them.

"Ah, victory," said Owens, leaning back in his chair and smoking a cigar. "It's a sweet, sweet thing. It's like a chess match, and I just called 'checkmate' on the Eagles. I must say I've played this thing brilliantly. This sould be a blueprint for other players. Guys, this is how you make it in the NFL."

Owens credited his agent, Drew Rosenhaus, for advising him throughout the long ordeal.

"I got the best agent in the business, baby," he said. "Drew guided me through this whole thing. When he advised me to go on *PTI* and badmouth my quarterback and my coaches, I thought he was crazy. But it turns out he was right. I can't wait till they come here and beg me to return. Andy Reid's gonna be eating out of my hand."

When Owens signed with Rosenhaus earlier this year, the Eagles braced themselves for the worst. Rosenhaus has a reputation for being a tough, take-no-prisoners negotiator. He took one look at Owens's contract and decided it was inadequate.

"So many people told me I was crazy when I advised T.O. to demand a new contract just one year after signing," said Rosenhaus. "But now I'm feeling some vindication. I have a feeling we'll be getting a call from them real soon. In fact, I already got one from [Eagles GM] Joe Banner. He said I was a scumbag and that I was worse than Hitler and that he would drop dead before giving T.O. an extra penny. Talk about playing hard to get."

If the Eagles want Owens back, they're not letting it on publicly. The team has stated repeatedly that it won't give him a new deal or trade him to a different team. When reached for comment, Banner had some choice words for Owens and his agent.

"What a couple of idiots. Jesus, how stupid can two human beings be?" Banner asked. "Do they really think we're going to give in now and sign them to a new contract? I'd rather shoot myself in the head. The only thing they are accomplishing, other than sabotaging our whole season, is ruining T.O.'s career. I haven't seen such misguided decision-making since last year when we agreed to sign him."

Now that his brilliant strategy is paying dividends, Owens can breathe a sigh of relief. Although Banner isn't letting on publicly that he wants Owens back, Owens and Rosenhaus are confident that "it's just a matter of hours before they come knocking with a new contract."

?

DID Y U KNOW

Enthusiastic tennis fans sometimes run onto the court and knife players.

First Base Coach Wonders If He's Even Making a Difference Anymore

LOS ANGELES, CA—John Shelby, first base coach for the Los Angeles Dodgers, is wondering if he's even making a difference anymore. After years of watching batters arrive at first base indifferent to his advice, Shelby has been forced to reassess his role on the team. Is he really needed? Is he having any impact at all? "This is sort of an existential question I guess," said Shelby. "All of mankind's greatest philosophers have dealt with the age-old question, 'Why are we here?' But I'm sure none of them have had to experience the soul-crushing experience of being a first base coach. I feel so . . . so impotent—though not in a Rafael Palmeiro sort of way."

Report: Some Professional Athletes Do Not Own Escalades

NEW YORK, NY—A recent report released by *The Sporting News* alleges that, despite popular perception, some professional athletes may not own Cadillac Escalade SUVs. The news comes as a shock to sports fans as well as many athletes, who are puzzled over the refusal of some of their colleagues to purchase one of the popular, luxurious vehicles. "That's insane," said the Washington Wizards' Gilbert Arenas. "Personally, I've never seen any professional athlete driving anything other than an Escalade, so I don't even know if this is true. But if it is . . . what are they waiting for? These trucks are garish, obnoxious, overpriced, oversized, and attention-getting. What's not to like?"

Wide Receiver Insists He Was Not Interfered With

CINCINNATI, OH—Bengals wide receiver Chad Johnson was infuriated Sunday when a phantom pass interference penalty was called on Minnesota safety Corey Chavous, giving Johnson's team an automatic first down. He pleaded with referees to pick up the flag in accordance with the honor system. "What? What are you doing? I wasn't interfered with!" screamed Johnson after the flag was thrown. "That's bullshit. That is fucking bullshit. Didn't you see what happened? I went up for the ball, but he had tight coverage on me. Sure, there was contact, but it was incidental. We were both going for the ball. Please, pick up that flag. I will not accept a first down under false pretenses."

Stuart Scott Caught Hiding in Broom Closet Practicing Ebonics

BRISTOL, CT—In a rather embarrassing situation for the hip young ESPN anchor, Stuart Scott was caught hiding in a broom closet, practicing ebonics for his nightly *SportsCenter* taping. Scott was discovered by a janitor, who had walked into the closet to get a new mop head.

"I just needed a new mop head, so I went into the supply closet, and there's Stuart Scott, sitting on a little stool with headphones on," said the janitor, Lee Stenson. "He didn't hear me come in, so he just sat there and kept talking in this urban street slang. I think he was getting it from the headphones."

Despite the accusations, Scott denies that he was listening to hardcore gangster rap in order to pick up on the latest urban slang and improve his "street cred."

"Nah, it wasn't like that," said an embarrassed Scott. "I just like to go chill sometimes in the broom closet, kick back and listen to some Method Man or Jay-Z or something. You know, its all quiet in there and shit, and it helps a brother get some rest. Y'all don't know how much pressure we be under doin' this shit, Dawg."

According to Stenson, when Scott noticed that he was watching, he attempted to cover himself by picking up the newspaper and pretending to read it.

Coworkers at ESPN were not surprised by Scott's actions. According to sources, many of Scott's acquaintances are suspicious of his hip urban slang, pointing out that it varies drastically from his natural conversational tone. He seems to be able to "turn it on and off," say coworkers.

"That's definitely an affectation of sorts," said Dan Patrick, ESPN anchor. "When he first started working here, he spoke the king's English. Then all of a sudden he started saying things like 'boo-yeah' during broadcasts. Then he started referring to everyone as 'dawg,' and it just sort of snowballed from there."

Scott defends himself by saying that his style has evolved naturally over the years and that his transformation in tone and attitude should not be interpreted as a calculated image change.

Many of his friends are confused by Scott's attempts to sound more "urban." They say he should be happy with who he is and not try to use hip slang to attempt to identify with a group of people he has nothing in common with.

"Look," said one associate anonymously. "He went to the University of North Carolina and got a bachelor's degree in speech communication. He grew up in a middle-class neighborhood. He's no ODB, that's for sure. He's more like Ted Koppel."

> "HE GREW UP IN A MIDDLE-CLASS NEIGHBORHOOD. HE'S NO ODB, THAT'S FOR SURE. HE'S MORE LIKE TED KOPPEL," SAID ONE ASSOCIATE.

Old-Fashioned Retro-Ballpark Has Futuristic Prices

SAN DIEGO, CA—At first glance, San Diego's Petco Park is a typical retro ballpark, complete with a brick warehouse overlooking the outfield, intimate seating, and a charming asymmetrical playing field. The atmosphere of Petco Park evokes a quaintness reminiscent of the grand ballparks of yesteryear. But one feature makes this beautiful bandbox stand out from its predecessors: the futuristic ticket and concession prices.

From $6 hot dogs to $9 beers to $45 bleacher seats, Petco Park boasts the prices of tomorrow in the ballpark of yesterday.

"Wow, I had no idea this place was so expensive," said Ted Loman, San Diego resident who brought his family of four to the ballpark and spent over $300. "We bought one of those game programs for $9.99. Then I went and got everyone a hot dog and a Coke, and the total came to $63. Imagine that. I thought this was a real old-timey ballpark, but prices like this make it a futuristic wonderworld!"

Another fan was wowed by Petco Park's amazingly high prices when he purchased an ice cream sandwich from a vendor.

"Holy cow, this ice cream sandwich cost $7," said Bill Montcliffe, 35. "That's an unbelievable price, especially for such a classic, old-fashioned place. Petco Park is like the ballpark of tomorrow . . . today!"

John Moore, owner of the San Diego Padres, is extremely proud of his new ballpark. He notes that the seats are extra-comfortable with lots of legroom, and the sight lines are second to none. But his favorite feature is the high prices.

"You really can't beat the experience of coming to Petco Park," said Moore. "We're really building a bridge into the twenty-first century here. And the best part is that with every purchase you make, we donate one dollar to the American Red Cross. It's the least we can do. Seriously. It was the absolute lowest amount they would accept."

Petco Park isn't the only retro park that charges ultramodern prices. Places like Camden Yards in Baltimore and Citizens Bank Park in Philadelphia may hark back to a kinder, more innocent time, but their prices hark forward to a stark, frightening future.

"Camden Yards is really the perfect juxtaposition of nostalgic surroundings and modern-day price gouging," said Orioles owner Peter Angelos. "When we built it, we wanted to evoke the memory of baseball past, when the tradition of the game meant more than dollars and cents. Then we wanted to combine that with the modern-day tradition of dollars and cents superseding tradition. People will always pay futuristic prices to recapture a piece of the past."

ON THIS DAY...

In 1936, Jesse Owens won four gold medals at the Berlin Olympic Games, much to the chagrin of Adolf Hitler, Mussolini, and Franklin Roosevelt, none of whom particularly liked black people.

Noam Chomsky Throws Most Depressing Super Bowl Party Ever

BROOKLINE, MA—Noam Chomsky, linguistics professor at MIT and well-known critic of the U.S. government, threw the most depressing Super Bowl party ever yesterday at his home in Brookline, MA. The radical left-wing intellectual reportedly spent the entire evening ridiculing the game as an "expensive public spectacle designed to divert the bewildered herd from the increasingly brutal policies of its own corrupt government."

"Worst Super Bowl party ever, hands down," said Glenn Hamrick of Cambridge, MA. "It was a great game, but Chomsky kept blabbering on about U.S. atrocities in East Timor and Central America or something. And he kept referring to us as the 'bewildered herd.' I don't know, maybe he's right, but I did have a hundred bucks on the over."

Hamrick attended the party at the insistence of his new girlfriend, Justine Densmore, who is in awe of her professor and assured Hamrick that the party would be "enlightening and life-changing."

"When I heard those words, I was a little skeptical," said Hamrick. "But Justine is pretty hot. I figured if I went with her to this little party, it would show her how smart and intellectual I am. But I wasn't expecting it to be as bad as it was. He had the game on in the corner on a little TV. Nobody was really paying attention to it, except to critique it."

According to Hamrick, the most uncomfortable moment came at the end of regulation when Adam Vinatieri kicked the game-winning field goal. As the ball sailed

"RIGHT ABOUT THE TIME WHEN EVERYONE IN AMERICA WAS WATCHING JANET JACKSON'S TIT FALL OUT, WE WERE HEARING ABOUT THE U.S.-BACKED SLAUGHTERING OF SALVADORAN NUNS IN THE 1980s."

through the uprights, Hamrick briefly lost his composure, much to the chagrin of his date.

"When that thing went through the uprights, I fuckin' just lost it," said Hamrick. "I jumped out of my seat and yelled, 'Yes! Fuckin' A, baby! Fuckin' A!' Everyone was staring at me. Then Chomsky, cool as can be, looked at me from under his little spectacles and said, 'Next time you want to stand up and cheer for your football team, think about the one million Iraqi children who died as a

see CHOMSKY, page 152

> CHOMSKY, continued from page 151

result of punishing U.S. sanctions.' That was like a punch in the stomach. A million kids is a lot. Then again, it *was* a really clutch kick."

Chomsky insists that the party was not depressing in the least. He regarded the gathering as an opportunity for a group of citizens to organize in the great democratic tradition, speaking freely about the powers that control them.

"My party was depressing? Maybe it was depressing to manipulators and controllers in the media, who seek to divert us. After all, if any significant segment of the populace had the slightest idea of what the government was doing in their name, they would no doubt be appalled. We live not in a democracy, but a corporate oligarchy designed to marginalize us, distract us, and remove us from the political process by bombarding us with bright colors, explosions, and violence. Remember, the smartest way to avoid democracy is to keep people distracted."

Other attendees reported being slightly disappointed by the ultraserious atmosphere of the Super Bowl party.

"So it wasn't your typical Super Bowl party," said Phil Davidoff, another student of Chomsky's. "I showed up with my football squares and a six-pack, but it was pretty obvious it wasn't that kind of crowd. But Chomsky was in rare form all night."

Chomsky mercilessly ridiculed the garish, expensive pregame festivities, the perfect example, in his opinion, of mass media mind control and corporate enslavement. Then during halftime he turned the television off to engage in a roundtable discussion of U.S. imperialistic policies and how the media supports them.

"That was pretty heavy stuff," said Davidoff. "Right about the time when everyone in America was watching Janet Jackson's tit fall out, we were hearing about the U.S.-backed slaughtering of Salvadoran nuns in the 1980s."

Fox's New Glowing Pitcher's Mound to Let Viewers Know Where Pitcher's Mound Is at All Times

NEW YORK—In a continued effort to appeal to casual baseball fans, the Fox network will feature a glowing pitcher's mound in its Major League Baseball broadcasts this season. The mound will be bathed in a bright yellow light similar to the one used to identify the first down yard-line in Fox's football broadcasts. Producer Susan Brightman explains: "We're looking to reach out to casual fans who have a hard time following the game. It can get mighty confusing sometimes, so we've developed this system to make things easier. If you can't find the pitcher's mound, just look for the gigantic glowing orb in the center of the screen with the pitcher perched atop it. That's the pitcher's mound. If you still can't find it, there's really not much more we can do for you."

MLB Owners Agree to Eliminate Steroids From Postgame Buffet

Sumo Wrestler Thinks New Loincloth Makes Him Look Fat

Randy Moss Confesses to Smoking Pot Next Week

Sideline Reporter Jailed for Refusing to Reveal Her Source

WASHINGTON, DC—CBS sideline reporter Bonnie Bernstein was jailed Tuesday afternoon after refusing to reveal the source of her allegations regarding running back Priest Holmes. Bernstein was subpoenaed by a grand jury on Monday but refused to budge, saying that her journalistic integrity was more important than her freedom.

The prosecutor in the case, Randall Fitzgerald, said Bernstein could be facing a long prison sentence if she fails to comply.

"Under federal law, Ms. Bernstein is required to disclose her sources to the government," said Fitzgerald, who is investigating Bernstein's claim that Holmes enjoys playing *Madden 2006* in his spare time. "If she continues to refuse, her short stint in jail could turn into a lengthy prison sentence, which would actually be great news for people who watch football."

Fitzgerald is hoping Bernstein's arrest will send a message to other sideline reporters.

"Sideline reporters have gotten out of control," he said. "Every time I turn on a football game, they are there spouting facts and figures that could very well be complete lies. Is Peyton Manning really a cutup in the locker room? Does Donovan McNabb help out at a community center once a week? Is Jamal Lewis *really* happy to be back on the field with his teammates? This is the kind of bullshit the American people need to know."

> "HER SHORT STINT IN JAIL COULD TURN INTO A LENGTHY PRISON SENTENCE, WHICH WOULD ACTUALLY BE GREAT NEWS FOR PEOPLE WHO WATCH FOOTBALL," SAID RANDALL FITZGERALD.

Bernstein's report was initially aired during the 1st quarter of Sunday's Jets-Chiefs game. Standing on the Chiefs sideline, she looked into the camera and delivered what Fitzgerald called "shockingly irresponsible" allegations about Priest Holmes.

"You know, Priest Holmes has been one of the NFL's top players on the field, but very few people are aware that he is also one of the top players *off* the field as well," Bernstein announced in the middle of a Chiefs scoring drive. "Holmes loves to play *Madden 2006* in his spare time, and rumor has it, he's the man to beat in the Chiefs locker room."

While Holmes has vehemently denied Bernstein's allegations, CBS Sports issued a statement in support of Bernstein and applauded her for upholding her journalistic integrity. According to the statement, "The job of sideline reporter is one of the most important jobs in our society. Like all sideline reporters, Bonnie is a tireless crusader for truth, and we applaud her for confronting those forces that seek to silence her."

Bernstein's lawyer, Alex Stein, says that his client is resolute and will stay the course, jail sentence or no jail sentence.

"I have spoken to Bonnie and she is resolute," Stein said. "She also wants her fans to know that she will issue her own statement next Sunday. It will be read by another sideline reporter, during a crucial moment of the Chargers-Broncos game. Stay tuned!"

Hurricane Puts Things in Perspective For Fantasy Football Owner

"MAYBE IT WAS JUST GOD TELLING ME, 'HEY, DON'T SWEAT THE SMALL STUFF. YOU CAN STILL WIN WITH THE ROSTER YOU HAVE,' " SAID GERALD WYMAN.

SACRAMENTO, CA—Hurricane Katrina which tore through the Gulf of Mexico yesterday, damaging homes in several states and killing untold numbers of Americans, put things in perspective for fantasy football owner Gerald Wyman of Sacramento. After viewing the harrowing news footage, Wyman began to reflect on the important things in life and realized that fantasy football is just a game.

"Wow, that was a pretty brutal hurricane," said Wyman, 33, an insurance adjuster. "So much destruction and chaos. I tell you, this really puts things in perspective. Thousands of people are homeless. Hundreds dead. Entire towns are submerged in water. Still, I can't help but feel a little bitter that I ended up with Kyle Boller at QB."

Just days earlier Wyman had endured a heartbreaking fantasy draft in which he missed out on almost every player he wanted. He stayed up all through the night playing it over in his head, wondering what he could've done differently.

"Why? Why? Why me? That's what I was saying," he said. "I was racking my brains to figure out what went wrong. I went in there with a plan, but the forces of luck, chance—of nature—foiled it. I was in an emotional tailspin. That's when I heard about the hurricane and all of a sudden my priorities were back in order. I can't help but think maybe that hurricane happened for a reason. Maybe

it was just God telling me, 'Hey, don't sweat the small stuff. You can still win with the roster you have.' "

Though he is shocked and stunned by the events in the Gulf, Wyman has vowed to move forward, and he has dedicated the upcoming season to the victims.

"It's hard to move forward, but I have to stay professional," he said. "This season is going to be special, because I'm dedicating it to the folks who are suffering down there with that hurricane. My thoughts and prayers are with them. New Orleans, Gulfport, Biloxi—this one's for you!"

In a further sign of their solidarity with the victims of Hurricane Katrina, members of Wyman's fantasy football league have decided to donate a portion of the entry money to the Red Cross.

"On behalf of our fantasy league, we are presenting a check to the Red Cross," Wyman said. "Sure, it's $55 that could have gone into the winner's pot, but there are folks out there who need this more than we do. I want those folks to know they are not alone. Man, it's a great feeling to give. This hurricane has really been a blessing in disguise for me."

Nation Mourns for NFL Player Who Didn't Get Paid Fair Market Value

SAN DIEGO, CA—Across the nation, grief-stricken Americans mourned for Philip Rivers, a first-round draft pick who did not get paid his fair market value by the San Diego Chargers. People of all ages, genders, races, and religious affiliations expressed solidarity with the embattled 22-year-old in his struggle to get exactly what he has coming to him.

"This is a black day for America," said Roy Fitzgerald of Tacoma, WA, a caller to San Diego's *Mad Dog Mike Show*. "What kind of world do we live in when a highly touted draft pick cannot get paid his fair market value by the team that drafted him?"

Loren Lapides of Grand Rapids, MI, struggled to keep her composure as she voiced her outrage at Chargers GM A. J. Smith.

"Mr. Smith, how could you?" she asked angrily. "This young man has overcome so much adversity in his life, worked his ass off to become a top draft pick, and you spit on him like he's some two-bit hustler? You only offer $14 million in guaranteed cash up front? Shame on you!"

Rivers's story has struck a chord in the heartland of America, where unemployment is at an all-time high and salaries at an all-time low. The desolate farmlands of the Midwest are fertile breeding grounds for mistrust of the corporations that care more about the bottom line than the needs of their employees.

But the heartbreak over Rivers's situation is not confined solely to one region of the nation. People from both coasts and every walk of life have come to see Rivers, who is being called "America's quarterback," as the embodiment of all those who struggle in this time of economic hardship.

"I have three kids and I can't get my boss to give me a raise," said 39-year-old Matthew Wilhelm of Keane, NH. "I make minimum wage and my boss is up there in his big office making millions off of my sweat. When I heard that Philip Rivers was not being paid his fair market value by the Chargers, I could immediately relate. We are one and the same. We are brothers. Fight the good fight, Philip. Hold out until you get the millions you deserve, you moderately talented quarterback."

In what was perhaps the most dramatic moment in the Philip Rivers saga, a crowd of over 1,000 people gathered outside his home in Athens, Alabama, in a candlelight vigil to offer support and strength to the young man. Before the night was through, Rivers made an appearance on the balcony and addressed the crowd below.

"I just want to thank everyone for their show of support through these difficult times," said Rivers. "Your strength and encouragement has inspired me to fight harder and win this battle so all Americans can earn a decent living wage and feed their children, and we can all get paid our 'fair market value.' I can assure you all that I will not budge from my original demand of a $15 million signing bonus with an incentive laden contract that could give me almost $20 million in up-front guaranteed money. Why? Because I'm an American, that's why. And what's more, I'm a professional athlete. We can do whatever the hell we want and people will still love us."

Inspirational Stalker to Never Give Up

PHILADELPHIA, PA—Stalker Rob Castillo, currently obsessed with tennis star Maria Sharapova, will never give up in his quest to win her love. The inspirational stalker even plans to travel to Philadelphia next week to watch Sharapova play in the Advanta Championship in hopes of meeting her and professing his undying love. "A lot of guys would've given up on Maria a long time ago," said Castillo, 38, an unemployed night watchman.  "But I'm going to keep stalking her until she falls in love with me. The word 'can't' isn't even in my vocabulary. I just hope I can be an inspiration to all the other stalkers out there. Never give up, guys. Remember: Whoever she is, she's just playing hard to get."

Next *Grand Theft Auto* Game to Include Baby-Killing

NEW YORK, NY—Fans of the popular video game series *Grand Theft Auto* received some exciting news yesterday from Sam Houser, president of Rockstar Games: The next edition, due to be released in 2006, will feature baby-killing. "We love to push the envelope with *GTA*, and the next edition of the game will feature enhanced graphics, better missions, and—drumroll, please—baby-killing," Houser said in an interview with Gamespot.com. "Killing adults is great fun, but after a while the novelty wears off and it starts to become routine. With baby-killing, you get to find babies all around town and shoot them. If you shoot 100, you unlock a really cool jet ski. Of course, it's all in good fun." Houser also leaked another exciting feature to be included in the next *GTA:* cannibalism.

Montreal Expos Lost in Poker Game

LAS VEGAS, NV—In yet another unfortunate turn of events for the doomed franchise, the Montreal Expos were lost in a game of no-limit Texas Hold 'Em Saturday night at Bally's Casino in Las Vegas. The game was played by Bud Selig, who was in town visiting with Vegas authorities about the possibility of relocating the franchise there.

"My wife always says that I shouldn't gamble," said Selig. "I tend to get carried away sometimes, and this is the result. Damn, I was really meaning to relocate them this year, too. I guess now that's the responsibility of the club's new owner, Frankie 'The Snake' Delucci."

The commissioner issued an apology to the Expos players and management following the debacle at Bally's.

"I want to express my sincerest apologies to everyone who will be affected by this," said Selig. "I know it's wrong to gamble. It's just that Texas Hold 'Em is so much fun, and once I start playing, I can't stop. A major league baseball franchise is too steep a price to pay for a game of cards, even if that team is the Montreal Expos. That being said, I'm sure the people of Montreal won't miss them too much. Bastards abandoned the team after the first chunk of concrete fell from the Olympic Stadium roof."

Delucci, a 32-year-old card shark from Amarillo, TX, has no experience running a major league franchise. He is a plumber by trade but is eager to learn the ins and outs of sports management.

"This is an exciting opportunity for me," he said. "I don't know much about baseball, but teams are generally worth a lot of money, aren't they? I'm not sure about the Expos, though. That Selig guy didn't seem too reluctant to give them up. He was like 'I don't have any more money. Will you take the Expos?' I really didn't want to, but I felt bad for him."

So the fate of the Expos now lies in the hands of Snake Delucci. He is expected to sell the team to the highest bidder, but he wants to explore all his options before making a decision.

"The most logical next move for me would be to sell these guys to whoever wants them," Delucci said. "But I'm also a little tempted to hold on to them, rename them, and start a franchise in one of these cities. I've always wanted to own a sports team and name it the Homos. Wouldn't that be funny as hell? I bet the players would get a kick out of it."

ON THIS DAY...

In 1947, Lou Gehrig began his decades-long streak of being dead.

NFL Players Vie For Gayest Touchdown Dance

SAN FRANCISCO, CA—These days, when celebratory dances have become an art form, players like Chad Johnson and Joe Horn, as well as several defensive backs, have made their signature end zone moves as much a part of the game as scoring itself. There's also a little good-natured competition between the star players about which touchdown dance is the gayest.

"With all due respect to those other guys," said Joe Horn of the New Orleans Saints, "I don't think there's anyone gayer than me. Have you seen my new move? It's pretty bold to do something that gay on the gridiron. But hey, I'm a bad motherfucker."

In his touchdown dance, Horn holds his arms outstretched to the sides, squats down, and slowly rotates his pelvis like an exotic dancer. Irish dance sensation Michael Flatley, the so-called "Lord of the Dance," who has made a career of prancing around in tights, says that Horn's dance is "pretty good," but leaves a little to be desired.

"Horn has nice form," said Flatley. "His moves, his style, his whole attitude is pretty

see GAY DANCE, page 160

"YOU DON'T GET MUCH GAYER THAN TERRELL OWENS. TO SEE HIM PRANCING AROUND IN THE END ZONE LIKE TINKER BELL IS TO WITNESS A TRUE SISSY AT WORK," SAID MICHAEL FLATLEY.

> GAY DANCE, continued from page 159

feminine. He looks gay all right, but he hasn't really crossed the line into flaming."

Members of the Miami Dolphins secondary have created their own "team celebration" that they feel sets a new standard of gayness. The team celebration is more effective, they say, because it allows the players to interact with each other like intoxicated females in a nightclub.

"Ever go to a club and see the way girls like to grind with each other when they get really drunk?" asked Patrick Surtain. "That's us. We get in a little circle, face each other, grab our crotches, and start going at it. Really, we stop just short of blowing each other. Take *that* Joe Horn."

The history of the end zone dance goes back close to twenty years. But for decades before that, any kind of excessive celebration was considered unsportsmanlike, and players kept their enthusiasm to a minimum. No one would be caught dancing in the end zone in the days of Dick Butkus and Deacon Jones. But that all changed in the eighties with Billy "White Shoes" Johnson. The Houston Oilers wide receiver began doing a garish dance in the end zone after every touchdown catch.

"I was just having some innocent fun," said Johnson. "I didn't realize it would turn into a goddamn homo-fest."

Unfortunately for Johnson, it has. But the days of Billy Johnson being the lone maverick player to dance in the end zone are long gone, and according to one Terrell Owens, there's a new sheriff in town.

"Billy was a trailblazer for sure," says Owens. "But with all due respect, his touchdown dance wasn't even that gay. It was just stupid."

Owens has created quite a stir the past few years with his gaudy, ostentatious dance routines. Some view them as harmless fun, some as shameless self-promotion, but almost everyone agrees that the touchdown celebrations are the gayest in the league.

"You don't get much gayer than Terrell Owens," admitted Flatley. "To see him prancing around in the end zone like Tinker Bell is to witness a true sissy at work. That guy makes Harvey Fierstein look like Clint Eastwood. And to do that on a football field, a place of unfettered macho aggression, is pretty ballsy."

Women's College Basketball Game Upstaged By Halftime Dancing Ape

CHATTANOOGA, TN—A women's college basketball game between the LSU Tigers and the Liberty Lady Flames Saturday was upstaged by a halftime performance featuring an awesome dancing ape. The game, won by LSU 90-48, was no match for the ape, which used a springboard to perform dozens of dazzling slam dunks. "Oh my God! Did you see what that ape just did?" asked Beth Mowins, play-by-play announcer for the game. "He just jumped off that little springboard, did a flip, and dunked the ball right through the hoop! And check out those funny shorts he's wearing. They have little basketballs on them! Ha ha ha. This is the most fun I've had all night. I hope this halftime never ends."

Teen at Party Pressured into Trying Steroids

IRWIN, IA—The Major League Baseball steroid crisis hit home Saturday night for Brittany Ludlow, a 16-year-old high school student who was pressured into trying tetrahydrogestrinone (THG) at a party. The teen injected a syringe full of the designer chemical into the meaty part of her thigh in an effort to fit in with the "A" crowd.

Afterward, Ludlow regretted her decision and vowed never to succumb to peer pressure again.

"I should never have done that, but all the kids were taunting me and calling me chicken," said Ludlow, a sophomore at nearby Roosevelt High.

The party was populated by popular students, and Ludlow said she felt enormous pressure to join them in their drug abuse.

"I just want to fit in like everyone else," she said. "All these people were sitting on the couch and doing THG and acting like it was the coolest thing in the world. Then this guy I like told me to stop being such a square and take the steroids. So I did. The needle really hurt. You know who I blame for this? Mark McGwire. He's been sending the wrong message to our nation's youth."

Others who attended the party said that steroid use is spreading among teens, in part because of the glorification of the drug in Jose Canseco's book, *Juiced*.

"Everyone at Roosevelt is doing steroids," said one student, a junior who asked not to be identified. "It's the latest craze. It all started when that Canseco book came out. See, today's high school students are obsessed with baseball players. We don't like 50 Cent

"ALL THE KIDS WERE TAUNTING ME AND CALLING ME CHICKEN," SAID BRITTANY LUDLOW. "NEXT TIME I'M JUST GONNA DO THE RIGHT THING AND STICK WITH ECSTASY."

or Eminem or anything. Nope, we emulate baseball players from the early nineties."

When the steroid scandal broke last year, officials were concerned about the mixed messages being sent to young people. It appears that those concerns were justified, as a recent survey suggests that over 87 percent of U.S. teens have experimented with the popular drug tetrahydrogestrinone.

"It's sweeping the nation. Our fears have been realized," said Eugene Montague, national director of D.A.R.E. "THG and other designer performance-enhancers have become extremely popular, and the concern is that they will replace ecstasy as the club drug of choice. If that sounds unrealistic to you, then you're not being alarmist enough."

In response to the growing steroid epidemic in our nation's schools, Major League Baseball is producing a series of public service announcements to warn children against using the drugs. The first round of spots will

see STEROIDS, page 162

> STEROIDS, continued from page 161

feature commissioner Bud Selig and union head Donald Fehr speaking out about the dangers of illegal supplements.

"Kids, I know you think that steroids are 'rad' and 'hip,' but you couldn't be more wrong," Selig says in the first PSA, which will hit the airwaves next week. "In fact, most base-ball players are clean and never use steroids at all. I know there's a lot of pressure at school for you to fit in, but steroid use isn't 'happening,' and anyone who tells you differently isn't your friend at all. So take it from me, Bud Selig, and my friend Donald Fehr: With the possible exception of a few track stars, a home run champ, and dozens of other millionaire athletes, winners don't use steroids."

Arab Female Olympian Exposes Ankles, Nose in Scandalous Magazine Spread

ATHENS, GREECE—Shock and disgust rippled across the Arab world Monday when Kuwaiti gymnast Alaa al-Boulmerka posed in *FHM* magazine with her ankles and nose clearly visible. The provocative and scandalous photos infuriated Islamic fundamentalists around the world, prompting one prominent Muslim leader to take out a "fatwah" on al-Boulmerka. "Harlot! Alaa al-Boulmerka has shamed her religion and must be killed immediately!" proclaimed Ayatollah Ali Sistani, revered Shiite cleric. "If she ever sets foot in the Holy Land again, she will be stoned to death and dragged through the streets. That is a small price to pay for acting like an immodest, Western whore. I just hope no Arab men view these photos. They will be so distracted by her ankles and nose they will forgo their afternoon prayers."

Black Guy Gives Up Trying to Appreciate *Hoosiers*

AMHERST, MA—Local black guy Dale Laramie, 32, gave up trying to appreciate the movie *Hoosiers* yesterday after trying in vain for years. "Okay, so a bunch of white kids win the state championship. So what?" asked Laramie. "I mean, it's an okay movie, I guess, but the way white people talk about it, it's right up there with *Scarface* and *The Godfather*. I guess they just get a rush out of seeing white guys beat up on black guys in a basketball game." For his next project, Laramie will attempt to figure out why everyone loves *Rudy,* the story of an annoying lit-tle turd on the Notre Dame football team who gets on the field for one play and has everyone chanting his name like he's some kind of hero.

Kordell Stewart Narrowly Edges Stephen Hawking for Ravens Backup Job

BALTIMORE, MD—Ravens fans expressed shock and disappointment Friday upon learning that Kordell Stewart had narrowly edged physicist Stephen Hawking for the team's backup quarterback job.

According to coach Brian Billick, Hawking beat Stewart in several categories, including decision-making, timing, and accuracy, but Stewart held the edge in the crucial category of not being in a wheelchair.

"It was a tough call. Both guys came in here and worked their butts off," Billick said on Friday. "I really have to tip my cap to Stephen. He outdid Kordell in a number of categories and there were many times that he looked more poised in the pocket. Unfortunately, it came down to mobility. Stephen just took way too many sacks. Plus, it freaked everyone out when he shouted out his signals with that electronic voice box."

Hawking, author of *A Brief History of Time,* has returned to his work in the field of quantum physics. He is resentful, however, and believes he was cheated out of the backup quarterback job.

"I've suffered some indignities in my life, but nothing as bad as this," Hawking said. "I think I might be the first person in history to lose out to Kordell Stewart. I couldn't even show my face in front of my colleagues at the Royal Society. They were like, 'Hey, here comes the big loser who's not even good enough to beat Kordell Stewart.' I really am

"UNFORTUNATELY, IT CAME DOWN TO MOBILITY. STEPHEN JUST TOOK WAY TOO MANY SACKS. PLUS, IT FREAKED EVERYONE OUT WHEN HE SHOUTED OUT HIS SIGNALS WITH THAT ELECTRONIC VOICE BOX," SAID BRIAN BILLICK.

ashamed of myself. Perhaps someday I will unlock the secret to time travel and prevent that whole thing from ever happening."

Until Kyle Boller returns, the Ravens will take the field with Anthony Wright as their starting quarterback and Stewart on the side-

see BACKUP, page 164

> BACKUP, continued from page 163

lines ready to play backup. Needless to say, everyone on the team is keeping their fingers crossed that nothing happens to Wright.

"If any harm comes to that gentleman, woe is us," said tight end Todd Heap. "Anthony is the only thing standing between us and Kordell Stewart. I guess it would've been pretty rough having to play with a guy in a wheelchair, but still, I think if they gave him a chance, Stephen could've contributed more than Kordell. At the very least he wouldn't have thrown as many interceptions. Plus he talks like a robot. It's fucking cool."

If his teammates are skeptical, Stewart himself remains as confident as ever. The 33-year-old has kept himself in tip-top shape and is ready to step in and carry the team.

"Hey, you know, I've been in this situation before," Stewart told reporters at his locker. "I know the offense, I know the plays, I've seen it all. I was confident that I could beat out Stephen Hawking if I just brought my 'A' game, and that's exactly what I did. Now I'm setting my sights on the starting job. All I have to do is beat out Kyle Boller and Anthony Wright. You think offensive coordinator Jim Fassel gives a shit anymore? That guy's dying to get fired."

ESPN Forces Its Way into Basement Poker Game

AURORA, IL—ESPN cameras forced their way into a basement poker game in Aurora, IL, last night and proceeded to film the game and broadcast it on ESPN2. The game was shown as part of ESPN's new *Real Poker* series, which portrays regular people playing poker in their homes. The owners of the house, Rich and Marie Straub, attempted to call police after the cameraman kicked the door down, but the line was already cut. "We were just sitting there playing and all of a sudden these cameras come charging in," said Rich Straub, who hosts the casual poker game every Tuesday night. "They told us to relax and keep playing, but it was pretty nerve-racking knowing it was all going to be on TV—especially since I was in my underwear and had a three-foot bong sitting next to me."

Shawn Green to Wear Funny Jewish Hat During Games

LOS ANGELES, CA—Rather than miss any more games due to religious holidays, the Dodgers' Shawn Green has announced that he will wear his hilarious little Jewish hat instead of his baseball cap for the remaining regular season games. The goofy little yarmulke thingy is part of traditional Hebrew garb and will give Green a way to pay respect to his religion without interfering with the team's pennant race. His teammates have come out in full support of him wearing the hat.

"Oh, I love that funny little hat," said third baseman Adrian Beltre. "It really provides comic relief and keeps the team loose. I never saw Shawn as a clubhouse cutup, but I guess he's trying to take on that role."

Manager Jim Tracy credited Green with keeping the team's spirits up during a difficult and grueling stretch run.

"Anytime we're feeling tense or anything, Shawn walks in the room with that hat on and everyone just lets out a big belly laugh," said Tracy. "What a card he is. He reminds me of my college roommate, Mohammed. He used to walk around with a tablecloth on his head. We would say, 'Tablecloths are for putting food on, you clown!' And then he would fake like he was mad and we'd all get a good laugh out of it."

Some of the veterans on the Dodgers pointed out that the team has never had a bona fide "class clown" on its roster. But Green's wacky antics have drawn comparison to some of baseball's most lovable funnymen.

"I've heard a lot of stories about guys like Bob Uecker, Roger McDowell, and Bert Blyleven, and now I think we can add another name to the list," said pitcher Darren Dreifort. "When Shawn walks in with that beanie thing on his head, it just sends me into hysterics. It's better than the old 'pie-in-the-face' routine."

Even the Dodgers fans are saluting Green's new hat, as yarmulkes have become all the rage at Dodger Stadium. Green has his own special section of fans called the "Green Crew."

"Oh yeah, the Green Crew," said Green. "I see them at the games sometimes. Their um . . . their hearts are in the right place, I guess. But still, it hurts to be laughed at for something that you hold so dear. It's just an article of clothing. It shouldn't be subject to such ridicule. And to think, I considered wearing my floor-length prayer shawl the other day for the Giants game."

? DID YOU KNOW

You have some stuff on the side of your face. It looks like mustard. Nope, other side. There you go.

Defender Flagged for Hurting Quarterback's Feelings

Novelty of Interleague Game Wears Off After First Inning

Conservative Coach Vows to Pull Out Some of the Stops

Jesse Jackson Calls for More Minority Ownership in Fantasy Football Leagues

MIAMI, FL—Civil rights activist and self-proclaimed rabble-rouser Jesse Jackson took a stand today against perceived inequities in the ownership ranks of the nation's fantasy football leagues. Stating that the playing field is "far from level," Jackson complained that not enough is being done to correct the imbalance, and that proactive steps need to be taken immediately.

"I'm here today to right a wrong," said Jackson at a press conference. "As I sit here and talk to you, thousands of young men from all over the nation are drafting NFL players to be part of their fantasy teams. The majority of those players are African American. And the majority of those owners are white. Is this fair?"

Jackson, who has been trying for years to improve the minority ownership situation in the NFL, has reportedly grown frustrated with his efforts and is setting his sights a little lower.

But some say this will also be an uphill climb. Since there is no single unifying body of fantasy football owners, it will be difficult to get the message across. Not only that, there are virtually no numbers to show what percentage of fantasy football owners are white and which are black. There may not even *be* an inequity in the ownership ranks.

"I'm not sure how he's going to go about doing this," said friend and fellow civil rights crusader Johnnie Cochran. "I'm all for advancement of minorities, and I, too, like a good fight, but this is ridiculous. How the hell are we supposed to know how many black kids run fantasy football teams? My friend Jesse, I believe, just wants a little face time."

And face time is exactly what he's getting. *Sports Illustrated* ran a cover story last week on Jackson's latest crusade, entitled, "Where Have All the Black Fantasy Football Owners Gone?"

In the article, Jackson rails against the injustices perpetrated against African Americans trying to get a foot in the door in the world of fantasy football.

"First, they don't let us own real football teams," shot Jackson. "Now, they're telling us we can't even own fantasy teams? What's next? Are they gonna arrest us just for *thinking* about football?"

Although he may be fighting some long odds, Jackson knows how to draw attention to a cause. Several news outlets have picked up the story, and the lack of minority fantasy football owners is starting to become a hot topic. Brandon Funston, ESPN's fantasy football analyst, weighed in on the issue:

"I must say I'm alarmed by this trend. I, like many others, had no idea that there was a problem with minority ownership in fan-

> "FIRST, THEY DON'T LET US OWN REAL FOOTBALL TEAMS. NOW, THEY'RE TELLING US WE CAN'T EVEN OWN FANTASY TEAMS? WHAT'S NEXT? ARE THEY GONNA ARREST US JUST FOR *THINKING* ABOUT FOOTBALL?" ASKED JESSE JACKSON.

see MINORITIES, page 168

> MINORITIES, continued from page 167

tasy football leagues. I don't even know how they could possibly figure that out."

When asked if he would take any action himself to help spur some change, Funston was adamant.

"Hell no! I'm not biting the hand that feeds me. Geez, look at me. I'm getting paid thousands and thousands of dollars to be a fantasy football analyst. Talk about stumbling ass-backward into money. I'm not doing anything to jeopardize this. Although, for the record, my official stance is: Yes, I think there should be more minority ownership in fantasy football leagues. There. That's all I'm saying."

As for Jackson, he's just getting started. He insists that change is coming to fantasy football, and he's going to be the man to bring it about.

Jordan Calls Kwame Brown to Remind Him that He Sucks

WASHINGTON, DC—Two years after retiring from basketball, hall of famer Michael Jordan called his former teammate Kwame Brown to remind him once again that he sucks. Jordan drafted Brown with the number 1 pick in 2001 and spent the next few seasons ridiculing him in order to toughen him up. He left a rambling message on Brown's cell phone late last night reiterating his position. "Kwame, you suck. You're worthless," said Jordan. "Look at you. You're a dipshit. You can't shoot, you can't rebound, you can't defend, is there anything you can do other than stand there and look stupid? I hope you take this message to heart and use it as motivation to get better. Because once again, let me state unequivocally that you are a piece of shit. And your hair looks gay, too. And I don't like your sneakers."

NFL Diversity Committee Confounded by Interview of Asian Coach

OAKLAND, CA—The Oakland Raiders have interviewed former offensive line-man Eugene Chung for their vacant head coaching position, sources reported Tuesday. The move was greeted with muted enthusiasm from the NFL Diversity Committee, which wasn't sure exactly how to respond. "Well, he is a minority, but he's not African American, which was kind of what we were going for," said Dan Rooney, president of the committee. "I guess Asians count. Does that satisfy the minority interview quota? Damned if I know." The committee was further confused when the Raiders interviewed former New England Patriots running back Mosi Tatupu, who hails from Samoa.

Royals Rebuilding Phase Enters Rebuilding Phase

KANSAS CITY, MO—The Kansas City Royals lost 105 games this season, marking the third time in the past four years the team has reached the century mark in losses. That's why the front office has decided to "blow up" the current roster and rebuild the rebuilding project that started in 1986.

"Our rebuilding phase is now entering its very own rebuilding phase," said Royals GM Allard Baird, in his fifth full season as general manager. "It was a great idea in 1986 for the Kauffmans to look to the future and start developing young talent. It was equally smart to continue that plan through the nineties and into the new millennium. However, the results have been unsatisfactory. We're blowing up the whole thing and starting over again. Hopefully, twenty or thirty years from now we'll start to see some real positive results."

Baird and owner David Glass have overseen the rebuilding project since 2000, when Glass took over as owner. However, after a series of mistakes and missteps, nearly everyone in the organization feels it's time to start over again—again.

"Once again, we're starting over again," said Glass. "The rebuilding phase of the past two decades has proven ineffective. We must rebuild again, only this time do it right. No more trading away of prospects. No more losing all-stars via free agency. No more losing 100 games. It's time for us to build a champion—at any cost! As long as it doesn't go over $50 million."

Players on the team, from the rookies to the veterans, know they could be cut or traded at any time. There is no such thing as job security now that the rebuilding phase is starting all over again.

The team's elder statesman, Mike Sweeney, has endured ten years of humiliation and failure. Shockingly, he has not yet demanded a trade.

"I really don't think about that stuff," said Sweeney, who has led the team in nearly every offensive category during his tenure. "Ideally, I would love to be around when this team finally wins another World Series. It would be really special after all the stuff we've been through. On the other hand, I wouldn't protest if they tried to trade me somewhere else. That's just part of the game. Did anybody hear that? I said I WOULDN'T PROTEST IF THEY TRIED TO TRADE ME SOMEWHERE ELSE. Jesus, do I have to spell it out for you people? Get me the hell out of here."

2006 will mark the first season of the Royals' rebuilt rebuilding phase. The front office is asking fans to be patient as they attempt to build a consistent winner from the ground up.

"Fans, please bear with us here. Rome wasn't built in a day," said Glass. "We remain committed to bringing a winner to Kansas City. It might take a year, it might take two years, it might take two decades. Hell it might never happen. But even if it doesn't, I can promise you that we will keep talking about it and pretending to care. It's the least we can do—literally."

> "FANS, PLEASE BEAR WITH US HERE. ROME WASN'T BUILT IN A DAY," SAID DAVID GLASS.

New NHL Rule Change Would Make It Illegal For Jeremy Roenick to Talk

TORONTO, CANADA—As part of hockey's new collective bargaining agreement, several new rule changes have been adopted to make the game more enjoyable for the common fan. In addition to eliminating the red line and reducing the size of goalie pads, the league has announced that, beginning in the 2005 season, it will be illegal for the Flyers' Jeremy Roenick to talk.

Commissioner Gary Bettman said the "Roenick rule" was instituted "out of sheer desperation."

Bettman is referring to Roenick's well-deserved reputation as a loudmouth, which was reinforced last month when he lashed out at hockey fans who called players greedy and spoiled. During a televised interview, Roenick told those fans to "kiss my ass" and suggested they stop attending NHL games altogether.

"We knew we couldn't go on like this," Bettman told reporters yesterday. "We need to keep Jeremy from opening his mouth in public, and we feel this new rule will accomplish that. From now on, if Jeremy Roenick even so much as cracks his lips open in public, he will be fined. If he does it a second time, his teammates will be fined. A third offense and we're going after his family."

Bettman chided Roenick for his inability to articulate his thoughts in a more bland, inoffensive manner.

"Jeremy needs to be more like his peers. He needs to learn all the age-old sports clichés and use them during interviews. Take me, for instance. I talk and I talk and I talk but I never actually say anything. That's what the fans want, that's what the media wants, and, most important, that's what the sponsors want. Just stop talking, okay, Jeremy? Actually, don't answer that. You'll be fined."

Surprisingly, Roenick has agreed to adhere to the league's new policy and will no longer make public statements about the NHL. When reached for comment, he had this to say:

"I accept the league's new mandate that I not make any public comments about the league. That being said, I am deeply saddened by the fact that players are being censored just days after signing a collective bargaining agreement that resulted in a 24 percent pay cut. These guys have been fucking with us for, I don't know, how many years now? Too many. This whole damn league is a frigging joke, and they can all kiss my fat ass, and yes, I'm talking about the fans, too, those white trash, mullet-wearing, cavemen who think they're such fucking geniuses. But I shouldn't get into it. I made a promise to keep my mouth shut."

THE BRUSHBACK GLOSSARY

POLE POSITION: You wanna hear about a pole position? I got a pole position for you right here, honey.

Worst Hitter Ever Wins Arbitration Case

HOUSTON, TX—Larry Dierkman, utility infielder for the Houston Astros and one of the worst hitters in history, won his arbitration case yesterday. The victory netted him a $1 million raise over last year's salary. "I'm glad it worked out for me," Dierkman told reporters after hearing the news yesterday. "It's funny, though. I really didn't do anything to deserve a raise. I hit .130 and made 12 errors, in like, 50 games. I was such a waste of space. But this arbitration shit is a great scam. What the hell do the judges care? It's not their money."

Police to Preemptively Blow Up Athens in Anticipation of Olympics

ATHENS, GREECE—Greek police have announced plans to preemptively blow up the city of Athens in anticipation of the summer Olympic games there. The move will help thwart any current terrorist plots against the city and disrupt any local terror cells that may have been active. "This is a sad but necessary action that we must take in order to keep one step ahead of those who seek to do us harm," said Athens chief of police Fotis Nassiakos. "Hopefully, by blowing up Athens we will eliminate any and all targets that the terrorists were plotting against." As of yesterday, the Acropolis tower and Parliament building were leveled by explosives. In the coming week the theater of Dionysos, temple of Olympian Zeus, and the Astor Hotel will be preemptively destroyed.

Carl Everett Still Can't Explain Where All Those Dinosaur Bones Came From

CHICAGO, IL—Outfielder Carl Everett, who vehemently denies that dinosaurs ever existed, still cannot explain the presence of thousands of dinosaur fossils around the globe. "Why are they there? I don't know," said Everett during an interview with *Maxim* magazine. "They're probably fake. They were probably made by scientists who don't believe in God and don't want anyone else to, either. And those supposedly real ones at the museum? Well, I don't know. They're either fake or they're . . . I don't know. I just don't. Can we talk about something else, please?" When told that modern-day birds are actually descended from dinosaurs, Everett became angry and stormed out of the room.

Man Playing Entire Season of *MLB 2004* Not Getting Laid Anytime Soon

DES MOINES, IA—Doug Greenbaum, a 31-year-old unemployed security guard from Des Moines, is in the midst of playing an entire season of EA Sports' *MLB 2004*. Despite the fact that his team, the Chicago Cubs, is in first place, even Doug knows there is a good chance he won't be getting laid anytime soon.

"I don't see myself getting laid anytime soon," says Doug, lying on his sofa with a five-day growth of stubble on his face. "It's just not gonna happen. It's cool, though. I still have PlayStation to keep me busy. I'm playing on 'all-star level' now, the highest level there is. So I have that going for me."

Greenbaum purchased the video game three months ago. Immediately after the purchase, he read the manual and learned about franchise mode, a mode where the user can choose his own team and embark on a season's worth of games that mimic the actual MLB schedule.

"I've improved by leaps and bounds," says Greenbaum. "When I first got the game I couldn't even field. I kept throwing to the wrong base. But I've totally taken my game to the next level. I have a great chance of making the postseason. And I've got plenty of time, since I'm not getting laid anytime soon."

Doug's friends agree with his assessment. John Morello, a friend of nearly fifteen years, spends a lot of time at Greenbaum's apartment and doesn't see any end in sight to his celibacy.

"Doug's just going through a rut right now. He spends a lot of time playing that video game. That's pretty much all he does. Sometimes I go over there and play with him. He kicks my ass every time. If you're that

"IF YOU'RE THAT GOOD AT *MLB 2004*, YOU MIGHT AS WELL WEAR A SIGN AROUND YOUR NECK SAYING, 'I'M CELIBATE,' " SAID JOHN MORELLO.

good at *MLB 2004*, you might as well wear a sign around your neck saying, 'I'm celibate.' "

The only other person in contact with Greenbaum is his mother, Edna. She lives across town and occasionally phones her son to check up on him. She worries about him sometimes, but said his current problems are nothing to be alarmed about.

"He's a good kid," says Edna from her home. "At least he's not out on the street selling drugs or anything. I know he'll be fine. It's just a tough job market out there right now. At least I don't have to worry about him getting some girl pregnant since he has no

see CELIBACY, page 173

> CELIBACY, continued from page 172

chance of getting laid ever. So that's one less thing to worry about."

Sources say that the closest Greenbaum has come to getting laid in the past six months was when his ex-girlfriend stopped by for a surprise visit in March. She reportedly was "totally grossed out" by his appearance and odor and has vowed never to return.

Marino Rips Teammates, Family in Hall of Fame Speech

MIAMI, FL—Former Dolphins quarterback Dan Marino used his Hall of Fame enshrinement speech to viciously rip his friends and family. As the audience watched in horror, Marino berated his wife and son and called his teammates "useless." "I'd like to take this opportunity to say that I hate everyone I've ever played with," Marino said during his speech Sunday. "It's been a nightmare having to carry all of you for my entire career. I hope you appreciate it. And to my family, thank you soooo much for supporting me. You really did a great job of spending my money while I risked my life on the football field. Thanks for nothing. God, how did I become a Hall of Famer surrounded by such losers?"

Bengals Complete Long Climb Back to Mediocrity

CINCINNATI, OH—The 7–8 Bengals celebrated a win against the New York Giants yesterday, but that's not all they celebrated. With a good offense, an okay defense, and a fairly effective head coach, the Cincinnati Bengals celebrated the end of their long climb back to mediocrity. Head coach Marvin Lewis lauded his team's efforts in the locker room after the game. "You used to be the Bungles. You used to be the laughingstock of the league," said Lewis. "You couldn't play offense or defense. Now, after years of struggling to pick up the pieces, we have finally achieved mediocrity. Nobody talks about us much anymore. We're not the subject of cruel jokes anymore. We're just another decent, middle-of-the-road team that will be forgotten about the minute the regular season ends. And you should be proud of it, men. Congratulations!"

Troy Aikman Apologizes For Grammatical Error During Football Broadcast

PHILADELPHIA, PA—Responding to widespread public outcry, Fox broadcaster Troy Aikman issued an apology today for a grammatical error he made during Sunday's broadcast of the Cowboys-Eagles game. The error came during the 2nd quarter and resulted in a flood of phone calls from angry viewers.

"I would like to apologize to anyone I may have offended by using that split infinitive," said Aikman, reading from a prepared statement. "As you know, color commentators work very hard and utter many words, and occasionally we are going to make mistakes. I promise it will never happen again. Please stop sending my family death threats."

The now infamous split infinitive occurred during an exchange between Aikman and broadcast partner Dick Stockton, following a Matt Hasselbeck interception. Aikman noted that, prior to the game, Seattle coach Mike Holmgren warned Hasselbeck "to not take those kinds of chances."

"I don't know what possessed me to say that," Aikman said after the game. "Obviously, the infinitive of 'take' is 'to take,' and the presence of the word 'not' makes it—

duh—a split infinitive. As soon as it came out of my mouth I wanted to jump in a hole and die. I especially feel bad for Dick. I think I really threw him for a loop. He spit his coffee out all over the place."

Stockton did manage to cover up for Aikman's embarassing gaffe by quickly changing the subject.

"Um . . . yeah . . . that's an interesting take on it," he sputtered, wiping the coffee off his shirt. "Um . . . anyway. Time for a commercial? No? Okay, well, it's 1st and 10 here on the Seahawks 20. Great game so far. Defensive struggle. A real slugfest. What do you think, Troy? Actually . . . forget it. I don't want to know."

Members of the media have taken turns blasting Aikman for his carelessness. Even his old teammate, Michael Irvin, criticized him on *Sunday NFL Countdown.*

"Now you know I played with Troy, and you know I love the guy, but you simply cannot make a mistake like that when you're at this level," he said. "Split infinitives, dangling participles, double negatives, we've all used them. Hell, even I've used them. But I'm not in the broadcast booth. I'm here in the studio with Mike Ditka. We operate at about a 3rd-grade level here."

Aikman's next game is on Sunday and he's looking forward to starting over with a clean slate.

"All you can do is put it behind you and move on," he said. "That's what I plan to do. I know the fans are on me right now. I'm sure on all the blogs I'm being made fun of . . . Damn! There I go again! I dangled a fucking preposition. You know, sometimes I just wish I'd studied more in school. Actually, no I don't. Then I never would've been a football player."

> "I DANGLED A FUCKING PREPOSITION. YOU KNOW, SOMETIMES I JUST WISH I'D STUDIED MORE IN SCHOOL," SAID TROY AIKMAN.

Scooter the Talking Baseball Denies Rumors He's Gay

NEW YORK, NY—Scooter the talking baseball denied rumors Monday that he is homosexual, despite the fact that he was caught Thursday night in Times Square fellating a transvestite prostitute. The arrest has sullied the reputation of America's most beloved talking baseball and led to a flurry of speculation regarding his sexual orientation.

"I would like to state unequivocally that I am heterosexual," Scooter told reporters in his high-pitched, girlish voice. "Just because I talk like this doesn't mean I'm gay. And just because I was arrested for blowing a male hooker doesn't mean I did it. I think the investigation will reveal that I was not blowing that gentleman. I was merely showing him how a curveball works."

Since his debut on Fox last year, Scooter the talking baseball has been the subject of rampant rumors about his sexuality. During the 2003 play-offs, Fox analyst Tim McCarver referred to Scooter as a "prissy little queen" during a commercial break. The comment was caught on tape and leaked to a tabloid, bringing further embarrassment to Scooter. McCarver apologized, but the damage had already been done. Scooter's sexual preference became the focal point of a national debate among sports fans until the 2003 play-offs mercifully came to a end.

This year, Scooter was hoping to start anew. Unfortunately, the fans have a long memory and he was subject to relentless heckling during Games 1 and 2 of the ALCS at Yankee Stadium.

"Why does everyone think I'm gay?" asked an exasperated Scooter. "I know I have a squeaky voice. I'm sorry, I can't help it. That doesn't mean I'm gay. And what if I was gay? Why should that even be an issue? The fact is that I am here to help children and morons understand the game of baseball. I've been hired by Fox to do this job and I believe it is an important one. If not for me, nobody would know that fastballs are fast and sinkers tend to sink."

After the arrest, Fox suspended Scooter from his duties. Meanwhile, the prostitute Scooter allegedly fellated is making the rounds on TV and radio shows.

Michael Chapel, aka Shawinda, described his encounter with Scooter on *The Howard Stern Show* Friday.

"He was walking around Times Square looking pretty drunk, and he was shouting out that he 'wanted some dick' to whoever would listen," said Chapel. "Then I walked up to him and asked him if he wanted to party."

"Okay," said Stern. "So at this point what are you wearing? What are you wearing when you first encounter him?"

"I had on this tight pink miniskirt, a lacy tank top . . ."

"Bra and panties?"

"No. No bra and panties. And he just looked at me and said, 'What are you packin'?' Then I lifted up my skirt and showed him, and he was like, 'Okay, let's get a room.' "

"Just like that? And then you went to the hotel room and he . . . uh . . . fellated you?"

"Yeah, he went right down on me and just went to work. And he made me call him 'bitch' while he was doing it."

see SCOOTER, page 176

> SCOOTER, continued from page 175

Scooter vehemently denies Chapel's account, claiming he is being targeted because of his money and fame.

"This is extortion, plain and simple," said Scooter. "Everyone knows I am not gay, nor would I ever solicit sex from a prostitute. This is all a big witch hunt. This is what I get for trying to do my job and make the game of baseball exciting and informative. It's not like Tim McCarver is going to offer anything enlightening. The guy's dumber than a pile of rocks."

Arena Football Season May Have Just Ended

PHILADELPHIA, PA—According to an Associated Press report, the Arena Football League season may have just ended. Nobody knows for sure if the report is true, but evidence does indicate that the 2004 season has drawn to a close. "Well, spring is coming, and I think Arena Football is played only during the winter," said *SportsCenter* anchor Dan Patrick. "Plus I just heard something about a really big game between the Philadelphia Soul and the Indiana Firebirds. Maybe that was the Arena Football Bowl, or whatever they call it. Frankly, I don't know, and I don't really give a shit." Calls to Arena League officials were not returned, but John Elway, owner of the Colorado Crush or Smash or something, indicated he would make an announcement as soon as he heard anything. Elway was golfing at the time, and thanked reporters for reminding him that he owns the team.

Chris Berman Has Crush On Deion Sanders

BRISTOL, CT—Chris Berman, host of *Sunday NFL Countdown* on ESPN, clearly has a crush on the Ravens' Deion Sanders. The jovial anchor almost creamed his pants while recounting Sanders's interception and subsequent touchdown against the Buffalo Bills on Sunday. "And who's that Johnny-on-the-spot? Why it's PRIME TIME!" shouted Berman, his face red with excitement. "He picks it off, he starts the high step, and he's off to the races! He could! Go! All! The! Way! Touchdown, Prime Time! And we know what's coming next, don't we? The end zone dance, as only he can do it. Welcome back, Prime Time. It's good to have you back."

Hamstring Injuries Linked to Being a Big Pussy

CAMBRIDGE, MA—According to a new study published in the *American Journal of Sports Medicine*, chronic hamstring woes are linked to being a big pussy. The findings could have a huge impact on the sports world, where these nagging injuries have become an epidemic.

"According to our study, a lot of the sports stars you see with so-called hamstring injuries are unbelievable pussies and crybabies," said Dr. Richard Freedman, who spearheaded the study. "We interviewed dozens of athletes and the results were remarkably consistent. A staggering 93 percent of them were pussies. My recommendation for these people would be to take off the skirt and get back on the field."

Freedman's findings have ruffled some feathers in the sports world. Many of the athletes interviewed for the study vehemently denied being pussies and instead said that they suffer from legitimate medical conditions.

"I am not a pussy. I resent that," said Cincinnati Reds outfielder Ken Griffey Jr., whose career has been derailed by chronic hamstring problems. "I've suffered terribly over the years when I did everything I could to

see BIG PUSSY, page 178

> BIG PUSSY, continued from page 177

get on the field, but my injury prevented me. I happen to have an extremely high threshold for pain. How else do you think I tolerated playing in Cincinnati all these years?"

Despite the protests, the study is expected to spur changes in the way hamstring injuries are treated. Instead of the traditional methods of rest mixed with physical therapy, trainers will use psychological tactics to get players back on the field.

"This is something I've suspected for years, that these guys are all just total pussies," said Al Brademberg, team doctor for the Jacksonville Jaguars. "So instead of being an enabler, I'm going to try to motivate them by appealing to their sense of pride. You know, something like this: 'Hey, pussy boy, got a sore hammy? Hey everyone, look at the big fairy with the boo boo on his leg. Let's get him a wowwipop.' See, that's pretty effective, isn't it? Plus it's a lot better than my old method of shooting them up with illegal steroids."

Dr. Freedman endorses Brademberg's new psychological approach and believes that hamstring injuries will decrease drastically if other teams follow suit.

"In caring for hamstring injuries, you need to employ nontraditional methods of treatment," said Freedman. "Remember, these are pussies we're dealing with here. They're not going to ignore the pain and go out there and play. They have to be pushed. If I were a trainer, I would be like, 'Oh, sorry guys. You're teammate can't play today. See, his leg hurts. No, it's not broken. Nope. Not even fractured. It just hurts. Don't worry. He'll be back on the field as soon as he gets around to it.' If that doesn't work, the patient should be beaten mercilessly. It won't help his hamstring, but it sure will be fun."

Coppenrath, Bogut, Redick, McNamara All Compared to Larry Bird

WORCESTER, MA—Vermont's Taylor Coppenrath, Utah's Andrew Bogut, Duke's J. J. Redick, and Syracuse's Gerry McNamara have all been compared to hall of famer Larry Bird, despite vast differences in their playing styles. Observers cite Coppenrath's post presence, Bogut's versatility, Redick's 3-point shooting ability, and McNamara's court vision as qualities that invoke memories of the Celtic great. "I don't know if Coppenrath is going to be the next Larry Bird, but he could be a poor man's version," said college hoops analyst Digger Phelps. "Just the way he goes out there and plays with, you know, that style that Larry played. Sure, there are many differences between him and Bird, but there is one glaring similarity: They're both tall." Phelps also noted that J. J. Redick, like Bird, has the ability to make his teammates better and that Gerry McNamara has a similar hair color.

Kellen Winslow Jr. Makes Triumphant Return to Motorcycle Riding

CLEVELAND, OH—The Browns' Kellen Winslow Jr. made his triumphant return to motorcycle riding today, a week after completing rehab on his right knee. Winslow suffered a torn ACL earlier this year when he was in a motorcycle accident. "Yes! I'm back everyone. It's really great to be riding again," said Winslow, perched helmetless atop his Honda. "A lot of people said it couldn't be done, but I just dug deep, prayed to God, and fought my way through it. I'm sure my team is proud of me. They know they didn't draft a quitter." Winslow then sped away and promptly slammed into a telephone pole. He will miss the entire 2007 season.

Bono Tours Baltimore Ravens Locker Room

BALTIMORE, MD—U2 lead singer Bono toured the devastated Baltimore Ravens locker room Sunday after the team's 21-9 loss to the Bengals, speaking with players and coaches along the way. He saw firsthand the decrepit condition of the offense and the total lack of morale on defense. Afterward he appealed for help on behalf of the pathetic group of losers.

"I've seen a lot of hardship and turmoil in my life, but nothing that could prepare me for the unparalleled clusterfuck that is the Baltimore Ravens offense," Bono, wearing his trademark wraparound sunglasses, told reporters. "While other teams enjoy having competent coaching staffs, skilled quarterbacks, and functional offensive lines, the Ravens are suffering needlessly from a complete lack of cohesion. Somebody do something. The inaction of the global community is shameful."

During his visit, Bono met with head coach Brian Billick to discuss the team's most immediate needs. Afterward, Billick called the meeting "productive."

"It was a frank, honest, and productive meeting," Billick said. "Bono really does care about this team and this city. Still, no matter how much concern he showed, no matter how much compassion he offered, I still could not bring myself to forgive him for *How to Dismantle an Atomic Bomb*. I'm sorry, but that album was wildly uneven and totally overrated."

The visit did very little to lift the team's spirits. Many of the players didn't even recognize him. The ones that did couldn't figure out what he was doing in their locker room.

Still, Bono's visit was a fruitful one since it did manage to call attention to the Ravens' plight. The singer said he would return next season to monitor the team's progress.

"I have seen the depths of human misery today, but I have also seen something else: hope," Bono told reporters outside the Ravens locker room. "With their resilience, these players make the Sudanese refugees look like total pussies. Of course, they also have it much, much worse than those people."

Controversial Female Olympian Refuses to Pose Naked

ATLANTA, GA—Sherri Kahn, a member of the U.S. Olympic beach volleyball team, has become a controversial figure after refusing to pose topless in a spread for *Maxim* magazine. She would have been another in a long line of female athletes who have recently agreed to bare all for men's magazines. However, Kahn refused, claiming that she has a right not to pose naked.

"Thanks but no thanks," Kahn said when offered the opportunity by *Maxim* chief editor Mark Merrill. "I don't see any reason why I should pose topless. I don't need a bunch of men drooling over my tits to make me feel empowered."

Kahn also explained that she has no desire to be subjected to one of *Maxim*'s mindless "interviews."

"I don't think it's really necessary to engage in one of those silly Q&A sessions with some horny editor," said Kahn. "I'm sure America would love to know what my naughtiest fantasy is, where the craziest place I've ever done it is, and whether or not I've ever kissed a girl, but that's my business, thank you very much. If you want to know something about volleyball or my master's degree in literature, feel free to ask. Anyone? Anyone? I didn't think so."

After Kahn's refusal, several of her fellow female athletes criticized her for being "prudish" and "uptight."

"Why would she say no? I don't understand," said Amy Acuff, Kahn's Olympic teammate, who posed nude in *Playboy*. "Doesn't she want to show the world that women can be both beautiful *and* strong,

"I DON'T NEED A BUNCH OF MEN DROOLING OVER MY TITS TO MAKE ME FEEL EMPOWERED," SAID SHERRI KAHN.

both sexy *and* accomplished? It's up to us pretty girls to be comfortable with our own sexuality, not hide it under all this so-called 'clothing.' This is a serious blow to the women's lib movement."

Kahn has been mercilessly ridiculed by other female athletes, as well as male athletes, for failing to shed the shackles of sexual repression. Even her parents have gotten into the act.

"Well, I never. This is not the daughter I raised," said Cheryl Kahn, Sherri's mom. "I raised my daughter to be a strong, powerful woman who is not intimidated by men and not afraid to express her own sexuality. In Muslim countries they force the women to cover themselves head to toe. That kind of sexual slavery does not exist here in America, where our women are encouraged to remove their clothes instead. It's empowering. What do you think those women's rights activists in Afghanistan are striving for anyway? The right to vote?"

NFL Cornerbacks Plead With Brett Favre to Return Next Season

GREEN BAY, WI—The cacophony of voices pleading for Brett Favre to return next season just got louder, as the NFL's cornerbacks have joined the fray in urging the star to play one more year. The group, led by Minnesota's Antoine Winfield, told Favre that the league wouldn't be the same without him.

"Brett Favre is an institution. He's an icon," said Winfield, who had one of his team's four interceptions in the wild card game against the Packers. "When you think about all he's accomplished, it's depressing to hear that he might retire. I sure would miss all those pretty, perfect spirals gunned right into my chest. Come back, Brett. You have so much more to give."

"I'm sure Brett is disappointed in his performance against us," said Ralph Brown, another Vikings cornerback who intercepted Favre that day. "Knowing the fiery competitor he is, he'll want to come back and make up for it. He's meant so much to this game, and to me personally. That was the only pick I had all year."

Brown then paused to recall his interception and subsequent 27-yard return.

"It was a cover-2, I think, although I can't be sure because we're not that organized on defense," he said. "Anyway, as soon as the ball was snapped, I saw Brett hand off to Ahman Green, only—now try and follow me here—he didn't really hand it off. It was a fake. He was trying to trick us! Unfortunately, I had already given up on the play, so while I was waving to my grandmother in the stands, I felt something hit me in the face. I was a little stunned, but my teammates pushed me from behind and told me to start running. Everything happened so fast. Anyway, 27 yards later I got tackled and finally realized

"BRETT FAVRE *IS* THE NFL. HIS NAME IS SYNONYMOUS WITH CLASS, RESPECT, AND EXCELLENCE. IT'S ALSO SYNONYMOUS WITH THROWING INTERCEPTIONS AT THE WORST POSSIBLE TIMES," SAID SHAWN SPRINGS.

that I'd been running with a football wedged into my face mask. My first interception! And I have Brett Favre to thank for it. Please, please return next year, Brett. The NFL needs you."

But it's not just Vikings defenders who are pleading for Favre's return. Dozens of other

see FAVRE, page 182

> FAVRE, continued from page 181

players have also benefited from his generosity and devil-may-care style. Cornerbacks, safeties, and linebackers from around the league are standing shoulder to shoulder in urging Favre to continue playing.

"Brett Favre retiring? Say it ain't so," said the Redskins' Shawn Springs, who intercepted Favre twice during a Week 7 loss. "Brett Favre *is* the NFL. He's the consummate professional, he plays hard week in and week out, and, most important, he's a role model off the field. His name is synonymous with class, respect, and excellence. It's also synonymous with throwing interceptions at the worst possible times. If he retires, I'll have no choice but to move to the AFC so I can play against Jake Plummer."

Though Favre did have a QB rating of 92.4 as well as 30 touchdown passes this year, it's his tendency to make crazy throws into traffic that has his opponents salivating every week.

"That guys is absolutely fearless, man," said Lamont Thompson, Tennessee Titans safety. "I really admire that quality in a quarterback. I only had four picks this year and two of them were against Favre. That just goes to show you what a gutsy, gritty player he is. The NFL needs more quarterbacks like him, and soon, because I'm coming up on a contract year."

Unsure what next season will bring, the league's cornerbacks are being forced to prepare for life without Brett Favre. For some, it would be a painful and awkward transition. "Life without Brett will be pretty grim," said Texans cornerback Aaron Glenn. "He embodies everything that a quarterback should be: He's tough, smart, athletic, and he's not worried about things like 'turnovers' and 'throwing into triple coverage' and 'completely taking his team out of the game by firing the ball to the nearest defender.' Ah, Brett Favre. They don't make 'em like that anymore. If they did, I'd be in the Hall of Fame."

Black Quarterback Disappoints Fans by Not Being Mobile

JACKSONVILLE, FL—Byron Leftwich, quarterback for the Jacksonville Jaguars, disappointed fans this season by being an immobile pocket passer. "I said when we drafted him that he was a pocket passer," said GM James Harris, who warned fans after the draft that Leftwich was "not a Michael Vick type." "I don't know why everyone thinks he can run around. I can't understand it." After Leftwich's first game on November 6, Jacksonville media and fans expressed confusion as to why he took so many sacks. "I guess I just expected . . . something else," said Dale Downing, host of WJXN's *Jag Hour*. "I can't put my finger on it, but the second I looked at him I thought he would be, you know, mobile, like those other um . . . quarterbacks that um . . . oh forget it. I guess I was just wrong. We all were."

One More Bet to Get Local Gambler Back On Track

TEMPE, AZ—After losing close to $500 on a total of four NFL games on Sunday, gambler Ray Watson admitted that he made some unwise, foolish wagers. Still he refuses to back down, and will now focus his energies on recouping his money with a blockbuster bet on Monday night. The blockbuster bet is expected to get Watson "back on track."

"Yeah I had a tough day on Sunday, but that's all in the past," said Watson, 29. "I thought for sure the Bengals would cover versus Baltimore and I figured that Green Bay would hang in against the Colts. In retrospect, I don't know what I was thinking. I lost everything. I have no money to pay the bookie. So it looks like I've got to really buckle down and make a good bet tonight."

Watson, a file clerk at a local hospital, has been gambling on NFL games for close to a decade. He is expected to draw on that experience tonight when he makes a "can't miss" proposition on the Washington Redskins.

"This is one of those games that seems like it's going to be close, but in the end I think the Skins will run away with it," said Watson. "I was watching the pregame show and they really did look fired up. LaVar Arrington was jumping around like that guy from the Under Armour ad. That's a clear sign that these guys will have the emotional edge tonight. That's why I'm taking the Skins and the under. If I lose, I pretty much have to leave the state. But that's not gonna happen. I won't have that defeatist attitude."

As a gambler, Ray Watson likes to study league trends as a way to gauge what's going to happen from week to week. He cites extensive research and study as the main reason behind his historic win streak of 2002, even though it was followed by a historic losing streak in 2003.

"2002 was a great year for me because I had the trends locked down," said Watson. "It was almost like I was clairvoyant. I just *knew* what was going to happen. In 2003 things changed and some of the trends started reversing themselves and I wasn't able to make the adjustment. But I'm going to have a huge year this year, starting with tonight's game. And if I don't win tonight, you probably won't be hearing from me for a while."

Watson's girlfriend, Karen Altman, has been urging him to stop making football wagers since the beginning of their relationship in 2003. She claims that his "historic winning streak" of 2002 has warped his perspective.

"God, he's always talking about how in 2002 he won like eight bets in a row," said Altman. "Every time I confront him about it, he's like, 'Don't worry. I'm due for another big streak. I just need to get back on track.' He's convinced that he can make 1 big bet and turn everything around. I hope he does, because I'm not about to give that bookie another goddamn hand job."

Latino World Cup Teams to Be Consolidated

NEW YORK—In the interest of alleviating an awful lot of confusion, all six Latino teams scheduled to play in the World Baseball Classic will be consolidated into one. Baseball commissioner Bud Selig made the announcement today and said that it "made sense for everyone involved." "We will be consolidating all the Latino World Classic teams into one team," Selig told reporters at a press conference. "This will make it easier for us to keep track of the players and organize the rosters. As we all know, there are many great players in the Latin world. Places like Venezuela, Panama, Mexico, and Puerto Rico are all baseball powers, and they are all basically interchangeable. So why not have one 'super team'? It'll certainly save us a lot of confusion and paperwork."

Continental Tire Fans Flock to Continental Tire Bowl

CHARLOTTE, NC—Last weekend, Continental Tire fans from across the nation made a pilgrimage to Bank of America Stadium in Charlotte, NC, for the much-anticipated Continental Tire Bowl. Decked out in the orange and black of their favorite corporation, they chanted slogans touting Continental's superior products and high-quality service. "Whooo! Continental Tire kicks ass!" shouted Tim McKay of Portland, OR. "I came all the way from Portland to see this! Seriously, these guys are, like, my favorite tire company, and I wouldn't miss this for anything. They have products for cars, trucks, SUVs, even school buses! They're so much better than those Goodyear faggots." McKay went on to say that his favorite tires are ContiSportContact 2 and the ContiTrac SUV3.

Panthers Coach Recounts Horror of Having to Use White Running Back

CHARLOTTE, NC—2004 was a trying season for the Carolina Panthers. The NFC champs got off to a 1-7 start and failed to make the play-offs, one year after appearing in the Super Bowl. The biggest reason for their disappointing season was injuries, especially on offense. Things got so bad that for two weeks, coach John Fox was forced to start a white man at running back. "I've been forced to make some tough decisions in my life, but that was the toughest," said Fox. "If you told me before the season that I would be forced to use a white guy as a featured back, I would've laughed in your face. But you know what the funny thing is? He did okay. I guess there really is parity in this league."

Football Coach Caught Lip-Synching Halftime Speech

NORWICH, CT—Dan Harwich, coach of the Division III Eastern Connecticut Bulldogs, was caught lip-synching a speech to his team during halftime of its game against the Charleston State Owls Saturday. Onlookers sat in stunned silence as Harwich embarked on a lengthy tirade that turned out to be George C. Scott's speech from the movie *Patton*.

"That was just despicable," said receiver John Zito. "I've always thought coach was a man of integrity and honesty, but now he's been exposed. The sad thing is I thought it was a really great speech."

Harwich, a big fan of the film, had the entire speech memorized and mimicked it in impressive fashion while hiding a tape recorder in his coat pocket.

"Now there's another thing I want you to remember," Harwich lipsynched, his eyes fixed in a steely gaze. "I don't want to get any messages saying that we are holding our position. We're not holding anything. Let the Hun do that. We are advancing constantly and we're not interested in holding onto anything except the enemy. We're going to hold onto him by the nose and we're going to kick him in the ass."

At that point, the players were mesmerized.

"Whoa, he said we were gonna hold them by the nose and kick them in the ass," said tailback Martin Bulger. "Then he called them 'Huns.' I was like 'Yeah, we're gonna kick those huns in the ass, baby!' But then things started to get a little weird. Coach sneezed. And when he sneezed, the speech kept going."

The sneeze occurred while Harwich was in midsentence. Unfortunately he was not prepared for the unforseen complication.

"He was really on a roll," said Bulger. "He said, 'We're going to kick the hell out of him all the time and we're going to go through him like crap through a goose,' and then came the sneeze. No big deal, right? Except that the voice kept talking. As coach was sneezing, the voice was saying 'We're not just going to shoot the bastards, we're going to cut out their living guts and use them to grease the treads on our tanks!' Then coach's face went white. All he could do was run the hell out of there. But by that time, we were already pretty pumped up. We went back out there and won. We held their noses and kicked them in the asses, just like Patton would've done."

> "I'VE ALWAYS THOUGHT COACH WAS A MAN OF INTEGRITY AND HONESTY, BUT NOW HE'S BEEN EXPOSED. THE SAD THING IS I THOUGHT IT WAS A REALLY GREAT SPEECH," SAID JOHN ZITO.

ON THIS DAY...

In 1162, chalk was invented. Chalk would later be used to line baseball fields.

Chess Club Hazing Victim Unable to Remove Rook From Asshole

"IF I WANTED TO HAVE SOMETHING SHOVED UP MY ASS, I WOULD'VE TRIED OUT FOR THE FOOTBALL TEAM," SAID VICTOR SHULTZ.

COLUMBUS, OH—Victor Shultz, 17, a student at Daley High School in Columbus, OH, may have to visit the doctor as a result of an ugly hazing incident he endured at the hands of the Daley High Chess Club. Shultz went to an "initiation night" thinking the experience would be harmless fun, but left hours later with a rather unique problem.

"I can't get this rook out of my ass," said a distressed Shultz. "I've tried everything. I'm really uncomfortable."

The rook was inserted in his anus during a bizarre hazing ritual performed by the other members of the chess club.

"I think they drugged me or something. I'm not sure," Shultz said. "I was totally out of it. I remember drinking a lot. Next thing I know, they're holding me down pulling my pants off."

The hazing started innocently enough, with the other members forcing Shultz to make a series of prank calls to Daley High teachers. That was followed by a drill on chess strategy.

Then, as Shultz says, "things started to get a little weird."

What followed was a cringe-inducing two-hour session of pain and humiliation that left Shultz with several chess pieces embedded in his rear.

"I've been shitting pawns all week," says a frustrated Shultz. "I'm going to have to go to the doctor now. Talk about embarrassing. What am I supposed to say to him? 'Hey, Doc, can you pull this chess piece out of my ass?' Actually, that's exactly what I'm going to have to say to him. Damn."

Needless to say, Shultz will not be joining the chess club and will never see the other members of the club in the same way again.

"Talk about a shock. Who knew a bunch of chess-playing nerds could be so cruel and twisted? I mean, I've heard of homoerotic hazing rituals before, but I wasn't expecting it from the chess club. If I wanted to have something shoved up my ass, I would've tried out for the football team."

Shooting Spree Upsets Fragile Clubhouse Chemistry

Terrell Owens Now Slightly Less Popular than al-Qaeda

Most Exciting Play Ever Immediately Placed Under Review

Little Leaguer's Life Peaks at Age 12

WILLIAMSPORT, PA—When 11-year-old Michael Smith hit a walk-off home run to win the Little League World Series, he felt like a real-life superhero. Smith experienced a feeling of exultation that he will never know again, because at the age of 12, his life has already reached its apex.

"Woohooo! Yay for me!" screamed Smith as he was greeted at home plate like a conquering hero. "I'm special! Everybody loves me! Everybody knows who I am! I'm going to change the world!"

It never occurred to Smith that his success would be fleeting and he would spend the rest of his life treading water in a sea of mediocrity. In fact, he's naïve enough to believe that someday he'll be a major league ballplayer.

"When I grow up I'm going to be in the big leagues," Smith said to ESPN's Harold Reynolds, ignoring the fact that only a tiny, negligible amount of Little League World Series participants ever make it to the majors. "I'm going to be just like my favorite player, Albert Pujols, only better. I'm going to be better than him! I am the king of the world! Nothing will ever change!"

Smith's manager, Larry Alivo, watched from afar as his team celebrated. He marveled at their jubilation, but acknowledged that such experiences are once in a lifetime.

"Enjoy it now, kids," Alivo said to no one in particular. "You're probably expecting to be here next year, too, and to go on to a life of triumph and greatness. It is more likely that you will experience all the crushing pain, fear, and anxiety that defines modern life, only your pain will be more acute because you have already been to the top of the mountain."

Alivo believes the constant, fawning media attention gives the kids an inflated sense of self-worth. As a result, they will have a difficult time accepting the fact that

"I'M GOING TO BE JUST LIKE MY FAVORITE PLAYER, ALBERT PUJOLS, ONLY BETTER. I AM THE KING OF THE WORLD! NOTHING WILL EVER CHANGE!" SAID MICHAEL SMITH.

they are unremarkable people whose lives have reached a thrilling, yet temporary, pinnacle.

"It's all downhill from here. I think that's what I'm trying to say," said Alivo. "It's nice to see the kids happy, but at the same time I pity them. They think ESPN cares about them. Ha! They are a commodity, a product, used to sell advertising. Let's see where ESPN is twenty years from now when they are grown-ups, sitting in their cubicles waiting

see LITTLE LEAGUE, page 189

> LITTLE LEAGUE, continued from page 188

for the day to be over. Actually, ESPN will probably be right there, filming a segment on the depressing lives of ex–little leaguers for *Outside the Lines.*"

Child psychologist Dale Schumann called on ESPN and other media outlets to curb their coverage of the LLWS and stop making superstars out of children.

"Look, the World Series should just be a fun little thing for the kids to enjoy, and then they should move on with their lives," he said. "These TV networks make it out to be the Olympics. Oh sure, they stress that it's all about fun, but they contradict that when they make it into a multimillion-dollar extravaganza, don't they? What I'm trying to say is that children are annoying, especially happy ones, and we should keep them off TV. I know that sounds a little strange coming from a child psychologist, but trust me on this one. I'm a professional."

Wheelchair Athlete Not So Inspirational When Trying to Negotiate Revolving Door

BEAVERTON, OR—Mike Bartlett, world famous wheelchair decathlete, has been an inspiration to millions during his career. But he was not so inspirational Friday while trying to negotiate his way through a revolving door at Nike headquarters in Beaverton, OR. One witness described the scene as "depressing." "Wow, I used to think this guy was such a hero," said 33-year-old Nancy Simmons. "But that wasn't inspirational at all. It was totally lame. All these people had to help him and it still took like ten minutes. To think that this is the man I cheered for when he won the wheelchair triathlon on ESPN last month." Simmons made up for her frivolous cheering by heckling Bartlett as he struggled to maneuver through the entrance.

Black Hole Fans Angered by Stephen Hawking's Comments

OAKLAND, CA—Raiders fans in the "black hole," the infamous bleacher section in Oakland's McAfee Coliseum, blasted astrophysicist Stephen Hawking for insinuating that black holes are not as destructive as he once thought. "Black holes do not destroy everything that enters them," Hawking told a conference of physicists last week. "They simply return the mass energy to the universe, but in a more mangled form." Raiders fans responded to the slight immediately. "Fuck you, pal! We destroy everything in sight! Nobody who ventures into this section walks out alive, man!" screamed Gary Welston, Raiders season ticket holder and black hole resident. "What the hell does he know about football anyway? He's a goddamn scientist."

Rob Dibble Visibly Aroused While Discussing Red Sox–Yankees Brawl

BRISTOL, CT—Rob Dibble, analyst for ESPN's *Baseball Tonight,* was visibly aroused while discussing Saturday's brawl at the Red Sox–Yankees game. The excitable Dibble, himself a hard-nosed, tough pitcher during his days with the Reds, clearly took great pleasure in the violent melee at Fenway Park. While commenting on the incident, he used adjectives such as "awesome," "thrilling," and "classic."

"That brawl is the kind of thing that can really bring a team together," he said, as a bulge slowly grew in his lap. "When Varitek and A-Rod were nose to nose, you could sense the excitement in the ballpark. It's moments like this that make the Red Sox and Yankees the classic rivalry that it is. If I see another fight like that, I may have an orgasm."

Dibble spoke to Karl Ravech on the air just hours after the game. He had to be restrained by *Baseball Tonight* staffers after he finished a lengthy diatribe describing the awesomeness of the brawl.

"Oh my God. Oh my God," shouted Dibble as Ravech and the other analysts became increasingly uncomfortable. "Yes! Yes! Yes! The rivalry has reached a new level. I'm telling you, the bloodshed in this game rivaled any game that I ever played in . . . like when Trot Nixon, David Ortiz, and Gabe Kapler beat the shit out of Tanyon Sturtze. That's the kind of thing that galvanizes a team."

Dibble then stood up, grabbed his chair, and hurled it against the wall before turning on analyst Tim Kurkjian, whom he attempted to strangle. It took several members of the camera crew to subdue him.

Cameraman Gus Dickey recalled the incident: "I've never seen anyone so worked up in my life. As he was strangling Tim, he was like, 'This is the kind of thing that can really bring this panel together! We're galvanizing as a team! This is the shot in the arm we needed!' It took 4 of us to pull him off the guy, and as we were dragging him away, I noticed something that will haunt me for the rest of my life. The guy had an erection the size of a Louisville Slugger."

Dibble was a relief pitcher for the Cincinnati Reds from 1988 to 1993. His hard fastball and propensity for brushing hitters off the plate earned him the nickname "Nasty Boy." But retirement appears not to have mellowed him. Dibble's colleagues at ESPN said that they could see the latest outburst coming a mile away.

> "THE GUY HAD AN ERECTION THE SIZE OF A LOUISVILLE SLUGGER," SAID GUS DICKEY.

"He totally gets a hard-on whenever a pitcher hits a batter," said Kurkjian. "He thinks that's the solution to everything. When we were discussing Kevin Millwood's problems this year, he said, 'What he needs to do is come inside on some hitters, brush them off the plate.' And when we talked about the A's bullpen problems he said, 'Their problem is that the hitters are too comfortable up there. They need to start knocking people down.' So you can imagine how excited he got during that brawl. I thought he was going to shit his pants."

Meanwhile, Ravech reported that immediately after the Sox-Yankees game, Dibble headed to the editing room to supervise the

see ERECTION, page 191

> ERECTION, continued from page 190

creation of the highlight reel. He stood with the producers and technicians and watched obsessively as they pieced together the clip package.

"He was watching the whole thing with these maniacal eyes," said Jeff Dirucco, *Baseball Tonight* producer. "While we were going through the footage, he kept reminding us to zoom in on the bloody face of [Tanyon] Sturtz. Then he complained that the background music was 'too tame,' and suggested 'Seek and Destroy' by Metallica. I was surprised at that. What, did he think we wanted to glorify the fight by placing an awesome heavy metal soundtrack in the background? That's not what we're about. Just kidding. It's exactly what we're about, and it was actually a pretty good idea."

The Brushback Presents:
QUICK QUESTIONS WITH THIS CHICK I MET AT AN OHIO STATE GAME

BB: Hey, how's it going?

C: Hey.

BB: Great game, huh?

C: Please leave me alone.

BB: Do you come to a lot of games?

C: My boyfriend's coming back in a minute.

BB: Can I buy you a beer?

C: Security!

Pistons "Accidentally" Leave Darko Milicic at Airport

DETROIT, MI—For the second time this month, the Detroit Pistons "accidentally" left 1st-round draft pick Darko Milicic stranded at the airport. This time it was in Boston, and the team insists that it will never happen again. "Well, I never," said GM Joe Dumars. "I just can't understand how it happened. We did a head count before we left and we thought everyone was here. I can assure you this was an accident that will never happen again." Milicic was reportedly sprinting behind the team, yelling, "Wait up," but to no avail. According to Milicic, the team looked back and started walking faster. "I was chasing them, but I guess they didn't hear me," said Milicic. "Perhaps I just need to improve my English. Yes, that is the problem. They must not have understood what I was saying."

Vince Young Doesn't Give a Shit that He's Failing Calculus

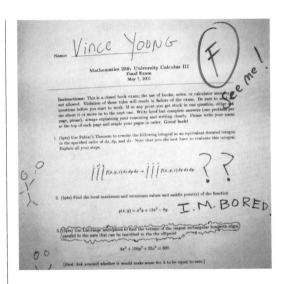

AUSTIN, TX—This week, University of Texas quarterback Vince Young learned that he was failing calculus. Don't expect him to shed any tears, though. The junior quarterback is on the verge of a long and lucrative NFL career and doesn't give a shit if he can *spell* calculus.

"I'm failing calculus? Ha ha ha ha, that's funny," said Young, who finished second in the Heisman voting behind Reggie Bush. "I guess I should stay after school and get some extra help right? Maybe I should get a tutor. I have a better idea: Maybe I should skip the rest of my classes and go on to be an NFL superstar. Gee, that's an attractive option."

Young has had a difficult time concentrating on his studies the past few months. His team is ranked second in the nation and will face USC for the national championship. It's also been Young's best season individually, something that would not have been possible had he studied or attended class.

"It's been an amazing year for me and my team," Young continued. "Academics are the furthest thing from my mind. Calculus? What do I care about that? I didn't even know I was enrolled in it. I'll get that homework in as soon as I can, though, Professor. Don't you worry. It's my top priority, right behind my interview with Bryant Gumbel and my massage."

Several other players on the Texas Longhorns have similar feelings about studying. If they're talented enough, they know they'll be in the NFL someday, and school will quickly become a distant memory.

Coach Mack Brown acknowledged the difficulties in getting his players to stay focused on schoolwork.

"Human nature being what it is, it's very difficult to get these kids to look at the big picture," Brown said. "Even if they do go to the NFL, getting a college degree is important. I tell my kids that every day. I sit them down, look them in the eye, and say, 'If you don't concentrate on your studies, young man, you'll be off this football team.' Of course, I only tell that to the role players. The stars can take a shit on their desks for all I care. They're keeping me employed."

Young has not said whether he plans to return to school next year, but if he does, he'll have the same lackadaisical approach to his studies. In fact, he might not attend class at all.

"Will I attend class next year? I don't know. I probably will once in a while. It's real hard to concentrate, though, when you've got a life like I do. Sometimes teachers ask me to hand in my homework. You know what I say? I say 'Sure, I'll hand in my homework as soon as I finish leading my nationally ranked team to victory in front of 100,000 people. Then I might get around to it.' I just love seeing the look on the teacher's face after I say that. It's probably the thing I will miss most about playing college football."

ESPN Receives Annual Government Grant to Distract Populace

BRISTOL, CT—ESPN, the Worldwide Leader in Sports, received its annual government grant today to continue distracting the populace with bright colors, loud noises, thrilling athletic feats, and mind-numbing banter. The popular sports network has been working closely with the government since the mid-1990s to lull the nation into complacency while civilization collapses around them.

"ESPN, simply put, gives people something to feel good about," said ESPN president George Bodenheimer. "It's a noble calling. When the Clinton administration came to me in '96 and proposed this deal to me, I was thrilled. What a great idea. Now, the Bush administration has taken it to another level. They've called on us to turn up the volume, increase the flow of information, and essentially scream our heads off so it's impossible not to pay attention. It's working great, and it's all for the benefit of you, the viewer. Seriously, you don't want to know what's actually going on right now."

Fox Announces New Reality Show *Guess Which Major Leaguer Is Gay*

HOLLYWOOD, CA—Producers at the Fox network have announced their latest venture into reality television: *Guess Which Major Leaguer Is Gay*. The show is the brainchild of Kirstin Catrell, who also produced *Playing It Straight*, the show in which female contestants must guess which of their male suitors is gay.

Guess Which Major Leaguer Is Gay will target much of the same audience as *Playing It Straight,* but will also appeal to sports fans as well. "People all over America are just dying to find out which baseball players are gay," said Catrell. "With this new show, we're going to make a game out of it. A female contestant will be introduced to dozens of seemingly normal baseball players, but with one twist: Three of them are homosexuals. Viewers can also chime in on their Sprint PCS digital phones. Who will it be? Barry Bonds? Jason Giambi? A-Rod? Chipper Jones? Tune in and find out. I think the results will surprise you."

Cowboys Fail to Consider Fantasy Implications Before Making Trade

DALLAS, TX—The Dallas Cowboys drew the ire of the fantasy community recently when they made a trade with the Cleveland Browns without first considering the fantasy implications. The Cowboys traded wide receiver Antonio Bryant to Cleveland in exchange for another wide receiver Quincy Morgan. After the trade, both clubs faced a barrage of criticism from the nation's fantasy owners.

"This is a pretty curious move. While it's true that Bryant was unhappy in Dallas, it's not likely that Quincy Morgan will be much of an improvement," said Michael Fabiano, senior fantasy writer for CBS Sportsline.com. "Morgan's fantasy value will drop considerably from this trade, so if you drafted him this

see COWBOYS, page 194

> COWBOYS, continued from page 193

year, you're pretty much screwed. Parcells is going to face a lot of heat for this move, and deservedly so."

The Browns are facing their share of ridicule over the deal, too, even though the trade will probably increase Bryant's fantasy value.

"A lot of people cut Bryant off their roster the past couple of weeks because he was unproductive," said Fabiano. "Now he's probably going to catch a lot more passes in Cleveland's offense. This would've been a lot fairer to the rest of us if the Browns had given some advance notice that they were going to make the deal. I, personally, just traded the guy the week before the Browns acquired him. This doesn't say much for Carmen Policy and the rest of Cleveland's front office. They really dropped the ball on this one."

Around the country, fantasy football owners are scrambling to repair their rosters. Those affected by the recent trade are furious with the two teams' failure to think about the consequences of their actions.

"I hope, in the future, that teams will consult fantasy football websites and publications before they start haphazardly making trades," said Larry Ulrich, 28, whose rotisserie team is currently at the top of the Yahoo.com fantasy league. "I had Quincy Morgan and now I'm going to have to trade him. If I knew this deal was going to happen, I never would have drafted him in the first place. Being a rotisserie GM is hard enough as it is without having to deal with these frivolous moves."

Commissioner Paul Tagliabue contacted both teams to express the league's displeasure. He called the move "irresponsible" but stopped short of levying any fines or penalties.

"Clearly both parties are guilty of being shortsighted," Tagliabue said during an interview on *Outside the Lines*. "Today's GMs often forget that one small trade can have far-reaching implications for thousands of people. Fantasy football is a multimillion-dollar industry now. Team owners and GMs must learn to think like rotisserie owners when making transactions. The player's individual numbers are more important than his overall value to the team. We need everyone to have that mind-set, not just Randy Moss."

Biochemical Weapons Specialist Psyched About Free Super Bowl Tickets

HOUSTON, TX—Vincent Maltell, an expert in biological and chemical weapons, is reportedly "totally psyched" about the free tickets to the Super Bowl he will receive as part of his job on the security force. Maltell's job will be to patrol Reliant Stadium with special chemical detection equipment to assure that terrorists have not infiltrated the building with weapons of mass destruction. "I have to walk around with this sensor and make sure there's no chemical or biological agents anywhere. It's a tough job, but as long as I don't find any anthrax or enriched uranium, I should be able to really enjoy the game," Maltell said. "I mean, how many people get free Super Bowl tickets at their jobs? Go Patriots!" Maltell will be clad in a bright orange radiation suit with gas mask in case of a terrorist attack.

Greyhound Bitterly Disappointed After Finally Catching Mechanical Rabbit

JACKSONVILLE, FL—"Aladdin," a greyhound that races at a dog track in Jacksonville, FL, was bitterly disappointed when he finally caught the rabbit he's been chasing all these years and discovered it was mechanical.

"I feel like such a fool," said the disheartened greyhound. "I've completely wasted my life chasing around this mechanical rabbit."

Aladdin has been running at the Jacksonville track for many years, chasing various mechanical animals along the way. After discovering that these were in fact decoys, he and the other racing dogs paused to ponder the meanings of their lives and wondered what the future would be like with no animals to chase.

"All my life I've been chasing this rabbit around thinking someday I'd be able to catch it and have a damn good meal," Aladdin said. "I became obsessed with it. And now, to find out it wasn't even a real rabbit after all, well that's just devastating. It's like Captain Ahab finding out that Moby Dick wasn't a real whale."

see GREYHOUND, page 196

> GREYHOUND, continued from page 195

Upon catching the rabbit, Aladdin immediately wrapped his large jaws around its head, only to suffer three broken teeth on the hard plastic surface.

"Look, I lost three teeth. See? I thought I was going to bite down and feel his soft, tender skull melt in my mouth. Instead I almost gagged on it. Now that was a rude awakening."

Now there are more dark clouds on the horizon for certain dogs. Those who "know too much" may be targeted for punishments aimed at protecting the sport's dirty little secret from exposure.

Said Franklin Hobert, head of the Greyhound Racing Commission of America: "I hate to do it, but we may have to put the bastards to sleep. I mean, if this thing gets out, how are we going to get these dogs to run? Would you chase after a mechanical rabbit?"

As for Aladdin, all that's left for him is to ponder what might have been.

"What a waste all these years have been," he said. "I hate to get all philosophical, but Shakespeare was right. Life really is a walking shadow, a tale told by an idiot, full of sound and fury, signifying nothing."

His trainer, Bob Pratt, scoffs at the notion of Aladdin's so-called wasted life.

"Wasted life? What else was he going to do, go to college? I'll tell you what he would've been doing had he found out early on: He would've been racing anyway. It's either race or get shot. We've got a million dogs just like him, and if he refuses to run, we can breed another dozen or so to take his place."

But don't tell that to Aladdin. Now that he knows the truth, he insists that this dog will have his day.

"I'm not going to keep chasing plastic bunnies for the rest of my life," he said. "There are real bunnies out there, waiting to be eaten. I'm seven years old now. That's forty-nine in dog years. It's time I started to live a little."

Peter Angelos Insists New Washington Ballpark Not Have Any Seats

BALTIMORE, MD—According to MLB sources, Orioles owner Peter Angelos has insisted that the new ballpark to be built in the Washington, DC, area not have any seats. The stipulation is part of a larger proposal that would compensate the Baltimore Orioles for any losses they would incur from the addition of a new franchise in the area.

"I know it's a difficult proposal, but it's something I must insist on," said Angelos. "I won't accept a new franchise that's going to draw crowds away from the Orioles. Therefore, I'm willing to allow the Expos to move into town, but the new stadium shouldn't have any seats. And I don't want any of the 'standing room only' bullshit, either. If they're gonna play, they're gonna play to an empty crowd. Don't worry. It's not that bad. We've been doing it for years."

Baseball Fight Marred by Actual Punches

Arizona Diamondbacks
Unveil New Slogan: "We Still Exist"

Simpleton Delighted by Touchdown Dance

Retarded Water Boy Not Sure Why He's Such an Inspiration

GLEN FALLS, IA—Frankie Roberts has been the water boy for the Glen Falls High varsity football team for ten years. The 32-year-old mentally challenged man's duties include distributing water bottles to the players and occasionally squirting the water into their mouths.

"We just love Frankie on this team. He's such an inspiration," said Ray Lawson, head coach of the Glen Falls High Tomahawks. "When we're feeling down, he just lifts our spirits. Just looking at him makes us feel better."

Roberts first started attending Tomahawk games in 1992. His family's home is located just across the street from the field, and Frankie would walk over with his dad, sit in the stands, and cheer wildly for his favorite team. After a while he became a staple at Tomahawk games, and the players began patting him on the head for good luck before each game. In 1994, Coach Lawson offered Frankie a job with the team, and he's been the water boy ever since.

"Frankie is just as much a part of the team as any of us," said Matt Montross, quarterback for the Hawks. "He's like family. Our old water boy was such a drag. He was just a regular guy who never overcame any adversity. It would've been nice if he was mentally challenged, or at least in a wheelchair or something, but no. He was perfectly normal and actually pretty smart. So we used to pick on him and beat the shit out of him during practices."

According to linebacker Terrance McAfee, Roberts has also become the de facto mascot for the team, rendering their old mascot, Chief Tomahawk, obsolete.

"If you ask anyone on the team who our mascot is, we'd say Frankie," McAfee said. "Some teams have lions, tigers, bears, or bulldogs, but we have a little mentally challenged guy. Chief Tomahawk was a great guy and all, but let's face it, nobody really gave a shit about his stupid Indian dances."

Roberts enjoys all the adulation, but admits to being a bit puzzled by it. Other than being a cheerleader and water boy, he does very little to help the team win. Still, they rub his head every Friday night for good luck and carry him off the field after big victories.

"It's fun being part of the team, but I don't understand why I'm such a big inspiration to everyone," he said. "They carry me around on their shoulders, they hug me, and they touch my head. I guess when they see a guy that's retarded, they think it's cute. It's not really that cute to me. I'd rather be normal and not so inspirational. Oh well, at least I get to hang around with the cheerleaders. Have you seen the racks on those chicks? Yaaaaaayyy!"

> "THEY CARRY ME AROUND ON THEIR SHOULDERS, THEY HUG ME, AND THEY TOUCH MY HEAD. I GUESS WHEN THEY SEE A GUY THAT'S RETARDED, THEY THINK IT'S CUTE. IT'S NOT REALLY THAT CUTE TO ME," SAID FRANKIE ROBERTS.

Seven-Dollar Ballpark Frank Made From the Finest Hog Anuses

SAN FRANCISCO, CA—Local ballpark vendors defended their decision to charge seven dollars for a hot dog yesterday, claiming that the franks were made from the "finest hog anuses" money can buy. "You pay more because we use the best ingredients," said Michael Wilson, president of KMG Foods, which handles vending at the new ballpark. "The hog  anuses you are eating come from the finest hogs in the land. The cow tongues, intestinal tracts, and various other meat by-products are absolutely top-of-the-line. Seven dollars is the absolute minimum we can charge, believe me." Wilson also defended his high-priced bottled water, claiming that it made all other water "taste like steaming dogshit."

Terrorist Arrives at Olympics One Day Too Late

ATHENS, GREECE—Hamsi Ratef, crazed suicide bomber, arrived at the site of the 2004 summer Olympics one day too late yesterday and was unable to commit the terrorist act he had planned. Ratef had traveled by bus from Ankara, Turkey, all the way to Athens in order to arrive in time for the closing ceremonies, where he intended to blow himself up, sending a message to the infidels and Satans. Unfortunately, the games were long over. "What happened? I was told to get here in time for the closing ceremonies," said an exasperated Ratef. "I knew I should have left earlier. I told my al-Qaeda handler that we were cutting it a little close. Now what am I supposed to do? I'm stuck with this stupid bomb around my waist and nothing to blow up. Perhaps I will approach that small café over there and destroy it. The owner is probably a Zionist pig anyway."

Jim Brown Has Little African Hat Surgically Removed From Head

CLEVELAND, OH—Jim Brown, Hall of Fame running back, underwent surgery yesterday to remove the little African hat from his head. Brown first wore the hat in June 1976 and has not taken it off since. It was removed in a simple two-hour procedure and will be donated to the Pro Football Hall of Fame. "Jim has had the hat for quite some time, and once he decided to remove it, he realized it was stuck to his head," said a spokesman for the Brown family. "It was all gross and sticky and just wouldn't budge, no matter how many people tried pulling it off. So Jim went to the emergency room, where they determined that surgery was needed. But he wanted everyone to know that he is still very fond of his hat, as it symbolizes his solidarity with Africans or something."

Danny Fortson Demands to Know Who Stole His Scrunchie

PHOENIX, AZ—Seattle center Danny Fortson had to be restrained by teammates Thursday night after discovering that his favorite pink scrunchie was missing from his locker. Fortson launched a profanity-laced tirade and threw a chair in a display that led to a two-game suspension. "Who the fuck stole my scrunchie?" Fortson yelled as teammates looked on nervously. "Who was it? Was it you, Allen? Was it you, Lewis? Whichever one of you motherfuckers stole that scrunchie is going to get a beatdown like you've never seen before! I got that thing from the fucking Lady Gap and I put it in my fucking locker and nobody was supposed to touch it!" Fortson was eventually forced to go online and order a new scrunchie in a totally different, lame color because they were out of the pink ones.

New Girlfriend Weirded Out by Derek Jeter Fanpage

ANTWERP, NY—Catherine Wheeler of Antwerp, NY, was reportedly "weirded out" upon discovering that her new boyfriend has his own fanpage dedicated to Yankees star Derek Jeter. The boyfriend, Carl Mellon, revealed the fanpage last Saturday during a dinner at his apartment.

"During dinner we were talking about the Internet and stuff," explained Wheeler, 29. "I was telling him that I know nothing about computers, and he said he was really into them. He said he's designed a few websites. When I asked him which ones, he brought me into his room and pulled up this Derek Jeter thing. I was like, 'Okay. I guess he's a big fan of Derek Jeter.'"

Wheeler's initial reaction to the fanpage was curiosity. Knowing little about the Internet and virtually nothing about web design, she questioned Mellon about how much time he spent maintaining the site.

"As soon as he told me he spends about

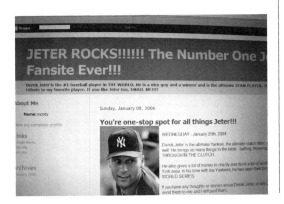

ten hours a week on his Derek Jeter fanpage, I was a little freaked out. Ten hours a week? That's a lot. I mean, how much can you possibly like Derek Jeter? And what's the point of having a fanpage, to let the world know you love Derek Jeter?"

The site, www.JeterRocks.net, has been up for close to two years and is, according to Wheeler, "pretty elaborate." The front page features a giant close-up headshot of Jeter with his batting helmet on, blowing a bubble. A caption below reads: *The pulse of the Yankees! This is your one-stop source for all things Derek Jeter. Images, quotes, links, trivia—we've got it all. Coming soon: shots of Jeter out on the town with sweetheart Lara Dutta!*

The bottom of the page features a ticker that scrolls by with factoids about the star shortstop.

"God, how much time went into this thing?" Wheeler recalls asking herself. "And how can a grown man be so obsessed with a baseball player? I really like this guy, but I had to stop and try to visualize him sitting in front of his PC uploading facts about Derek Jeter. He must be pretty obsessed to know all that stuff. He even told me he was working on a message board so the 'Derek Jeter fan

see JETER, page 202

> JETER, continued from page 201

community could have a place to meet and chat about all things Derek.' Ew. Weird."

Mellon, 32, insists there is nothing weird about the website. He says he is just a big Jeter fan who started the site as a hobby.

"I've always appreciated the talent of Derek Jeter and how much he brings to the table when he takes the field," said Mellon. "Some people are into cars, some people are into music—I'm into Derek Jeter. What's the big deal?

"The main reason for creating this site was to put my appreciation for the man into words and images," he continued. "There are thousands of people just like me out there, and they want a one-stop place where they can get their Jeter fix. Believe me, I get tons of e-mails every day telling me what a great job I do. But it's just a hobby. I'm not obsessed with the guy or anything."

Wheeler begs to differ. After browsing the site briefly at Mellon's house, she probed more deeply the following day at work. Among the horrors she discovered was a Derek Jeter quiz, a Derek Jeter opinion poll, details about a Jeter lookalike contest, and, worst of all, poems about Derek Jeter.

"What have I gotten into?" Wheeler thought to herself as she peeled away layer after layer of creepiness. "I clicked on this 'Rate Derek Jeter' thing, and you know what? It was all 10s. That was the only option."

According to Wheeler, the poetry page featured only three poems, two of which were penned by Mellon himself.

"Oh for fuck's sake, that is so gay," Wheeler said. "Not that there's anything wrong with that, but I'm not dating a guy who is more into Derek Jeter than he is into me.

"It's over," she continued. "It's disappointing, because he really seemed like the most normal guy I've met in a while. Boy, was I wrong. I guess my ex-boyfriend's painkiller addiction wasn't so bad after all."

Jeremy Shockey Passes Asshole Torch to Kellen Winslow Jr.

ALBANY, NY—In a ceremony held at the New York Giants training camp facility in Albany, tight end Jeremy Shockey officially passed the asshole torch to rookie tight end Kellen Winslow Jr. The brief ceremony marked the changing of the guard for asshole tight ends out of the University of Miami. As Winslow accepted the title, he vowed to carry the torch with dignity, pride, and respect. "Being the NFL's biggest asshole is something I take very seriously," said Winslow in his trademark sneering, arrogant tone of voice. "Since I am the greatest tight end who ever lived, I expect to be the greatest asshole who ever lived also. Jeremy has done a great job thus far, but it's time for a changing of the guard. There's a new sheriff in town."

Griffey Completes Punch Card, Gets Free Surgery

CINCINNATI, OH—Yesterday afternoon, Reds outfielder Ken Griffey Jr. completed the punch card provided to him by Beacon Orthopedic Hospital in Cincinnati and is now entitled to one free surgery.

"I've really earned this," Griffey said of the freebie. "It's been, what, five surgeries since leaving Seattle? I kind of lost track. But when I scheduled this latest one, I presented my card to the receptionist and noticed that all the holes had been punched. I'm getting a free surgery! Ouch, I think I just tore my rotator cuff!"

Griffey will have arthroscopic surgery on his left knee, which is not to be confused with his right knee, which he had surgery on in 2002.

Griffey was such a regular at the hospital that hospital administrators presented him with the punch card, never thinking that he'd actually fill it up and be able to redeem it.

"Ken has been a faithful, returning customer for us," said Dr. Robert Martello, director of Beacon Orthopedic. "As a thank you for patronizing our hospital so many times we offered him this free surgery punch card. It was just a gesture. We had no idea he would use it. I've never seen somebody so injury prone in my life. That's what he gets for not doing steroids."

Griffey's latest surgery comes on the heels of his best season in years. He plans to spend another off-season rehabbing so he can return next year at 100 percent.

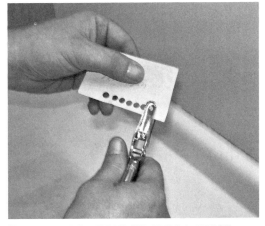

"WHEN I SCHEDULED THIS LATEST [SURGERY], I PRESENTED MY CARD TO THE RECEPTIONIST AND NOTICED THAT ALL THE HOLES HAD BEEN PUNCHED. I'M GETTING A FREE SURGERY!" SAID KEN GRIFFEY JR.

"It's frustrating because this has really been a great year for me," Griffey said. "Hopefully next year I'll be back to the shape I was in when I played in Seattle. Remember that? Man, I had it good there. I guess that old saying is true: 'Leaving Seattle is great until your whole goddamn career goes to shit.' "

Pussy Cries During Hall of Fame Enshrinement

CANTON, OH—John Elway, former quarterback and complete pussy, cried during his Hall of Fame enshrinement ceremony at Canton, OH, Saturday. Elway started his acceptance speech strong but crumbled midway through, shedding tears and blubbering like a schoolgirl. "It's been a great run," Elway began. "It's hard to believe that a young kid from . . . from . . . I'm sorry. I told myself I wouldn't do this but . . ." Elway carried on like that for close to an hour before finally stepping off the stage. He was followed by fellow inductee Barry Sanders, a true man who did not shed one tear during his entire speech.

Ethiopian Eats Zero Hot Dogs in Three Days to Win Starving Contest

ADDIS ABABA, ETHIOPIA—In a unique twist on the popular American fad of competitive eating, Ethiopians have developed a competition to see who can starve the quickest. This year's winner was 30-year-old Negaso Woldegiorgis, who consumed a record zero hot dogs in just under three days to become Ethiopia's hungriest human being. "Congratulations, Negaso," said judge Addis Worle. "You have consumed zero hot dogs in our hot dog not-eating contest and are now the hungriest person in Ethiopia, which, if you think about it, is saying a lot." "Thank you," replied the pencil-thin Woldegiorgis as the judge placed a ribbon around his bony neck. "It is an honor to be so hungry. If only the prize were some food. The ribbon—is it edible?"

"Tremendous" Voted Most Popular Word by Nation's Sportscasters

NEW YORK, NY—Fans of the word "tremendous" celebrated yesterday as it was voted the most popular word by the nation's sportscasters. The fun, versatile word came in far ahead of "swagger" and "adversity" in the poll, conducted by ESPN.com. " 'Tremendous' is a wonderful word, a tremendous word," said CBS sportscaster Dick Enberg. "It's just a tremendous honor to be able to say that word over and over again during the course of a game. My colleagues and I are extremely happy to see this word finally get the recognition it deserves. This is a tremendous day for us, and a tremendous day for 'tremendous.' "

MLS Commissioner Invited to Steroid Hearings Out of Politeness

WASHINGTON, DC—The House Commerce, Trade and Consumer Protection Subcommittee extended an invitation to Major League Soccer commissioner Don Garber to attend this week's steroid hearings. Though soccer has no discernible steroid problem and nobody would care if they did, the committee decided to invite Garber out of politeness. Garber will testify on Wednesday, even though nobody will be listening to him.

"We wanted to interview all the commissioners from the major sports leagues," said Cliff Stearns (R-FL), chairman of the subcommittee, "so we immediately thought of the obvious guys—Stern, Tagliabue, Selig, and Bettman. Then somehow this Garber guy found about it. He called and was like, 'So . . . when should I show up to testify?' I felt so bad. I was like, 'Oh, you didn't get a call? Um . . . yeah, we want you to show up Wednesday.' So now he's testifying during the afternoon session. It's no problem. It'll give me an opportunity to run to the bank and do some errands."

Stearns purposely scheduled Garber as the last speaker so he and his colleagues could have the option of cutting out early during his testimony.

"We have a chance to get an early dismissal on Wednesday as a result of Mr. Garber speaking," said Stearns. "I think a few people should stick around just to keep up appearances, but most of us will probably take off, especially if it's a nice day. I hope he doesn't take offense to it. After all, we were nice enough to invite him in the first place. He should just be happy that he got to come to Washington and meet a real congressman."

Garber's testimony is expected to shed little light on the steroid problem in sports or offer any solution to that problem. In fact, some members of the committee were surprised to find out that the United States has its own professional soccer league.

> GARBER WILL TESTIFY ON WEDNESDAY, EVEN THOUGH NOBODY WILL BE LISTENING TO HIM.

"We have a soccer league? Wow, I didn't know that," said Fred Upton (D-MI). "All this time I thought only children and foreigners played soccer."

Stearns defended his decision to invite Garber, suggesting that the commissioner's testimony might even provide a little comic relief during the slow proceedings.

"I don't think it's such a bad thing that we have this guy testifying," said Stearns. "It could be really funny, especially with [Tim] Murphy (R-PA) and [Mike] Ferguson (R-NJ) cracking jokes the whole time, like when we had that FCC guy in here talking about Janet Jackson's tits. Remember that? I spit coffee all over my goddamn shirt. Not that steroids are a laughing matter. It's just that soccer is."

Former X Games Champ Promoted to Shift Supervisor at Krispy Kreme

LIFE DIDN'T SEEM LIKE IT COULD GET ANY BETTER FOR HARTMAN, AND TO HIS CHAGRIN, IT DIDN'T.

LONE TREE, CO—When Josh Hartman won three gold medals at the 1999 X Games, the 21-year-old thought he had reached the apex of his career. Turns out, he was right. Like his favorite hobby, skiing, everything's been downhill for Hartman since February 2000, when he injured his back in a snowboarding mishap. With no college degree and no job skills, Josh was forced to take a job at Krispy Kreme in Lone Tree, CO. But after three years of employment, things have taken a turn for the better, as Hartman has finally been promoted to shift supervisor.

"It's about time. I think I really deserved this promotion," said Hartman, now 27 and living with his girlfriend and her daughter. "I've been sort of the de facto shift supervisor for some time now. I do the most work, I have the most seniority, and when the new kids have questions, they come to me. I've really established myself here, which is pretty good for someone with no college degree."

The manager of the Lone Tree Krispy Kreme, Larry Fitzgibbons, decided to promote Hartman after he impressed him with his work ethic and punctuality.

"Josh is a good kid. He's always here on time and he's the only one willing to clean the toilets at the end of a shift," said Fitzgibbons. "Plus, he's been here forever. Most kids work here for a few months during high school, but he's making a career out of it. Pretty soon he'll be making ten bucks an hour like me."

Hartman's current lifestyle is a far cry from 1999, when he was a celebrity on the extreme sports scene. Life didn't seem like it could get any better for Hartman, and to his chagrin, it didn't.

"Now those were great times," recalled Hartman. "You should've seen me in '99 during big air. To get the gold, I threw this sick backside 360 with a mute grab, and on the next run I stomped consecutive switch 90 rolls, which is something I'm real proud of. But there's a downside to reaching the peak of your life at age 21. There's still a whole lot of years left after that."

Hartman spent the majority of his teen years learning to ski and snowboard. His mother, Sheila, often warned him that sports alone wouldn't take him through life, but after his success in '99, she had second thoughts.

"I used to give him a lot of grief about all that snowboarding and stuff," said Sheila, "but when he got to the X Games and won all those medals, I had to eat my words. He was, like, famous for a while. Well, locally famous. And for a very short while. And then he hurt his back, and that's when reality set in. As exciting and thrilling as 'mute grabs' and 'switch 90 rolls' are, they don't help much in real life. The bright side is I don't have to listen to those stupid expressions anymore."

see KRISPY KREME, page 207

> KRISPY KREME, continued from page 206

After his X Game career ended, Hartman was unable to find work and couldn't afford to go back to school. And his reputation as X Game champ wasn't opening doors for him.

"I walked into a job interview in Aurora for some kind of mutual fund company, and I figured my reputation would precede me," recalled Hartman. "My résumé didn't say much, but it did mention that I won gold medals in slopestyle, half pipe, and big air. The manager was like, 'Okay, you won some events at the X Games, but what else have you done?' Then he pointed out that I had 8 spelling mistakes on my application. He didn't like that it was written in longhand, either. Or that it was on a cocktail napkin."

Fitzgibbons, Josh's current boss, says he is impressed by his feats at the X Games but doesn't have much use for those talents at Krispy Kreme.

"Winning three gold medals is quite an accomplishment," he said. "I told him that, too. But now he's part of America's workforce, and he must strive to attain success in other fields. We here at Krispy Kreme like to think of our donuts as 'totally rad' and 'gnarly,' and sometimes people even get 'stoked' when they eat them. See? You just gotta talk their language. That's why the kids respect me so much."

Unselfish Player Puts Winning Ahead of Family

MIAMI, FL—Jeff Bigbie, second baseman for the Florida Marlins, is the ultimate team player. In four years in the big leagues, he has consistently sacrificed his own self-interest for the good of the team. He has also sacrificed the best interests of his wife and children, who have taken a backseat to his insatiable desire to win.

"For me, winning is the most important thing," said Bigbie, who is part of an infield platoon with Luis Castillo and Damion Easley. "I don't know, that's just the way I was brought up. It's not all about me and my well-being and my family. It's about the group of guys in that clubhouse, and the fans who support us every day."

Even in the off-season, Bigbie spends time studying game film, taking grounders, and tweaking his swing. He also plays winter ball in Venezuela while his wife raises the children and takes care of the household. For Bigbie, it's all worth it.

"Hey, I know it's hard for them, but I've got teammates to think about," he said. "It's not about the name on the back of your shirt, it's about the name on the front. A lot of guys have families, but when you walk into the clubhouse, you leave that stuff at the door—literally. My wife and kids are outside right now. Just tell them I'm not here."

Football Fans Purchase Chunky Soup Just to Shut Donovan McNabb Up

PHILADELPHIA, PA—Donovan McNabb finally got his wish today when football fans across America agreed to purchase Campbell's Chunky Soup in order to shut him up. McNabb and his mom, Wilma, have been promoting the soup relentlessly in a series of television commercials and viewers are finally crying *no mas.*

"Okay. Okay, I'll buy the frigging soup, all right? Jesus, just shut the fuck up about it," said Philadelphia resident Ted Thorlakson, 32. "Every time I watch football I have to endure about two dozen Chunky Soup commercials. It doesn't even look that great, but if it'll shut these people up I'll buy it. Mmmm . . . yum yum. I love Chunky Soup. There, now can I be left alone?"

Convenience stores all over the country have reported a sharp increase in Chunky Soup sales over the past week as the will of the nation's football fans has finally been broken. The ferocious ad assault, once considered excessive and annoying, is now paying big dividends.

"Holy fuck, okay! I'll buy it!" yelled Gene Reddik, 24, of Mount Vernon, NY, after viewing yet another McNabb commercial on Sunday. "I swear to God I will purchase mass amounts of this gruel just to shut that asshole up. That Wilma McNabb is one persuasive broad. I bet she never had any trouble getting Donovan to clean his plate when he was a kid. She probably just annoyed the shit out of him until he cracked."

McNabb went on the air to thank consumers for purchasing Chunky Soup. While in the spotlight, he took the opportunity to point out that the soup comes in a variety of flavors, perfectly suitable for everyone in your family.

"You got classic chicken noodle, minestrone, clam chowder, Italian wedding, and even chunky beef stew," he said. "There's a flavor for everyone. Personally, I like the chunky beef stew, because it fills me up and gives me the energy I need to excel on the football field."

To many consumers' dismay, the soup commercials will continue to run during NFL games until the company's quota is met.

"If we don't see at least half a million units sold by January, then we have to conclude that these ads aren't working," said Shannon Irby, director of marketing for Campbell's. "If the ads aren't working, then we'll need more of them, and we might even get a new spokesman. I'm thinking maybe Ray Lewis. Everybody loves that guy, right?"

> "MMMM . . . YUM YUM. I LOVE CHUNKY SOUP. THERE, NOW CAN I BE LEFT ALONE?" ASKED TED THORLAKSON.

Spelling Bee Champ Tired of Being Disrespected

EDINA, MN—12-year-old Tyler Maxwell, last year's national spelling bee champ, is tired of being disrespected by his family members and peers. Though he won the competition handily and is considered one of the best spellers in the nation, the youngster feels he's still not getting the credit he deserves.

"Nobody respects me. Nobody gives me any credit," said Maxwell. "You hear all the time about little Sarah Lipman, who won it in 2002, and that Indian kid who fainted last year and recovered to spell the word, but you never hear about Tyler Maxwell. He-llo! I spelled 'chiaroscurist' like it was a day at the frigging beach. I didn't even ask for the definition. But for some reason, I'm still underrated. The spelling business is a harsh mistress."

Maxwell has taken a backseat to many of his flashier peers this year, such as 11-year-old Maria Macias, who wowed judges in the semifinals by spelling "acrocyanosis" both frontward and backward. Then there was Sanjeh Mehta, who spelled each word in three different languages. Neither, however, had the staying power to win the championship. That honor belonged to Maxwell.

"I'm just the kind of kid who flies under the radar," Maxwell said. "No matter what I do, no matter how much I accomplish, there are always going to be haters out there. Like today when I went to the bookstore, the lady at the desk didn't even know who I was. How can you work at a bookstore and not know

"I SPELLED 'CHIAROSCURIST' LIKE IT WAS A DAY AT THE FRIGGING BEACH. I DIDN'T EVEN ASK FOR THE DEFINITION. BUT FOR SOME REASON, I'M STILL UNDERRATED. THE SPELLING BUSINESS IS A HARSH MISTRESS," SAID TYLER MAXWELL.

who the national spelling bee champ is? Please. Do your homework, lady."

At home young Tyler says he is treated like any other 12-year-old, even though he is the 2004 national spelling bee champ. Apparently his parents are among the people who are overlooking his accomplishments.

"I love my mom and dad, but they're treating me like shit," Maxwell said. "They made me clean out the garage the other day. Do you know how messy it was in there? Just moving my dad's porn collection took two hours, although I did learn a few new words I'd never heard of."

Tyler's parents deny that they disrespect their son. In fact, they claim to have an entire room set aside for his trophies and awards.

see SPELLING BEE, page 210

> SPELLING BEE, continued from page 209

"We couldn't be more proud of Tyler," said his father, Darren. "He's worked extremely hard to get where he is today. He's one of the best spellers in the country—sorry, *the* best speller in the country. I don't know why he has this hang-up about being disrespected. He is so sensitive. Just the other day we were playing Scrabble and I was trash-talking, you know, just joking around about how I was going to beat him. Well, he got really mad and started yelling at me, saying I was being disrespectful. Then he just went into this state of Zenlike concentration and kicked the living shit out of me the rest of the game."

Tyler says it's not his place to determine where he ranks among the world's best spellers, but he hopes that someday people will see him as one of the greatest of all time.

"I can't say that about myself. That's for other people to decide," he said. "All I can do is go out there and do my best and hope that people recognize me for it. There will always be someone out there who is trying to bring you down, someone sad and pathetic who is jealous of all your success. In my case it's my dad. But that's okay. I knew when I became spelling bee champ that I'd be a lightning rod for controversy."

Coors Lite Under Fire for "Here's to Date Rape" Ad

GOLDEN, CO—The Coors Brewing Company is under fire from women's groups over a new ad campaign that glorifies violence against women. The first "Here's To Date Rape" ad shows a group of men heading to a bar, drinking dozens of Coors Lites, picking up a waitress, plying her with beer, then violating her as she lies unconscious. The ad is set to the same lite-metal song as the "Here's To Football" ads, with the last sentence changed to "Here's To Date Rape!"

"This is completely unacceptable," said Lydia Montcliffe, director of the National Organization of Women. "We're used to beer commercials *implying* violence against women, but this outright depiction of it goes too far. They're not getting away with this one."

However, Coors spokesman Will Cirano adamantly defended the company's latest campaign. "This ad in no way glorifies date rape," Cirano insisted. "We are simply reiterating the theme from our previous ads. Beer, heavy metal, football, and bitches go hand in hand. Sometimes 'guys night out' can get a little out of hand, and this commercial is an honest depiction of that. You know, boys will be boys." Cirano also pointed out that the ad ended with the responsible slogan "Think before you drink."

Randy Moss Wins Trash-Talking Match with 8-Year-Old Packers Fan

GREEN BAY, WI—The Vikings defeated the Green Bay Packers in impressive fashion Sunday, but that wasn't the only victory the club celebrated. They also celebrated Randy Moss's impressive trash-talking victory over Jeremy Pickens, an 8-year-old Packers fan.

"Hey you, with the faggot haircut, you want a piece of me?" Moss shouted to the horrified Pickens after he heard the boy cheering for the Packers. "Come on down here, bitch! I'll fuck you up! You think you bad? Check the scoreboard, motherfucker! Check the scoreboard!"

When Pickens began to cry, Moss only grew more aggressive.

"Hey, bitch, why don't you come down here and say 'Go Packers' to my face!" shouted Moss. "Yeah, you want a piece of this? You want a little of this? I didn't think so. That's right. Go on and cry to your mommy, bitch."

> "YEAH, YOU WANT A PIECE OF THIS? YOU WANT A LITTLE OF THIS? I DIDN'T THINK SO. THAT'S RIGHT. GO ON AND CRY TO YOUR MOMMY, BITCH," SAID RANDY MOSS.

Moss's teammates praised his effort and said they were inspired by his aggressive, in-your-face attitude.

"Randy just went out there and played with a lot of intensity," said receiver Nate Burleson. "You can tell he was real emotional by the way he laid the smack down on that little punk in the front row. He just went head-to-head with the kid, *mano-a-mano*, and the kid totally freaked out. He had no chance."

Moss said that he was simply trying to get his team fired up. He also denied being a bully, insisting that he acted in self-defense.

"Man, that kid was sitting right behind the bench and he was screaming 'Let's go Packers! Let's go Packers!' right in my ear," said Moss. "So when I stood up for myself and fought back, I think the guys really responded to it. In fact, a few minutes later, Onterrio [Smith] spit on some old lady. We were like 'Yeah! We're bringin' it to the house, bitches! We're bringin' it to the house!'"

Outside the Vikings locker room, Moss doesn't have much support. He is being lambasted in the national media for his perceived arrogance and boorishness.

"That was a disgrace," said Chris Berman on *NFL Primetime*. "One thing you've got to have is respect for the game and respect for the fans. Randy Moss, great receiver, but he needs to learn how to play the game the right way. Am I right, Tom Jackson?"

"To an extent, yes," Jackson replied. "But to be fair to Moss, the child did have gay hair. However, that does not justify making the child cry. He should've just made fun of him behind his back instead, like we do to Ron Jaworski."

Black NASCAR Driver Pulled Over During Race

AUSTIN, TX—Bill Lester, an African American NASCAR driver, was pulled over by the cops during the Ford 200, held April 4 at Miami Speedway. The cops said that Lester was speeding and insisted they had no ulterior motives for pulling him over. "Our job is to prevent people from speeding, and Mr. Lester was going 156 miles per hour," said Officer Lance Hendrickson of the Florida State Police. "That's speeding where I come from. He needs to just admit his mistake and pay his fine. To try and play the race card right now is just shameless."

Hendrickson also defended the decision to order Lester out of the car and taser him. "The suspect was extremely agitated and we were having a hard time calming him down," he said. "We told him to step out of the car, lay on the ground, and put his hands behind his back. To our surprise he did not want to do this. That's when we utilized our nonlethal taser stick to subdue him. We then carried him off as quickly as possible so as not to interfere with the race."

Lester indicated that he plans to fight the ticket in court. He believes the traffic stop was motivated by race, not speed. "Look, I don't mean to sound alarmist or anything, but there was something fishy about me being pulled over," he said. "Why didn't they pull over any of the white guys? They were all speeding, too. And that tasering, it brought back dark, painful memories . . . of last week, when I was tasered by that department store security guard. I'm starting to really dislike the south.

Report: Some Americans Not Ready for Some Football

NEW YORK, NY—A recent study commissioned by the NFL indicates that some Americans may not be ready for some football. The alarming report is expected to serve as a wake-up call for NFL fans as well as for the media, which is being blamed for leaving the nation woefully unprepared for the start of the 2006 season.

"We here at ESPN accept our share of blame for this lack of foresight and will lead the way in preparing all of our nation's citizens for some football," conceded ESPN president George Bodenheimer during an interview on *Outside the Lines*. "That way, when Hank Williams Jr. yells 'Are you ready for some football?' the answer will be a resounding 'Yes.' But it's not time to push the panic button yet, America. If you get on the ball now, you should have time to enroll in fantasy football, sign up for my office football pool, and get a handle on the preseason power rankings. Let's get to work, folks!"

ACKNOWLEDGMENTS

Special thanks to Tony Ashton, original *Brushback* webmaster; my entire family, for all their support both financially and otherwise; Chris Raymond, Joe Dirusso, Pat Burke, and Bill Cordaro—all for posing for pictures, no matter how embarrassing; and my editor, Kate Hamill, for discovering *The Brushback* and working tirelessly to make it into the treasure you hold in your hands today.

ABOUT THE AUTHOR

DAVE SARAIVA is the creator of *The Brushback*, the online sports newspaper he has written since 2003. He lives in Massachusetts and enjoys watching television.